Words of Endorsement

"If you are an adoptive or foster parent at the end of your rope, *Wise Adoptive Parenting* is the book for you! Imagine chatting with an expert who has helped hundreds of families in a desperate situation like yours. That's what it's like to read this book. I couldn't put it down. It has my highest endorsement and thanks to Ron for making this much-needed contribution to the field of adoption literature."

-**Sherrie Eldridge**, Author, *Twenty Things Adopted Kids Wish Their Adoptive Parents Knew*

"Understanding is rather cognitive; acceptance is a matter of the heart" – one of many profound and impacting lines that flow throughout another book by Ron Nydam, titled *Wise Adoptive Parenting*. It combines the values of honesty and justice, mercy and grace, understanding and empathy, truth and reconciliation into new guidelines for engaging hurting relinquished and adopted children.

"Ron presents different understandings of change in the hearts of the adoptees with deep appreciation for the challenges these children sometimes face as they address early-on losses as well as the traumas of neglect and abuse. He challenges parents to discover their children as different from children by birth, especially in terms of the way in which they are best parented. This book is a must-read for hurting adoptive parents and another bright light for all of us!"

-**Delores Teller**, M.A., Post-Adoption Psychotherapist and Educator, University of North Carolina

More!

"Ron Nydam is a hero of mine. He has opened his heart to allow his mind to understand the experiences of others. Nydam is neither an adoptive parent nor an adoptee, yet *in Wise Adoptive Parenting...when kids struggle to adopt their parents* he writes with a deep understanding of the needs of struggling adoptive parents. He writes as if being an adoptee in his landmark book, *Adoptees Come of Age: living within two families.*

"Even more than his having "insider" knowledge, he approaches this emotional topic of family disruption in adoption with love, compassion and the absolute belief that adoptions, although fraught with extra layers of loss and shame, can become loving and fulfilling.

"Our culture fails to place the challenges of adoptive parenting in high regard. When all around them are simply singing their praises, not knowing their struggles, this makes it nearly impossible for these adoptive parents to ask for help or receive the support they need.

"Therapists and social workers are not yet trained to be attuned to the special needs of an adoptive family, let alone of an adoptive family in crisis. *Wise Adoptive Parenting* is a breakthrough guide that will become a must-read for all adoptive families and the mental health professionals who are called upon to help them heal."

-**Amory Winn,** MA, LMHC,
President, American Adoption Congress

Wise Adoptive Parenting

When Kids Struggle to Adopt Their Parents

Ron Nydam Ph.D.

Adoption Dynamics Publications

Denver, Colorado

2018

First Printing: 2018

ISBN 978-1-387-74847-1

Adoption Dynamics Publications
480 South. Marion Parkway
Suite 1603-A
Denver, Colorado 80209

www.wiseadoptiveparenting.com

Dedication

for my colleagues in the American Adoption Congress,

for dear friends who are adoptive parents, and

for my father, John, an unwanted child

Acknowledgements of Appreciation

Maxine Glaz, theologian and pastoral educator, colleague and friend, was well aware of my interest in relinquishment and adoption. In a very thoughtful manner, Maxine told me that there was more to be written about this subject. Her words of encouragement to write more about the dynamics of compromised attachment have stayed with me in the years of counseling and teaching that I enjoyed. So thank you, Maxine!

I want to express my deep appreciation for the chapter-by-chapter critique that **Chris Schlauch**, my colleague and friend who teaches at Boston University School of Theology, offered to me over the past two years of crafting *Wise Adoptive Parenting*. Chris could see what I could not see about both theory and practice as these relate to caring for wounded children. He helped me to keep the adoptive relationship primary in responding to children who often feared this most important experience of bonding. His wisdom is there between the lines.

Thank you to **Carol Willis**, my copy editor, who helped me to write less words and make them sharper. An adoptive mother herself, she was able to really "get" the message that this book seeks to present to adoptive parents who sometimes feel like pulling their hair out when adoptive family life is especially difficult.

In the early stages of writing, **Linda DeYoung**, an English teacher by trade, helped to move me along with thoughtful reflections about both the wider content and the better writing of chapter after chapter. Her guidance and encouragement were helpful maintaining the momentum needed to stay with the project.

Also, thank you to **Rich Urlaub** and **Beth Paddock**, adoptees themselves, who taught me so much about the shadows of relinquishment and loss in the dynamics of adoption. They shared with me their own life stories as these relate to the challenges of naming and owning their relinquishment and adoption realities.

And a special word of thanks to **Mr. Ryan Klotz**, the graphic artist who offered the artwork for the front cover as well as paintings and sketches throughout the book. Ryan, as an artist, has captured that questioning look on the faces of young people. They may be some of the relinquished and adopted children and youth who are puzzled by their personal life experiences. Thank you, Ryan, for your contribution to *Wise Adoptive Parenting.* He can be reached at <<rcklotz@gmail.com>>.

And, thanks as well to the many adoptees and birth parents and adoptive parents who told their stories with passion and pain and eloquence. I continue to learn from you all, conversation after conversation. In a very tangible way, you are the writers of this book. Thank you all for your willingness to open your wounds and to trust the healing process that points to a hopeful future!

Ron Nydam Ph.D.

Table of Contents

Prologue

Adoptive parents often take a hit in the lifelong processes of the relinquishment and the adoption of their children. Few adoptive parents are prepared for their child's resistance to the familial love that they so desperately wish to offer.

Over the past 25 years of counseling, researching, reading, and writing about adoptive dynamics, I have often observed the pain that lives in the eyes of adoptive mothers and fathers who quietly live with the disappointment of having adopted children who struggle to love them back. Oh, how they wish it could be different!

Somewhere in the continuum between healthy connecting and troublesome not-connecting, adoptive parents sometimes grieve the loss of the dream of who their adopted child could have become. The wish, of course, was for the adoption to really "work" in such a way that the adoptee's life could have gone forward in a more or less normal fashion, whatever "normal" means— you know, just the usual loving moments as well as the usual bumps and bruises of growing up. But for some adoptive parents such is not to be the case.

They have realized that they must discover their children as much as form them. They have learned that their own adoptive-parent expectations needed to be for the most part shelved as they experienced distance and conflict more than closeness and calm with their little boys and girls. New expectations needed to be

11

realistically in line with the nature of the relationship that would develop between parent and child.

This relationship, this connection with the relinquished and adopted child, takes on many forms that often surprise and disappoint adoptive parents. But **these relationships are precisely the "place" where substantial change must occur for adoptive family life to be better.**

First, consider the relinquished and adopted son who is genetically set to be so musically talented that he excels on the violin, quite different from the wished-for son of the athletic father who could hit home runs on the baseball diamond.

Or, the relinquished and adopted little girl who is not the wished-for daughter who loves to excel in school. Instead, she dislikes going to school, struggles to study, and does not do well academically no matter what the pressure or reward may be. Rather, she excels artistically and draws with a pencil in ways that stop your breath.

These are stories about children different from the wished-for adoptees, different from the early-on homed-for child whom adoptive parents first imagined. But over time these differences usually become accepted and managed, and sometimes even enjoyed and celebrated.

However, **other stories are much more painful and difficult to manage**. Very much the focus of this book are those children at the low end of the continuum of connection to their adoptive parents, children who sometimes even hold parents and siblings--their adoptive family—hostage by very difficult, unruly, even violent behavior. This behavior may serve as an important defense against the fear of getting close in their early years with parents who seek to love them.

These adoptees who fear intimacy may defend themselves in many different ways. And their primary defenses may make happy family life nearly impossible. Sometimes, amid such frustration, parents struggle to find a way to metaphorically shake them (because of course children should never be actually shaken!) to somehow get through to the children that their love for them is real.

As sad and as tragic as it may be, it is true that sometimes hearts, very little hearts, appear to have turned to stone and are not very available for parental affection—even to the point of a failed adoption. (Chapter 8 is a presentation of this tragedy.)

One of the purposes of this book is to take these adoptive parents off the hook, so to speak, and bring forward some understanding of the challenge that they face that few people outside of the adoptive family circle are able to appreciate.

Too often adoptive parents live with quiet disappointment, desperation, and personal shame as they are viewed as failures with children so difficult to manage. Too often adoptive parents take the rap for the difficulties that their children by adoption sometimes face. At least this is disheartening; at most it is tragic and profoundly unfair.

One way to define tragedy is to think of it as never living the life that we should have lived. For those of us who are spiritually interested, it is never living the life that God intended us to live. It might be thought of as a life derailed from the tracks leading toward a fulfilling existence.

Tragedy can mean getting hung up by the circumstances of even early life in such a way that one's potential is never fully achieved and healthy intimate connecting is usually compromised. In this way some adoptees never live the life that they should have enjoyed with a smile.

Please be clear that I am not speaking to the fantasy of the life that an adoptee could have lived with his or her birth parents. Here I refer only to the life the adopted had he or she been able to adopt his or her parents in the earlier years of development.

The lack of this early relationship in sufficient depth, this plain old oxygen that is needed to survive both emotionally and spiritually, usually compromises the quality of a child's life. How sad for both the adoptee and the adoptive parents who may try so hard to get near to the hearts of their children.

These pages unfold in a manner that proceeds from some basic understandings of the processes of relinquishment and adoption, especially as they relate to the importance and the power of solid connection with parents. We'll also review different parenting methods so that adoptive parents—and all parents for that matter—know why they are doing what they are doing.

Parenting by way of knowing is much better than parenting by guessing. Parents can be held hostage by the way in which they see their relinquished and adopted children. Giving up a wish is always painful. They may struggle to truly allow their children to be real and to really "see" these children for the real persons that they are.

With new understandings of the adoptee's struggle and new ways to engage them, I hope that reading this book will lessen the guessing. Again, I have seen deep sadness in the eyes of parents who worked to construct a family, having been quite unaware of the difficulties that would come along.

So together, as writer and reader, let's see how much understanding we can bring to the challenge of turning things toward good for boys and girls—even very little boys and girls—who are looking for love but struggle to let it be.

Why this book?

The web of relationships within which I live is what matters the most to me. I have taken down the plumage on my office wall, all those certificates of honor, framed in wood. And in their place now hang photographs of our grandchildren. **People matter most.** Belonging means loving and being loved; this is what makes our lives rich.

I wrote this book because relinquishment and adoption put belonging at risk.

Hopefully this book will serve to bring deeper understanding and new parenting skills to adoptive parents who have been frustrated by both relinquishment and adoption.

Ron Nydam, Ph.D.

Denver, Colorado

April 16, 2018

1

Introduction: Her Arching Backbone

In deep distress, Sally Anne arched her back as this stranger, her adoptive mother, tried desperately to comfort her, to sooth her angry outburst as well as her fear of the many unknowns before her.

Are infants fearful of the unfamiliar? Well, yes, they are.

At three months of age, Sally Anne was refusing to go along with the program--to make this transition from her first mother to her second mother. Tears and rage and tears and rage and tears and rage went on until finally, about 20 minutes later, she relaxed that arched back of hers and, exhausted, gave in to the protective blanket of sleep. She had no fight left in her for the moment, but what might still be to come?

Sally Anne's adoptive mother was weeping. She, also exhausted, was just beginning to realize how difficult, how much of a struggle it could be for their newly claimed and newly named daughter to become her daughter.

Let's not overlook how helpless, how powerless her adoptive father felt. Fathers must be brought into this story. They have such an important contribution to make in the lives of their children. But this father could not bring comfort to either Sally Anne or his wife.

This new dad now had lots of questions--questions he had never thought of before about what might be going on with his infant daughter. He had watched carefully as Sally Anne's little backbone arched backward and fought the very arms that could comfort her. Her entire body was screaming, "No!"

Why such profound resistance and distress? Why would this little girl not take great comfort in the warmth of her new mother's embrace? Why would she fight the new deal, the new arrangement with these new parents? Dad wondered in deep disappointment about what might be next.

This protest serves as the subject of our conversation about the struggle that adoptees sometimes have with the challenge of learning how to tolerate, then get along with, then begin to love and bond to new parents who stepped forward and signed up to be the guardians of their bodies and their souls, the deepest parts of personality.

By way of introduction, some basics about this protest need to be explained. They each ground our study of how some adoptees have such a hard time making love work. From these building blocks we start to construct effective parenting methods with relinquished and adopted children who protest their adoptions with great strength.

We'll examine ten core values and four foundational assumptions.

Ten Core Guiding Values

First, this protest against being adopted must be respected. This might sound surprising because adoptive parents might wish to and even assume they can overpower this push-back with their love.

We can understand these second parents wishing to wear down this profound emotional defense against them and all the differences that they stand for in these early moments of connection. After all, these second parents talk differently, smell different, eat differently, and hold this baby differently than the first parents or foster parents did for the first three months of their child's life.

Consider this: Even at eight days of age a newborn can sense the difference between the breastmilk pads of its birth mother and those of another mother.[1] Consistently, the infant turns its head in the direction of its own mother's milk. Also, we might even wonder about prenatal bonding and forever guess about the impact of an infant's prenatal environment and experience as part of the earliest stages of development. So little is known about prenatal emotional development—to what extent is there an experiencing self that feels?

So, respect for these moments of protest in early life before one's adoption must be the first word in this

---

[1] Daniel Stern, *The Interpersonal World of the Human Infant.* New York: basic books, 1985, 39.

discussion. Respect for birth parents and other caregivers involved is also vital. To denigrate adoptees or birth parents or former foster caregivers, or to cast birth story and birth family history in a negative light--all forms of disrespect--would certainly contribute to the beginning of the breakdown of a possibly good relationship between parents and children by adoption.

Put positively, **respect for this protest against what happens with relinquishment and adoption is foundational and critical for positive adoptive parenting outcomes.** Here are the words of an adoptive mom as she and her husband receive a Chinese infant from an orphanage where this little girl had certainly bonded with one of the orphanage workers:

My dearest Keira,

> You were so mad and sad the first day we met you, honey. So mad. And you had every right to be. Someone had loved and cared for you with all her heart and now she was taken away. My heart broke for you as you searched the waiting room hoping to see her face. Hoping this was a bad dream. You would look into our faces,..wondering who we were. Our paths have been planned by God and He is so much wiser than we are. I am just so sorry it has to involve pain and loss. But I will hold you as you cry...hold you knowing I can't take the loss away. I can only let you know that I am here to love you as you walk through it. I am so happy

to be your mom. And time will melt our hearts together.[2]

Second, and certainly the central focus of this book, **understanding what the newborn or older adoptee is experiencing in the transition to new parents is essential.** But really, how could we ever know for sure the answer to the many questions we would have about their earliest phases of development? How could we ever know what that baby is dealing with, even in the delivery room when second parents are present for the "handing over" of an infant child to its new parents? We will never know exactly what the baby experiences.

Understanding relinquishment from the perspective of the child is a very difficult challenge not anticipated by adoptive parents, who are seldom prepared for the struggles of the relinquished and adopted child.

Consider, for example, a boy who is relinquished and released from a country in Eastern Europe, often at the age of 18 to 24 months. He has already had tens of thousands of moments in his life. Tens of thousands of experiences have formed his basic perceptions of the world in which he lives. Sometimes, dealing with the edges of abandonment or the trauma of physical or sexual abuse or the agony of neglect leaves that little boy deeply wounded before ever finding a home in America.

The task of parents and caregivers is to understand, as best they can, how that child is experiencing life. This, however, will always be an approximation to some degree. Dealing with these sometimes profound

---

[2] Thank you, Susan and David Harrell from Grand Rapids, Michigan.

difficulties leaves adoptive parents exhausted and discouraged, guessing about this protest much more than knowing how to understand it or how to respond to it.

Nevertheless, only working toward a better understanding of the mind and the heart of the child will change guessing into knowing. That's why this book will spend so much time exploring the mind and heart of the adoptee.

Third, and what looms above this entire conversation, is the critical importance of acceptance. Understanding is rather cognitive; acceptance is a matter of the heart. Here, adoptive parents face the challenge of continuously mustering up acceptance of the adoptee for who the adoptee really is. At times, in moments of negative behavior, this can be incredibly difficult. Nevertheless, as soon as personal judgment against the child or the child's behavior begins to raise its head, the adoptee will quite understandably back away.

As we shall see, the challenge for the relinquished and adopted child is that of allowing new parents into his or her life. This is the central difficulty that this book seeks to explore and explain. As odd as it may sound, accepting another's acceptance may be very frightening to children who for a variety of reasons have learned to protect themselves by staying away, keeping the distance, even starting a fight to maintain that distance. Or, they present a well-protected adaptive/false self to their parents and the world, keeping the real and true carefully hidden and well protected.

The fourth core value in this review of adoptive development is trust. All of us know that risk comes along with the need to trust. People often talk about the fear of getting hurt again as a reasonable explanation for difficulty with trusting. That means that the person--in this case a very little person–has somehow been hurt before.

This first-time hurt is usually buried in the mix of memories that are conscious or, even more difficult to deal with, memories of early-on injuries that are too painful to remember consciously. These are the blows to the human heart that are so difficult for a child to know.

Instead, their sufferings are acted out in troublesome behavior. One purpose for difficult behavior may be simply to maintain distance from adoptive parents. Clearly trust is hard to come by in the relationship between an adoptee and his or her new parents. Feeling safe may be in short supply for the wounded child.

The fifth core value is honesty. But honesty has been difficult to come by in the practices of relinquishment and adoption. Decades ago, minimizing shame and embarrassment around unplanned pregnancy guided the professional practice of relinquishment and adoption. Adoption agencies, birth parents, and adoptive parents, especially in white North America where shame was a primary concern, colluded to act "as if" the unplanned pregnancy never occurred, thereby protecting everyone involved from shame.

It was thought, too, that completely separating adoptees and their birth parents was in the children's best interest, clearing the way for a singular experience of bonding to their adoptive parents. And so, yes, sometimes adoptees were told that their birthparents died in a car accident. An untruth like this was thought to be the best way to facilitate separation between first parents and child. Honesty was not a value highly held in those decades. We need to understand this.

Today, however, **a significant shift toward openness and honesty has occurred in the practice of relinquishment and adoption**. For this we give thanks because one can only create an identity out of the building blocks of reality, of truth about one's birth parents and family history, of honesty about the genetic blueprint that comes with each relinquished and adopted child.

In these present days when birthparents are very much in charge of the choices for the placements that aIre made, their common insistence on truth telling and a more open adoption practice has put honesty forward as an important value. Thank goodness for this!

One adult adoptee recalls the long and extensive search process through which he hoped to locate and meet his birth mother. After several years of searching, he successfully located her in a state mental hospital. She was suffering from paranoid schizophrenia. She had no memory of him, at least at the time of his visit.

This was, of course, a very sad outcome, but this young man now knew his truth. He could say, "Hello, my name is Mark and my truth is that I was relinquished and adopted soon after I was born. My birth mother is a person with paranoid schizophrenia. She does not know me and, really, she never will." This was his reality, and he could name it and now move forward to strengthen his own identity by knowing more about the story of his relinquishment, as sad as it may be.

I often say that **even bad news is good news because it is real news**. For this reason, honesty is a very important value in our considerations about the difficulties that surround adoptees' experiences of separation from their birth parents and transition to their new second parents.

Put simply, honesty matters.

The sixth value is justice. We all quickly understand what justice means. Concern about justice will open up a review of the injustices that may occur in adoption practice. In this regard, we wonder what is fair, what human rights may have been overlooked in the practice of relinquishment and adoption in North America.

In the closed adoption system of recent decades, birth parents had, in fact, a restraining order put upon them[3]. They were not to contact the adoptive parents of their relinquished and adopted children. Adoptees, similarly, were forbidden to seek information about their own birth history, about their own medical history, genetically speaking, or about the whereabouts and the names of their birth parents. So, to some degree, they were denied knowledge of important parts of their own identity.

Remember that this was understandable because these decisions were made in the interest of minimizing

---

[3] Thanks to Rich Uhrlaub for this insightful way of describing the boundaries set in place between birthparents and adoptive families within the system of closed adoptions.

shame, even to the point of giving birth mothers fictitious names in the "homes for unwed mothers" of yesterday. Avoiding shame through secrecy was more important than notions of fairness to all the parties involved. Understandable but sad.

Justice is a value that has played little in the laws and procedures of adoption practice. In our conversation about carefully parenting relinquished and adopted children, we will pay attention to the importance of the fairness that triad members–adoptees, birthparents, and adoptive parents–may have been denied.

The seventh core value is mercy. Simply defined, mercy is the experience of not getting the negative judgment that you do deserve. We all know the term as that for which the plaintiff usually pleads in the courtroom. A moment of mercy usually ends with a sigh of relief that the consequence or even punishment for a certain infringement of some law, some standard, or some expectation has been avoided.

In the context of this conversation, mercy is the gift of care that adoptive parents often need to extend to their children in order to hold the relationship which is so critical for transformation. For example, adoptive parents are often called to absorb the anger of their children. More about this later. And measuring mercy is certainly one of the challenges of being an adoptive parent. At times what looks like mercy from the side of the parent is experienced by the child as success in manipulation. So, the dispensation of mercy becomes a problematic judgment call for adoptive parents.

Eighth is the consideration of the concept of grace. Simply defined, grace is the experience of getting something good that you do not deserve. It can be a gift of care to the adoptee as the parental response that is not merited. A child doesn't earn it. It is simply given, most often as an action to express love and affection for no other reason than the giver cares deeply. It is not dependent on one's human, and therefore often troublesome, behavior. So, grace is a gift that is given irrespective of what the receiver may do or not do.

Note, however, that sometimes such a gracious response to a child may be an error in parental judgment when the structure of rewards and consequences needs to be primary in the parenting method. Parents may wish to be gracious, but a troubled child may see such as response as, once again, success at manipulation. This is a challenging discernment.

Every child, of course, needs to be carefully understood in order to be carefully parented. Here again, parenting by knowing is qualitatively different from parenting by guessing.

Ninth on our list of core values, and, perhaps the most important in terms of responding to the struggles of the adoptee, is empathy. The word literally means "feeling into." Historically, the term comes from the history of art whereby we look upon the work of the artist, all the details of the painting, and seek to determine the experience of the artist.

For example, Vincent Van Gogh painted dark, ominous clouds over a wheat field pushed by the wind, with dark birds coming forward toward the artist. It's entitled, "Birds over the Wheat Field." He created this painting several months prior to his alleged suicide. As we look at it, what do we see that gives us a sense of his personal struggle at that time? Attempting to answer this question is the exercise of empathy, entering emotionally into the life experience of another.

Empathy should be distinguished from sympathy: "feeling with" or "feeling next to." Sympathy is the report of our own feelings as we face the suffering of another. Put simply, sympathy is still about us. Empathy is the skill of leaving ourselves and experiencing the life of another. Sympathy is of little use in caring for our children because we can be sympathetic and never understand what life is like for them. Chapter 5 describes empathy in detail.

The challenge of parenting relinquished and adopted children is that of learning to "feel into" or "live into" the experience of the child. In this way, we look at the struggles of growing up from the perspective of the child as well as from the perspective of the parents. As parents, we must wonder what it is like to be this little boy or this little girl.

To practice this skill of empathy, that is, feeling into the life of another person, we must put ourselves aside. To listen carefully to the life experience of a child as adoptive parents, we are challenged to put aside our assumptions, our opinions, and our judgments and simply listen.

Listen to the often-troublesome behavior the child is presenting when the child is fearful. Listen to the raw and sometimes primitive gut reactions to this new environment. Listen to the words spoken and seek to understand the emotional experience between the words.

These are the challenges of becoming empathic to the child's struggle. Yet this experience of becoming empathic to the relinquished and adopted child is one of the pathways that will transform guessing into knowing.

Seeing the challenges that come along with relinquishment and adoption from the perspective of the child is the primary challenge of this book.

Finally, **reconciliation stands as the tenth core value that guides this book.** We may recall seeing another meeting at the local airport. The news media would, every now and then, film the moment of reunion between an adult adoptee and a "lost" birth parent. We all witness this incredible moment of reunion. We see a bouquet of flowers. Hugs and hugs and hugs and tears flow freely as these two people meet for the first time since their separation years ago. This meeting, showcasing the joy of that emotional moment, is so powerful that it makes the 6 o'clock TV news.

Well, why such a big deal? Why all these tears? What is their source? Certainly, something profound, deeply embedded in the hearts of these two people, was tapped and brought to light, to a new reality in that moment at the airport.

In our recent past, given the restrictions of the closed adoption system of the last several decades, remember that a legal restraining order was set in place whereby adoptees and their first parents were not allowed to pursue each other. These restraining orders also forbid birth parents from pursuing adoptive parents in any way.

As you can tell, adoptive parents were carefully protected. And relinquished and adopted children were very carefully disconnected from their first parents, even though no crime was ever committed that should result in laws of legal restraining.

Slowly, North American Society has begun to see the long-standing difficulties that have resulted from such secrecy and restraint. Core values such as honesty and justice and empathy for the suffering child and the suffering birth parents were put aside in the interest of avoiding shame for the birth mother and relieving the unfortunate embarrassment of infertility.

Reconciliation stands as one of the core values today that drives the very human interest in search and reunion. Birth parents find relief by knowing the stories of their relinquished children, and adoptees are now given access to original birth certificates and the opportunity to discover birth parents in a manner that is healing and respectful.

People sometimes wonder how confusing this might be for the child. Well, consider this: none of us has too many people to love us.

In successful search and reunion experiences, adoptees find so much to gain. Many report that they "finally feel real." Notice the importance of that word, real. As difficult as it is to explain, adoptees outside of reunion often report that they do not feel entirely real, that they have a partial sense of self. And, of course, this is a significant disadvantage that plagues them from childhood onward when they do not know their story or cannot relate to the very important people who gave them life.

Remember the comment, "even bad news is good news because it is real news"? For adoptees, **these experiences of being reconciled to their relinquished past, their relinquished people, and sometimes their relinquished culture are moments of significant restoration.**

We are also seeing a significant healing shift for many adoptive parents who have all along been quietly and secretly fearful of the power that birth parents might have in terms of intruding upon their adoptive family life, despite the legal restraints that may be in place to protect them. They fear the birth parents as unknown adversaries who might return to take back their children.

The negative fantasies held by adoptive parents about birth parents can now shift in significant ways. Emotionally healthy birth parents, who will always be grieving the loss of their children at some level, come to be friends, not enemies. They become partners in their common concern for the well-being of the adoptee. Those fears subside.

So, it's easy to see that reconciliation, bringing together people who have been separated from each other, is usually a common good for everyone involved in the adoption story.

Four Guiding Assumptions

One: Adoption is to be first for children.

This may sound odd, but the practice of adoption has not been first for the children. I know this is a provocative statement, but the truth is that the voice of the adoptee, that little girl or little boy, has not been heard in the practice of adoption. There has been little, if any, advocacy for the adoptee.

Putting the needs of the child first means putting the various needs of the parents second. Making the needs of the child first is critical for healthy adoptive development.

At first we might notice that within the closed adoption system of recent history, adoption was a way of making the family complete by the presence of children. For some, adoption was thought to be a solution to infertility. If we think about it carefully, however, we will notice that certainly this is not the case. Adoption does not solve infertility.

Not being able to have a child by birth is a grief that still must be grieved, Otherwise, negative dynamics may emerge whereby a child is seen as a replacement. For example, no child would vote for being a so-called "replacement child." (See Chapter 4 for a review of roles played in adoptive family life.) Each of us certainly wants to be his or her our own person.

Because decision-making is no longer shame-based as it was in earlier decades, birth parents are insisting on more active participation in the placement of their relinquished children. Today, in the various forms of open adoption, birth parents choose adoptive parents presented as a page from a portfolio of possible second parents for their children. Here, once again in the process of relinquishment, what is primary for the birth parents, becomes the guiding variable in the practice of placement of a child.

We should consider the possibility that the best thing for the child is to stay with his or her birth mother and/or father, and that Church and Society should do as much as they possibly can to maintain and nurture that primary connection. In this case, the decision not to relinquish may be in the best interest of the child. And, of course, when relinquishment and adoption are clearly the best option for an infant or young child, then those needs of that child should be primary.

All of this means that the needs of the adoptive parents for a child or the needs of the birth parents for a certain kind of placement must be secondary to the primary vote that that little adoptee might make, were he or she able to cast a vote.

Two: There is a wound.

This guiding belief needs to be explained in some detail. An assumption is usually a basic understanding that we cannot prove–we assume it and go from there, constructing a theory of some sort. How could we ever prove that an infant or a neonate, still not born to this world, could in some way be emotionally distressed–yes, even before birth? This is quite a jump to make.

A person could also assume the opposite, namely that there is no wound of which to speak. This would be based upon the belief that the neonate or infant is not developed enough neurologically to experience some kind of fright or loss or corresponding wound in any meaningful way. The denial of such an early wounding would allow us to see the baby, born or not yet born, as more of a "blank slate" who becomes able to take things in, to experience emotion as development proceeds.

Others might say that the truth lies more in the middle between these two opposite assumptions. And that may well be the case.

One way to describe the concern here is to wonder about whether a neonate or infant could be described as an "experiencing self." Then, to the degree that this is the case, those experiences, even very early ones, would inform the earliest perceptions of being alive.

These are interesting possibilities to wonder about anecdotally. Consider the story of the so-excited first mother who after 29 years was reunited with her relinquished daughter.

During the first conversation that they had together, they started talking about music. Her daughter told her that one of her favorite musical pieces was Handel's "Water Music." When the birth mother heard this, she began to weep and remembered that in the maternity home where she was placed to await giving birth, she would sit in a rocking chair and listen to that very same piece, Handel's "Water Music."

What do we make of that? Pure coincidence? Or is there more that we might learn about prenatal development?

Hopefully, we can see the risk of choosing to minimize the possibility of early childhood wounding. Nancy

Verrier, an adoptive mother herself, made the term *primal wound* a common descriptor of the adoptee's experience by writing a book about this very thing.[4] In it she details the struggles that her relinquished and adopted daughter presented to her and, in trying to make sense of these relinquishment struggles, draws the conclusion that there must somehow be a wound for each adoptee, a wound that is sometimes too painful to know.

This is how she describes this injury:

> When the natural evolution [of birth mother and fetus bonding] is interrupted by a postnatal separation, the resultant experience of abandonment and loss is indelibly imprinted upon the unconscious mind of these children, causing that which I call the 'primal wound.'[5]

Verrier gave us language to discuss this possible reality of adoptive development. Her assumption flies in the face of our culture that has been quite interested in maintaining a very different assumption, namely that the exchange of caregivers at birth is "no big deal." Accordingly, without the assumption that pain is involved, that an adoptee is, first, a hurt child, adoption can then be seen as an easy and painless solution to the problem of the orphaned child.

But, as I say so often, **you cannot fix a problem if you say it's not there**.

---

[4] Nancy Verrier, The Primal Wound: understanding the adopted child. Baltimore: Gateway Press, 1993.
[5] Verrier, p1.

Every now and then we see a news report about the first union of a relinquished child with her new family, gathered with smiles and balloons and fuzzy little animals. And the news reporter usually features the joy, even the delight, that everyone nearby is taking in seeing this child for the first time.

But be careful to look at the child's face. Everyone is happy except the child. New people, new language, new food, new dress, new smells, new everything! So, when this rather frightened infant sees all of us for the first time in this new land, we can see fear in her eyes.

From the beginning of this new relationship, there is pain and suffering that is seldom noticed or is quickly overlooked. Usually the needs and the protections of the adoptee are not noticed in that news report. Nor until recently have they been noticed in our culture in any significant way. Denial works--until it doesn't!

But again, you cannot fix a problem if you say it's not there. The reality of this initial life injury needs to be named and carefully responded to in a fashion that fits with what that little girl needs. So, our assumption is that there is a primal wound.

Three: Relinquishment and adoption are different!

Adoptive parents really get tired of hearing the oft spoken and usually insensitive comment that "adopted kids have problems." I always find it upsetting when I hear it because I know the pain that these words sometimes create for adoptive parents and for adoptees themselves.

This statement is quite problematic because it covers over precisely the issue that needs to be addressed for adoptive parents to do well in engaging their children. It would be much more useful and accurate to say that "relinquished children have problems."

Of course they do. Why wouldn't they?

Let's look carefully at what's happened here. We are tampering with the most important relationship in human development and experience. Donald Woods Winnicott, a physician in London who studied infants and children who lost their parents in World War II, calls this exchange of parents a "muddling"[6] of the relationship between parent and child.

From the beginning of their lives together, when so much is fragile and tender to the touch, these infants or young children lose the familiar, the foundation of their security. The props are knocked out from underneath them in their young lives just when they need strength and support for the task of bonding, of becoming a person.

Of course they have problems–or maybe we should call them challenges--that the rest of us in the non-adoptive world never have to face or understand. Few of us can identify with them. And, obviously, most adoptive parents are not at all prepared to see these challenges. The word bushwhacked comes to mind, a total surprise coming out of seemingly nowhere that slaps us from the side. Adoptive parents sometimes feel this way.

---

[6] Donald Woods Winnicott, "Two Adopted Children", in *Child and the Outside World: Studies in Developing Relationships*. London: Tavistock Publications, 1957, 54.

You may have already noticed that relinquishment and adoption are two words that I always say together when describing the adoptee. In our society, even our usual language betrays us on this issue. When we say only "adopted children," all the difficulties that come along with relinquishment or the termination of rights by the court may be neatly ignored. The reality of the first parents and birth family history and culture as well as the many variables that come along genetically in the development of a child–these are all swept under that rug of denial. They are not seen because they are not named. That's why in this book you will always read the mouthful, "relinquished and adopted children," as the fitting way to describe adoptees.

When we first think about the term relinquishment, we usually think about a moment in time, a legal moment before the judge of whatever jurisdiction who signs off on the termination of parental rights of the first parent(s). It is an important moment that becomes a memory. However, this is not the best way to think about this term.

Much better, **let's look at relinquishment as a lifelong process**. I say process because this exchange of parents always plays in some way in the development of the child. Relinquishment continues as a very real part of an adoptee's identity. And it is certainly lifelong for adult adoptees because identity formation continues throughout our lifetimes.

Put differently, losing first parents, for whatever reason, is a very important reality that needs to be regularly named and regarded as an important part of the adoptee's story. When we neglect the impact of being relinquished, our understanding of the adoptive experience will always be both incomplete and inaccurate. With relinquishment, it is always the case that much more is going on. And that "much more" deserves careful attention.

Similarly, it is so with the term adoption. From a legal standpoint, once again, this can be thought of as a single moment before the judge when parental rights are bestowed upon adoptive parents. Legally speaking, they become mother and father, the second parents of the child. They assume the rights and responsibilities and of course the challenges of being mom and dad to a new child when the judge signs off on the adoption. And certainly, remembering that moment in a child's history is an important thing to do. Celebrating "adoption days" openly and thankfully is usually good parental practice. It's honest.

But the term adoption carries so much more than that courtroom memory. **Adoption, too, is a lifelong process of relating to second parents, hopefully in a manner that is successful.**

Put differently, the adoptive relationship, the vital connection between parent and child–that's what adoption is about in a lifelong way. To think of it only as a moment in time is to truly miss the important influences on the relationship between parent and child.

So, best we begin by saying that relinquishment and adoption are wisely thought of as separate, parallel lifelong processes that both inform and sometimes impact the development of the adoptee. With this understanding of both relinquishment and adoption, adoptive parents can engage their children with greater appreciation for the challenges they face. This in turn will facilitate a healthier connection, a more comprehensive and accurate fit between parent and child.

Let me offer several examples that will help clarify this important distinction. Sometimes an adoptee will ask the very normal question, "I wonder where my birth mom is and I wonder if she's okay. Do you think she is?" This clearly is not a matter of adoption; this is a matter of relinquishment.

Curiosity and grieving are usually healthy responses to the adoptee's experience of loss. This very important dynamic put in place by an adoptee's relinquishment continues to inform the way that child sees the world. Such an inquiry impacts development when a child gets stuck in anxiety and fear around asking the question. The only thing in this case that has to do with adoption is the way an adoptive mother or father responds to this relinquishment question from the child.

Now consider the scenario when a child remembers an experience in an airport some years ago: "We were walking in the airport, and there were lots and lots of people, and I remember that my mom was squeezing my hand really hard, and I wondered why. So I asked her, and she told me she didn't want to lose me in the airport."

This memory is not, first of all, about a child being relinquished; this is about the adoptive parent's overprotective response coming from a deep feeling of anxiety around losing the very child that she was given by another parent. This mother may be feeling insufficiently entitled to this child, to be its mother day in and day out, for better and for worse. Her fear, less than conscious, may be that somehow the child will be "taken back" by birth parents who have changed their minds about the decision to relinquish in the first place. In this relationship, this matching between adoptee and adoptive parents, this dynamic might correctly be thought of as an adoption issue.

Hopefully, we can now see that relinquishment and adoption present qualitatively different dynamics going on in the relationship between parents and child.

Four: Adoptive Development Involves a Catch-22.

One last consideration for us to make by way of introduction is that of a description of what we might call the Catch-22 of adoptive development. Put simply, because of the impingements of relinquishment--the possible injuries of sustaining loss and a basic sense of insecurity that may come with the loss of first parents and/or foster care--the adoptee may be hard-pressed to appreciate and even access the nurture that second parents stand ready and wanting to offer.

Sometimes we call this "biting the hand that feeds you." This is the dilemma that usually lies at the core of the struggle to trust, the struggle to allow parental love, the struggle to melt into the bosom of the parent. To the degree that this is the case, to the degree that the adoptee is defended against closeness because of past painful experience, the ability to bond to new parents may be significantly compromised. The pattern of

41

expectations that the adoptee may already have from past experiences may inhibit the risk of vulnerability.

Again, here lies the heart of the problem. The relationship, the attaching between parent and child is where personal growth begins. This connection is the space and place where transformation happens, where, for example, a child develops the capacity to fall asleep because he or she feels safe.

How much hurt can an infant or a young child handle before that little heart starts to harden and be less available to care? For some such children, it takes a great deal of courage to reach out for the hand of another, for the warmth of another's skin, for the mirroring, being noticed with a smile, that all of us need not only in childhood but also in adolescence and adulthood.

So, you see that **this Catch-22 dynamic may be the most important challenge for the adoptive parents to face in order to establish significant connection with their son or daughter.** These new parents must find a way to "tune in" to the minds and hearts of their children so that their children can find a way to "tune in" to the minds and the hearts of their new parents.

Remember Sally Anne? At three months of age she had already had thousands of moments of experience. She arched her little back against her new mother because melting into her tender arms was most frightening. She had already learned that caregivers abandon her. Whatever bonding had occurred was now broken and simply hitting the reset button did not work for Sally Anne. She was a frightened little girl and had to protect herself against the unfamiliar second parent and the corresponding fright that comes along with losing the security of the familiar first parent. Nurture from another caregiver, a new parent, as warm as it was, was too frightening to accept. When you are hurt, trust is a scary thing.

Sally Anne was caught in that moment in the Catch-22 that I am describing. She could not let a good thing happen. At that moment, she was unable to access the physical and emotional warmth and care that she needed to be well. Sally Anne was frightened. All she could sense was the danger of the unfamiliar. She closed her eyes and her mouth to the very nurture that she needed to live life well. Put differently, in that initial meeting she could not bond even though her future development depended upon it.

By the way, we often hear the phrase bonding and attachment. Today it simply sounds redundant. But the history of the term bonding has to do with what infants do somewhat like the "imprinting" that baby ducks do to a mother duck (or dog or cat, or whatever is walking close by) when, at around three weeks or so, ducklings begin to follow the mother duck. That's bonding.

This moment of bonding is sometimes a very distinct event when the baby first allows herself to release herself into the warmth of her mother's chest. But sometimes this takes years, as difficult as that may be to live with and survive.

Recently one adoptive father told me that he remembers the moment when his son bonded to him and to his wife. This boy, one of the "lost boys of Sudan," was adopted at age 12 after having survived horrific conditions in a war zone. The ensuing 10 years were marked by conflict and distance with only rare moments of vulnerability. And then, at age 23, as four years of college were ending, he wrote a letter to his second parents.

Not only did he say thank you for their years of staying with the challenges that he had put before them, he also was finally able to profess his appreciation and his affection for them both. Finally, he broke through from his side of the relationship. The tears in their eyes were witness to this moment of finally bonding, this wonderful moment of grace.

The term attachment initially had to do with what the parent would offer the child, therefore the phrase "bonding and attachment." Whatever adoptive parents can offer to their children in terms of their affection and care and counsel – this is the attachment they offer.

As we shall see, the quality of this primary connection is the most critical variable in determining the future health–physically emotionally, and spiritually–of the relinquished and adopted child. And here precisely is where adoption practice most often drops the ball and leaves adoptive parents without an in-depth understanding of how they must find a way, usually a new way, to present themselves to their hurt children.

These parents, just like the parents of Sally Anne, need and deserve some basic understandings of adoptive parenting with children who protest their new and different circumstances. Sad to say, at times their children are certainly biting the hand that feeds them.

2

Troubles with Glorifying Adoption

At first look, it's just natural to celebrate the creation of a family for the orphaned child. Here we have a mother and father, most usually, who step up to the plate and commit to the nurture and ongoing care of the relinquished child in need. Or, it may be a single mother-to-be or a single father-to-be who volunteers, or a same-sex couple, committing to giving their hearts as best they can to a child--a little boy or girl in need of parents. You just can't grow up without them.

Adoption brings a certain relief to the responsibility that all of Society has to respond to the unusual needs of adoptees at whatever age and/or with whatever disability. The decision to parent such children is a wonderful response to the moral imperative to "attend to the orphans in their distress."[7] It is also a great undertaking, a life-changing, very big deal for everyone involved.

Relief certainly stirs the wish in Society at large, agencies of adoption, and most importantly for our conversation, adoptive parents not only to celebrate, but also to glorify adoption as such a noteworthy choice.

---

[7] James 1:29 in the New Testament Scriptures.

By *glorifying* I mean making something more wonderful than it really is.

So everyone usually celebrates. We may all join in the party with balloons and gifts and the best of well wishes. We may smile with both relief and delight on the occasion of the first days of an adoption.

There may well be other emotions as well, maybe just below the surface, a little less conscious. For adoptive parents there may be some ambivalence–anxiety and even fear about what it will be like to raise this child. For everyone involved there will be hope that the future of this family will be good all around. But first, of course, there is celebration.

Everyone celebrates...except for the adoptee. This infant or young child, perhaps from another country, usually begins adoption with a variety of different affects. This term means gut-level reactions to the environment, fear and confusion for starters. If we look carefully, we will see some of that fearfulness written on the face of the child, sometimes along with tears.

You may recall that brief television video where so many people come to greet the relinquished and adopted infant at the local airport with smiles and celebration. But the face of the baby speaks the truth about relinquishment. It tells us this is a frightening experience. This sobering reality just does not quite fit with the celebration. The adoptee is noticing things differently.

The adoption process always begins with loss. Somebody loses somebody.

Obviously, first of all, the relinquished infants or young children lose the most in terms of the disconnection with their birth parents and all that goes along with the loss of such people and their history and their culture.

Second, healthy birth mothers and responsible birth fathers never get over the sadness and disappointment of their loss, the relinquished child. We must take notice that with relinquishment we are tampering with the most important human connection in life, a profound link between a mother and her child.

And third, some adoptive parents lose the child that they hoped to conceive with all the genetic blueprinting and family history that would forever have been part of that child's identity. As I will say over and over, wishes die hard. Adoption is no solution for infertility; there is still loss of the wished-for baby-by-birth. This sadness needs to be named and mourned.

Certainly, adoptive parents are also losing life as they have known it, and, in beginning the process of adopting a child, each of these losses may bring sadness that sits just below the surface.

But where is there room at home or in Society to be sad and disappointed within the processes of adoption? As we shall see, part of good adoptive parenting is the task of helping relinquished and adopted children to be both sad and angry, joining them empathically in their losses.

And, of course, any celebration is usually short-lived when there is significant protest in the form of tears and screams and stubborn refusal to be comforted. After the ride home from the airport, Sally Anne, whom you met in chapter one, was inconsolable, taking her new parents down a different road, far from celebration.

The adoptee is the biggest loser in this story because she is challenged to face a world, a beginning life experience, where there is a great unsettling.

Before she arrived in her new home in America, Sally Anne had spent nearly 12 hours in an airplane, flying from Seoul, South Korea, to Denver--hours of noise and confusion and foreign voices and different food and people fussing over her in ways that only made her more fearful. Everything was strange.

Clearly, Sally Anne would not learn to glorify her adoption, and few adoptees do.

Think about it this way: From the beginning there is an understandable mismatch between the experience of the child and the experience of the adoptive parents. Sally Anne had to first endure her own relinquishment, first from her birth parents, and second from her fostering parents in an orphanage north of Seoul, followed by the long plane ride to America. All this occurred without the involvement with her parents-to-be. Her third step began with the process of adoption: being placed with her new parents in America.

But for her adoptive parents, this is their first step, and so they begin this adoptive experience out of kilter with and then two big steps behind their little girl who has taken a hit before simultaneously trying to and trying not to rest in her new mother's arms.

As life goes on, the adoptee may learn to be thankful for her adoption, especially if she is able to put her relinquishment in realistic focus as part of her very normal lament. But initially, adoption is hardly an experience for the adoptee to celebrate.

The story is not only about the adoptive parents' good and honest joy of receiving a child. At some point such festivities usually subside into sober reflection on the challenges ahead. Then room needs to be made for sadness or anger or fear of the unfamiliar around these losses for everyone involved.

Adoption Workers Must Pay the Bills

Agencies of adoption are charged with the responsibility to carefully oversee the process of transferring a child from one set of parents to another. This process has come to be carefully regulated to protect the child from further disruption. Once again, we start with the assumption that the child, fearful of all the new surroundings, has already been hurt, wounded emotionally and spiritually.

Adoptions are certainly enhanced by carefully screening potential adoptive parents for placement in their homes. Pre-adoption education is an important part of facilitating successful adoption practices, and post-adoption resources that need to be increasingly available to adoptive parents.

These agencies then serve a very important role in Society. With less regulation, as is the case with private adoptions in some jurisdictions, troublesome adoptions remain at greater risk.

All of this oversight costs money as the professional cadre of adoption workers need to be paid for their services. Administrative costs, legal and otherwise, add significantly to the bill. And further, if a trip or two occurs to Russia or Romania or Ethiopia or Korea or China, that costs money as well.

Usually, adoptions from local social service agencies are less costly–anywhere from $0 to $10,000. The expense of private non-agency adoptions, in states where they are allowed, depends first upon the fee of the attorney. Such arrangements, now with more open adoptions, sometimes include the promise of paying living expenses and even providing further education to the birth mother if and when she agrees to relinquishment to a given person or couple. From there, however, the price usually increases to higher numbers, $30,000 and up. The price for most adoptions continues to escalate.

Obviously, this is a significant expense for prospective adoptive parents to pay. For many middle and lower income couples it is prohibitive. Nevertheless, for so many would-be parents and adoption agencies, this is the necessary cost of doing business.

So, how do I say this gently? This leads to a troublesome conflict of interest for agencies of adoption. Beyond donations and other forms of assistance, they depend upon the fee that is collected for the placement of a child.

Many agencies also offer extensive pre-relinquishment counseling to soon-to-be birth mothers. They assist in the process of making a decision about whether to keep a child or whether to relinquish that child to new parents. As careful and as conscientious as an adoption worker may be about facilitating neutral space for this decision, and certainly most are sensitive to this, there remains a systemic conflict of interest between serving the pregnant mother well and covering the agency's budget.

Glorifying Adoption Creates Blind Spots

Occasionally, I have been called the "Darth Vader" of adoption practice. For some I have come to express the "dark side," the underbelly of adoption practice as practiced here in North America. I have come to accept that description as probably pretty accurate. I will live with the critical remark. But, Ouch!

Because, put simply, **there is indeed a dark and painful side to the separate, parallel processes of relinquishment and adoption**, pretty much for all the players in the family circle of the adoptee. In one way or another everybody in the adoption story faces unusual and sometimes very difficult challenges.

So, let's look together at seven different blind spots. Only when our core values such as openness and honesty and justice shine some light on these blind spots can we have the sensitive wisdom to begin adoption reform guided by adoptees.

Blind spots are usually understandable oversights where things get missed for a variety of reasons, some innocent and some less so. The changes that could occur, were these blind spots removed, could be far-reaching, especially in terms of putting the child to be adopted first.

Blind Spot #1- The adoptee has no voice.

Between 1856 and 1929 over 150,000 children were taken from the streets, alleys, and old abandoned buildings of New York City and put on what came to be called Orphan Trains.

Charles Loring Brace, a Presbyterian seminary student, observed these children's troubling circumstances and believed that they would be much better off in the "rural Christian homes" of America's West[8]. Year after year the trains went to all 48 of the continental states to bring these children to the farms and ranches of America where they could lend a helping hand. They were "put up for adoption" on the top of railroad crates so that the townspeople, the farmers and ranchers, could walk by and examine them, to pick and choose any of the children whom they thought might become part of their families and good working hands on the farm.

But this so-called good idea was a bad idea in many ways. Young children would often run away once they realized the use and abuse that they were to receive in these families.

These children had no voice in what was happening to them. They were stripped of all identifying information--a

---

[8] See *The Orphan Trains,* produced and directed by Janet Graham and Edward Gray, PBS home-video, 1995.

letter or a name or an address, for example, that might relate to any family connections in New York City and later other urban centers of America. **They were considered to be "bad seed," and the less that people knew about their tattered history, the better for them**.

No one thought to listen to their protest as children. No one advocated for them or represented them in formal or informal fashion. Their voices were not heard.

Even today, adoptees–neonate or baby or older child– have no voice. Who speaks for the child?

Today, power has shifted in the so-called "adoption triad" of birth parents, adoptive parents, and adoptees in terms of who makes the major decisions. Historically, adoptive parents, who usually paid the bill, were the primary decision-makers. Their voices were heard the loudest because they paid the adoption fee.

Now, first parents have insisted that their voices be heard as well, even in a primary way, since the long history of shame-based decision-making has come to an end in North American Society. In domestic agency adoptions, adoptive couples are now "put up for adoption" before these first parents who pick and choose from a portfolio of usually 4 to 6 different couples presented to them by the agency. So, today the voice of the birth parent is being heard.

But still, not that of the adoptee.

Again, who speaks for the child? Were the infant or child able to cast a vote magically looking ahead to the struggles of staying with her birth parent(s), how would that vote be cast? Someone needs to at least ask that question. Someone must advocate in such a way that this question is primary in the decision-making process around relinquishment and adoption.

Adoption must first be for the child. The interests of both first parents and second parents should be secondary to the needs of the child. That's what good parenting is all about. Plans for adoption would then be considered only after every effort is made and every resource is considered that might help to keep children with their first parents. This should almost always be the first consideration. Were it impossible, then and only then would a plan for adoption be chosen. Yes, this could well be how an adoptee in the ongoing process of adoption would cast her vote.

Blind Spot #2: The suffering of the adoptee goes unnoticed.

Having eyes that see is always a challenge. When everyone else is celebrating, it is quite understandable that the suffering, the sadness, the anger, and the fear that may be part of the adoptee's experience goes unnoticed or ignored.

When everything is so unfamiliar, it just makes sense that this child would be anxious about the goings-on. How could a child feel secure when everything is different? It's understandable that children like Sally Anne are frightened, and it's understandable that we cannot face the pain, so we turn our heads away from the suffering right in front of us.

But of course, that leaves the adoptee all alone in her struggles. And **then part of her is still an orphan on the inside.**

Consider Amy, for example. Her adoption was from a local branch of Lutheran Family Services. As her life proceeded in her new family, she was a careful child-- very adaptive to the expectations of her parents. She was a no-problem child, at least in terms of defiant, problematic behaviors. She went along with the rules and was able to feel safe in her new home.

Teachers reported that Amy did her work well in the classroom but tended to isolate herself from her classmates, choosing to be by herself rather than joining in with others to work or play. Then there was that one day when her teacher had recess duty and observed Amy, all alone in the corner of the recreational field looking through the chain-link fence as if searching for something or someone.

By the first or second grade, adoptees usually figure out cognitively what adoption means in terms of the wonderings and hurts of relinquishment. They "get it" that they lost someone. **As children like Amy become aware of the reality of other parents "out there," usually sorrow ensues.** Attentive parents may notice that at this age adoptees in both closed and open adoption proceedings sometimes become sad, wondering about their first parents. Then again, this sadness over relinquishment is often unnoticed.

Precisely at this point in the processes of relinquishment and adoption, adoptive parents have an opportunity. They can take the lead and engage their children in a conversation about birth parents and birth story, and, with domestic open adoption, about the whereabouts and possible access to parents by birth. But usually parents miss this opportunity because they want to see and focus on the good without seriously engaging whatever sadness someone like Amy may express or whatever angry acting out adoptees may do to signal the depth of their own suffering.

In this situation, if adoption is glorified as simply a wonderful experience for everyone involved, then the child's suffering remains unnoticed yet stays alive, quietly, sadly, or angrily in the heart of the adoptee.

Adoptive parents sense this. But often such suffering is minimized, viewed as a phase that a child will get through. This is seldom true. Even counseling professionals, if they are relinquishment-uninformed, may miss the boat on what a child is facing. They often focus on the adoption and collude with society by ignoring the location for the difficulties that may be driving problematic behavior. If this occurs, the unnoticed part of the heart of the adoptee where there is pain will be hardening.

The relinquished and adopted child is a hurt child.

Accordingly, adoptive parents need to understand this suffering and respond empathically in a manner that facilitates healthy attachment. Entering the heart of an orphaned child means that the parents must be able to lament and join the child in her suffering.

Such empathy, entering the world of the adoptee, is the gold of adoptive parenting. But this can only happen when parents have eyes that can see.

58

Blind Spot #3: The fears and anxieties of adoptive parents are minimized or disallowed.

When adoption is presented as a glorified good, it certainly makes sense to anticipate that a wonderful family life will follow. All of Society, for the most part, and certainly adoptive parents are thus set up to look to the future with high hopes for familial happiness and good bonding and attachment. Somehow, adoption is supposed to work.

Well, this high expectation of only goodness clouds the vision, the ability to really see the challenges that adoptive parents have yet to face. Normally, new adoptive parents will suppress the fears and anxieties that go unmentioned at the beginning of an adoption experience.

Sometimes these parents will wonder how much they will be able to love this child without the profound experiences of pregnancy and birthing a child. But this goes unmentioned in the glorifying of adoption.

Some adoptive parents may be fearful of birth parents and see them as threats to the family instead of partners that build their family. Will these birth parents return and retrieve their relinquished children?

Sometimes adoptive parents even feel insufficiently entitled to their children. They may also have doubts about their parenting abilities with these new and different children.

And, as the process of adoption proceeds and difficult behaviors occur as part of the protest of the child, new anxieties about parenting and new fears about a healthy match come to mind--not to mention the personal heartache when adoptive parents are perceived as poor parents because of the misbehavior of their children. This is the unfair "rap" that adoptive parents often get which is uninformed, but nevertheless a painful reality.

Obviously, adoption brings pain to adoptive parents in so many ways. Collectively, people turn their eyes and hearts away, unprepared to see, really see, suffering adoptive parents.

Blind Spot #4: Injustice is done to adoptees, adoptive parents, and birth parents.

Issues of justice are missed when adoption is presented in an unrealistically positive light. From all three points of the adoption triad, matters of fairness ought to be noticed. Even when fairness seems impossible, naming these injustices is essential to the healthy lament that comes with learning to be an adoptive family.

Starting as we should with concerns for the relinquished child, we notice, for example, the action of amending the original birth certificate of the child to record his or her new parents "as if" they gave birth to the child. Simply not true. It is not a birth certificate; it is best named and called a certificate of adoption. And when possible, **the original birth certificate (OBC), the truthful record of birth, is a document that belongs to the relinquished child.**

We remember and understand that shame-based decisions led to such dishonesty and secrecy. Understandable. But such secrecy leads to a violation of the human right to know your story, whoever you are and however painful the story might be.

Despite the considerable efforts of many groups such as the American Adoption Congress that represent folks within the circle of adoption, legal statutes still exist that maintain this injustice against the rights of the adoptee in the majority of our United States. (Canada to the north has been much more progressive.)

For birth parents, injustice also takes the form of not knowing. In my experience as a therapist, healthy birth mothers never get over the relinquishment of their children. There will never be a day when these relinquished offspring do not matter to birth parents, who for whatever reason let go of the adoptee.

Documents signed within the closed adoption system were "one- way ratchet" legal releases. Birth parents promised never to interfere in the life of the adoptive family. They legally committed themselves to entirely disengage from the future story of the relinquished child. But nothing was promised back to the birth parents for the release/gift of their children to new parents--no information, no medical reports, and no news about the welfare of the child. The vast majority of birth mothers today want that information and ask for it since shame no longer runs the legal decision-making.

All the needs of birth parents have not been considered. In terms of justice, birth mothers and birth fathers are at significant disadvantage in dealing with their own sorrow, their own lament, when they have no knowledge of the health and well-being of their children who were surrendered at birth. This leaves their wound more open and more long-lasting. They face the unfairness of not knowing something they need to know to proceed without their relinquished children.

The story of adoptive parents within closed adoptions contains certain injustices as well. For example, consider all the questions that adoptive parents cannot answer regarding the birth story and birth family history of their children, all foundational to the personal identity of the adoptees. Adoptive parents need to know where these first parents may be and how they are doing.

Our identities are built upon the reality of our stories. They cannot be composed of the fantasies that children or adoptive parents may have about the how and the whereabouts of birth parents. So clearly, adoptive parents are at a disadvantage in parenting their children, helping them know their own stories, develop their identities, and become strong on the inside with sufficient self-esteem.

The injustice to the child then becomes an injustice to the adoptive parent. This is an unfair and unfortunate but seldom noticed result of glorifying adoption and believing that stories of relinquishment do not matter. Ask any adoptee what he or she thinks.

With international adoptions, usually very little or perhaps nothing at all is known about the birth story and family history of children. Chinese adoptees, for example, may be infants who are left on the doorstep of the church. This is usually a difficult pill for relinquished children to swallow and puts adoptive parents, once again, at a disadvantage in parenting their children. Their questions about their first parents, once they cognitively appreciate their relinquishment and adoption, are very normal, and it is painful for both parent and child to learn to live with voices empty of answers.

Now, with the onset of varying degrees of openness in adoption, certainly less is lost. For this we are thankful. Openness and honesty help to erase the negative fantasies that both children and second parents may have about first parents. Open adoption is usually the clear expectation of birth parents today as they are in the driver's seat of adoption practice.

There will still be lots of questions but there will be more answers, and those answers will be redemptive. Remember, even bad news is good news because it is real news.

Blind Spot #5: Society's lack of attention to the inherent difficulties of relinquishment and adoption is reinforced.

The central concern of this book is that the protest of an adoptee to his or her own adoption needs to be clearly understood and anticipated by everyone involved in adoption. As long as the dynamics set in motion by relinquishment continue to be swept under the rug by the broom of glorification, adoptive development will be impaired in one way or another.

Society turns its face away from the difficulties around relinquishment and adoption for a variety of reasons. For one, it is rather normal to blink in the face of suffering. It is the usual thing to do when we see pain--especially in the eyes of little children. We may want to minimize or even deny it because it makes us so uncomfortable. We would see the good, sometimes at the price of not seeing the bad.

Becoming empathic to the lament of the adoptee, to that fearful, anxious face on the screen, demands something from all of us. We would have to join the child in her emotional struggle to stay alive on the inside where there may be much distress.

We would have to "get it" that the baby may be frightened by all that is so unfamiliar. We would have to "get it" that the baby would struggle to trust this new environment that is so strange and confusing. We would have to "get it" that the ongoing tears of sadness and the muscle-tightness of anger at the airport makes sense in terms of the experience of the child.

Understandably, we do not want to go there, and so staying within the bright light of the goodness of adoption, a much more comfortable place to be, we continue to reinforce our societal preference for eyes that stay blind.

We see these blind spots reflected in our educational communities, where very few graduate programs for professional counselors, social workers, psychologists, or psychiatrists offer anything of significance in terms of training these people in the realities of relinquishment and adoption. Ask any of them. The absence of such professional education speaks volumes about the way Society continues to turn its eyes away from the tearful challenges of the struggling orphan.

Why would very intelligent, highly trained professionals passively accept the lack of awareness of relinquishment and adoption? When training sustains blindness, communities of students are never challenged to "see" the adoptee.

Sometimes, inquiring minds do not want to know. Yet keeping adoptive development struggles a secret avoids the sometimes painful truths that challenge everyone in the circle of adoption.

What are the secondary gains of not knowing and not seeing? For one, as adoption continues to be glorified in our communities, agencies of adoption are not charged with the responsibility to carry adoptive parents forward in their parenting challenges. Now life can go on as if nothing much is different.

Initially, at least, whatever shame there may be on the part of birth parents or second parents is quietly put to rest. Although shame is much less of an issue than it was in decades gone by, it is still a reality at some level for both first and second parents. When an eye for the reality of the challenges in the adoption story is kept shut, honor is protected.

Blind Spot #6: Adoptive parents are unprepared for the protest that may certainly come their way.

The specific concern of this book is not about relinquishments and adoptions that have gone well. These stories of open conversation, of strong connection, of empathic appreciation of disappointments certainly exist, but they hardly need this book.

Rather, this conversation is specifically for adoptive parents who have been bushwhacked, surprised by the awkwardness and difficulty of parenting their children who struggle to adopt them. And given the variables presented in this chapter thus far, it is certainly understandable that such parents would be ill prepared for what is to come.

Some of these parents are good friends of mine and some have struggled to exhaustion, **feeling held hostage by a frightened, obstinate adoptee.** Some come to final defeat in a failed adoption (see Chapter 8). These stories result in guilt and sadness for years to come.

The blinding spotlight of glorification makes it difficult, if not impossible, to see what is so unexpected to see. Adoptive parents can certainly anticipate discovering who their children are in ways that may be different from that of their own genetic and cultural family stories. They might expect the importance of being patient and spending lots of time with children who will be working to warm up to them and love them back.

But no matter what adoptive parents are told, even in the course of good pre-adoption training and conversation, **the variable of their own denial remains,** driven by the wish and belief that all will be well, that all will be love, not unlike the limited value of premarital counseling when couples believe there will never be any problems in their glorious love-struck affection for each other.

It is an entirely new step to venture into the challenge of obstinate protest, always a surprise no matter how much one might consider its possibility. Sally Anne's new parents stood there surprised and troubled by her refusal to be snuggled. The adoptee's resistance opens a painful wound that brings tears of sorrow to the eyelids of parents who seek to love but cannot find the way.

This kind of parenting is difficult duty; it feels like a slap in the face. And when it happens over and over and over again, it becomes profoundly disheartening. If success at being a parent is measured by the obedience and good nature of the child, then adoptive parents usually look like parents who fail big time at parenting their children--tragically and unfairly so.

What remains to be literally seen, correctly interpreted, and empathically appreciated are the signs and sorrows of the hearts of these hurt children. Remember the assumption that there is a "primal wound." Well, the difficult, obstinate and resistant acting out that relinquished and adopted children sometimes do is the red flag that they are struggling way deep down with lots of anxiety, anxiety that covers over the fears and confusion that they are experiencing. As days and months go by in their development, they act as if they can never trust again.

All of this is an immense load that sometimes stops the breath of adoptive parents. Addressing these difficulties is the primary goal of this book. Because although glorifying adoption would work to limit our noticing such difficulties, sooner or later the glory wears off and the unplanned, unpolished journey of parenting struggling children begins.

Blind Spot #7: The legal statutes that favor secrecy and discrimination against both adoptees and birth parents are reinforced.

The laws of the last 100 years in the United States that keep citizens away from each other, young and old, have for the most part stayed on the books. Kansas and Hawaii are the only two states that have always had a system of open adoption (and, for the record, rather low abortion rates.) The other 48 states have statutes going back to 1917–in Minnesota–that were put in place to minimize the shame around unplanned pregnancy. Although progress is being made in several states today to facilitate more open access to adoption records, changing these statutes is a slow and tedious challenge.

As stated in the first chapter, legislation to close adoption records was primarily an issue in white, shame-based America. People of color were much less inclined to secretly put such children away. Years ago, the price for an unplanned pregnancy in white America was usually the loss of the child, as painful as it might be. It served as a form of heart-breaking punishment.

Accordingly, laws were put in place that protected the child–hidden from his or her own history–from becoming a symbol of "bastard" shame. And these laws, supposedly, protected the birth mother and birth father from the public shame of pregnancy without marriage.

Birthmothers were hidden away in maternity homes with names like "Home of Redeeming Love" that were anything but that. Supposedly after that, birth parents could go forward "as if" they had never conceived a child. Many made the attempt, but many also found it impossible to do so.

These laws also offered many adoptive parents relief from the public and personal embarrassment of infertility, if indeed that was the case. Understandable as the statutes may have been at that time in American history, few were able to look ahead and see the longer-term sufferings, the struggle of adapting when adopting was on the horizon. **All three players in the adoption**

triad would be set at a disadvantage to make their lives work in a healthy productive manner.

Denial is sometimes so powerful as to shut our eyes to the ways in which we sometimes hurt ourselves. In the legal statutes of yesterday regarding relinquishment, we shut our eyes to what the adoptee experience would be like. We shut our eyes to the ongoing, everlasting grieving of birth parents. We shut our eyes to the challenges of being adoptive parents who, in turn, would be so very unprepared for the protest soon to come their way.

Surprised by the power of disruption, surprised by the struggles of bonding with the child, surprised by the challenge to make human connection with the heart of the orphaned little boy or little girl, parents then learn that statutes have been set in place that make connection, reconnection, and repair so very difficult. What a disappointment!

The laws that seemed to be for the benefit of all have turned out to undermine everyone in the long run. And the glorification of adoption has kept these laws on the books. Certainly, the need to deny painful realities has been a driving force in maintaining that glorification.

To conclude this chapter, here is one more story.

Shirley is a registered nurse who decided to adopt two boys, full brothers, from an orphanage in Ethiopia. She knew that as a single mother she would have her hands full. But she delighted in the idea of becoming a mother and sharing her love with these two little guys who needed exactly that. These boys were two years apart. The youngest was nearly a year old when the process of adopting began.

Eighteen months later she flew to Addis Ababa for the second time to bring them to their new home. She had spent $28,000 in the process and an additional $6,000 in travel to make these adoptions happen. And, yes, there at the airport were her friends and family and neighbors to celebrate with her and, unfortunately, to end up frightening the boys. Toys to unwrap, the sweetness of candy, and lots of noise, all were part of their introduction to America. And so the story begins.

These boys, Raymond and Randy, now ages 2 ½ and 4 ½, kept Shirley very busy. At first, she was wonderfully surprised at how adaptive and even docile these boys appeared to be. They seemed to be accepting of their new surroundings and the new white-faced people in their lives. The boys ate well. Potty training was a difficult struggle but Shirley anticipated something like that.

They both had difficulty falling asleep and staying asleep. Shirley wondered about this, but her heart was warmed by their presence in her life. Then one evening she came into Randy's room where he was banging his head against the wall. So surprising--why would a 4 ½-year-old boy want to hurt himself by this head-banging behavior? It made no sense to her.

Shirley sought out post-adoption services at the agency that she had used. One of the adoption workers visited and talked with her about Randy's head-banging, which is sometimes connected to early neglect. **(Sometimes feeling pain is a better option than feeling nothing at all)**. Shirley was told to be patient with the hopes that this behavior would slowly subside.

But that did not happen. She sought out another therapist, more informed about issues of bonding and attachment, who suggested to her that when she noticed this behavior she should rub Randy's head gently for a while to sooth his anxiety. This so-called intervention eventually brought good results as Randy's head-banging slowly subsided and months later finally ceased. Interesting. She wondered why.

Neither of these boys ever snuggled much in the nape of their adoptive mother's neck. They kept their distance in a way that disappointed Shirley. But she attributed this to their gender, thinking that perhaps this is the way boys are. With both boys, eye contact was hard to come by. She wondered about this as well. She continued to seek that contact, asking for it directly when speaking to the boys. But it did not come easy.

As they continued to grow, she noticed, more with Randy the older than with Raymond the younger, that he did not seem to have much of a conscience. She saw no sense of personal guilt or the sadness of remorse when he was confronted about fighting with his younger brother. When he began to throw things at Raymond, Shirley became uneasy with his quick draw to violence when he was upset. It was as if Randy could not rein himself in once his anger was triggered.

Shirley found herself increasingly angry at her older son, and when that anger began to spill out into bitter words toward Randy, she once again sought counsel. The glory of adoption, as we have called it, had certainly faded far away and the sometimes heart-breaking struggle of helping her boys manage themselves in appropriate ways became increasingly overwhelming.

71

In the counseling conversations with her relinquishment-informed therapist, Shirley began to learn about the significant difficulties that are set in motion by the loss of first parents at such a very young age. These boys had sealed themselves off from their own suffering, constantly acting it out instead in increasingly difficult behaviors. This meant that they sealed Shirley off as well in what might be called a compromised attachment to her.

It was disappointing to learn that love was not enough. Her naïve belief that offering her sons her affection would be all that was needed to make them whole fell flat. So much for glorifying adoption.

With limited access to their hearts, Shirley had to learn important cognitive responses. Daily rewards and consequences were absolutely necessary to help her sons move from angry outbursts and increasing withdrawal toward a more disciplined home where ongoing conversation and very strict structure were the best medicine.

This was not at all what she anticipated; it had to be learned as something quite new and quite different from what she wished to offer these two boys.

Raymond and Randy responded to the reward and consequence system that Shirley set up. She began to see that survival was the single most important value in their lives. And if this meant telling a lie or stealing another student's iPod in order to be cool, these boys might do so.

Shirley had to look behind the glorification of adoption and learn that the love she had for her two sons could

not get through to their hearts. Her love was unrequited-
-a disappointment she learned to live with along with
grief for what she had dreamed would be. But with open
eyes, she could adjust her parenting to meet their needs,
something we'll look at closer in the next chapter.

3

Different Kinds of Adoptees, Different Kinds of Parenting

Of all the chapters in this book, this one is probably the most important and practical for the purposes of parenting by knowing in contrast to parenting by guessing. This goal will be accomplished by assessing the struggles of the child and matching them with parenting styles.

Certainly, this can apply beyond parenting relinquished and adopted children; it also speaks to parenting in general. And certainly, generalizations only go so far. Each story of relinquishment and adoption is unique, as is the personal identity for each adoptee. Accordingly, parenting each adoptee presents a unique challenge of its own.

To begin, **there is no substitute for getting to know your child as intimately as possible**. Quality time, as important as it certainly is, is not enough; there must be quantity of time as well. Early-on day care is not a good idea. The goal here is not only to help a child feel safe, but also to develop a sense of who this very young person is.

Parents need to learn what works to sooth and what does not work, what makes an infant feel safe and what is frightening, what food is pleasurable and what food is distasteful. They need to discern the meaning of a given cry that beckons in contrast to a different cry that quickly moves to sleep, and what sleeping habits develop in ways that work for the child (not necessarily for the parents!) All these kinds of observations, in moments of closeness as well as moments of distress, are important input into sizing up how well this child is connected to her parents.

One negative example clearly makes the point. Some years ago I was the guest in a home where the parenting method used for a six-month-old infant was regulated by the clock. For a clear, predetermined period of time, despite the cries of the infant, the parents would not respond. And once that period of time, intended for sleep, was over, the baby was picked up and the needed parental response was provided. It was agonizing for me to listen as this infant cried out for care for many minutes, obviously in some distress.

Now think about this with me. This method of parenting certainly serves the interest of the parent in terms of defining sleep time. **But what of the cries of the infant** when, for whatever reason, this baby has a significant need for warmth and care and a return to the calm of sleep?

Not unlike some children in orphanages in Eastern Europe, for example, this child finally returned to sleep weary and exhausted after failure to retrieve the parent. The lesson learned was so negative, namely that the only response to distress is to disconnect and rest unassured that parents/caregivers will respond consistently with care. Of course this spells difficulty for this relationship in terms of future emotional and spiritual development.

This is the cry of the orphan–what do you do when no one is there?

There is no one kind of child. We sometimes get the impression that all the books on parenting begin with a basic assumption that one kind of child exists who behaves in a great variety of ways. And this "one-kind-of-child" idea would certainly promote the notion that there could somehow be one best kind of parenting approach that would work for this one kind of child--a "one-size-fits-all" method of good parenting.

Well, **this parenting theory needs to be laid to rest quickly.** This is not a helpful way to think about parenting methods in general, and much less helpful for the specific and unique challenges of parenting relinquished and adopted little persons, whose minds and hearts maybe wounded by trauma and neglect.

It may certainly appear to be simplistic, but for our purposes I am suggesting three ways to categorize children in terms of the strength of the bonding of the child towards his or her adoptive parents. Although I am going to use three different boxes here to put adoptees in, please remember that these markers of bonding strength fit just as well on a continuum from very strong to very weak. Sometimes categories are helpful. The legitimate concern, however, is that when people are in boxes their uniqueness may not be noticed. Hopefully, we can manage that concern.

The first category that we might use as we think about a child, especially a relinquished and adopted child, is the "love is pretty much enough" category. This describes children who cuddle up well in that special spot on the side of the adoptive mom's or dad's neck--that very specific warm spot where infant face skin meets the warm skin of a parent's neck. Here, all is well in the world of this child. Warmth describes well how this child enjoys that kind of skin-to-skin closeness to his new parents. This is something crucial to all children, in fact. (Obviously, this is **not** a description of Sally Anne at the beginning of her adoption at three months of age.) We might think of this neck-hug as a marker for "love is enough."

In the beginning of life for a child in this group, hundreds and hundreds of smiles are reflected back and forth with the smiles of mothers and fathers. This is a joyous relationship in which the strength of the bonding of the child and the attachment from the parents' side is considerable.

As this child grows up, she allows her parents to be her parents. She accepts their instructions and their authority in general. Usual guidance and discipline are part of daily life in a way that is healthy. In this case, we might say that this little girl is well connected to her parents. She would deal with conflict in a way that usually defers to the rules and expectations of her parents.

And exactly why would this well-connected child warm to the skin of her parents, pleasantly obey their requests and seem committed to pleasing them? Simply put, the love and the affection of her adoptive parents has gotten through to her heart. She knows that she is loved. The warmth of parental care is strong enough, and the adoptee's capacity to access that warmth is sufficient.

A healthy relationship is born. She wishes to please her parents because she loves them and seeks their pleasure in her behavior. Her motivation is not a subtle attempt at manipulation; she sincerely seeks the smile of the parents to whom she is bonded. Parents would never need to pay her money for good grades. In fact, she might take that as a subtle insult, a misguided response since she seeks no other reward than the pleasure of pleasing her parents.

Sonja Joy is such a child. At six months of age she was released from a Chinese orphanage where she had been well attended to. The caretakers there wept deeply as Sonja was sent off to an entirely new and different life in America. Now came the biggest transition in her entire life. Coming to America some 4,000 miles over an ocean deep into an entirely new culture with new sounds, new smells, and new people–all these foreign things contributed to the frightening trauma of becoming an American adoptee.

This was an experience of shock, plain and simple. Everything was dangerous. But her response was very different from that of Sally Anne. Certainly, Sonja was frightened. Nothing now was familiar, nothing at all. At first, nothing in her environment could make her feel safe. But as anxious as she was, Sonja was capable of accessing the warmth of her second mother's skin in that neck hug, that special spot on her new mother's neck.

Rather than being inconsolable, she could be comforted during her distress.

Like Sonja, this category of children would most likely experience successful and joyous adoptive relationships. This is the kind of warm connection to an adoptee for which all adoptive parents would wish and pray.

The primary tool of parenting these boys and girls is the relationship that lives between them and their parents. In their early years, because this connection is so important to them, these children will be relatively happy and relatively obedient to their parents.

These are not children who are manipulators, nor are they what Betty Jean Lifton has termed the "good adoptees"[9] who behave well out of fear of abandonment, a fear they live with that if they misbehave they will once again be taken away, relinquished again, rejected.

No, these children have gotten through their fears. They are able to live trusting their new parents as permanent replacements. They will behave and misbehave within the context of a solid relationship. We are describing a safe place in which these adoptees can grow up.

Little Kerry, for another example, came to the United States through Holts Children Services in Seoul, Korea, at the age of nine months. As her adoptive parents report things, she came from a very good foster home where the attendant foster parents were very engaged in

_____

[9] See the book by Betty Jean Lifton entitled *Lost and Found,* (New York: Crown Press, 1976) in which In chapter 9, entitled "Good Adoptee–Bad Adoptee", [pp.46-58], Lifton describes how both approaches to adoptive parents serve as a defense against the fearful true self of the adoptee that remains carefully hidden.

responding to the physical and emotional needs of the children there. Her connection to her adoptive mother, Susanne, was steady and strong.

At age five Kerry came home from a very white kindergarten bringing her everyday questions to her mom: "Why is my face flat?" "I wish my hair was blonde," and "Where is my birth mom?"

Obviously, questions like these carry serious weight in terms of Kerry's sense about herself. Her adoptive mother answered these questions honestly and not defensively, taking them in stride as they continued to bubble up in the consciousness of this little girl. And here again, the relationship is the primary tool for parenting.

Put differently, the heart-to-heart connection between Kerry and her parents is sufficient. Further, Kerry is healthy enough to be connected to her own heart; she knows her own emotions and can name them as she continues to develop. This personal heart connection is the indicator of solid mental health and spiritual well-being in the life of every child. Kerry's adoptive parents are quietly very proud of their little girl. They talk about Kerry with an automatic smile.

What about children who for different reasons are not well connected to their own hearts? This is the second group of adoptees. Given the catch-22 challenges of development outlined in the introduction, it is quite likely that relinquished and adopted children may have needed to cut some "emotional nerves" to their own hearts, while all along being pretty much unaware that they have separated themselves from their own emotional inner life.

Staying tuned in to their fearful gut feelings becomes such a difficult and maybe even impossible emotional task that to survive, some children push their pain so far away that they cannot feel it. And in so doing, the ability to be close to others, especially second parents, is sacrificed to some degree in order to feel safe.

To whatever degree this is the case, those who parent by knowing will adjust their methods to more cognitive efforts at persuasion.

We might call this second category the cognitive-oriented child. Of necessity, their own hearts are not very available to them. These children operate not so much by attending to matters of their hearts or what we might call the center of their emotional and spiritual lives. Instead, their primary method of getting around in life with people is that of thinking through their choices, considering their options, wondering in a cognitive way what to do next to survive and feel safe in their family situation.

For these children, we now must default backwards developmentally to a more challenging parenting experience.

Jonathan is such a child. Although his birth mother was clearly planning on relinquishing her child, his birth father fought this decision, making things complicated for the first several months of Jonathan's life. After two very different experiences of foster care, he was adopted when he was eight months old.

The first foster parents were quite attentive to his daily needs and were usefully skin-close to Jonathan. They gave what they could give to him in a very useful and appropriate way, attaching to Jonathan as richly as they could.

At five months of age, he was assigned to another set of foster parents who, as it turns out, were especially interested in the financial support given to them as foster parents. They had been foster parents for many years. Their attentiveness to Jonathan was compromised by the busyness of their family and the lack of attention that sometimes comes when a foster family well knows that the child will not be with them for very long. And so, they minimized their own attachment in order to lessen the grief that would come with more closeness to the child. They cared for themselves, but not so much for Jonathan.

Therefore, for the next three months, Jonathan unfortunately experienced a good deal of isolation and the fear that comes with the unfamiliar. He managed this distress by withdrawing, both into himself and away from the people around him. His facial expressions were increasingly blank as he fought the battle within himself to survive with minimal warmth.

All this occurred before his adoption at eight months of age, before he was received by so-excited parents who were so pleased to have Jonathan as their son. Yes, there were balloons and cake on his adoption day and the extended family all appeared to welcome him into his new third family. As is usually the case, everyone was happy in that moment...except for Jonathan.

The stimulation of all this busyness and all this newness frightened him. Quite wisely, his adoptive mother did not allow this baby to be passed around into everyone's lap. Doing so would have only solidified more of Jonathan's fright. She held him close to her body and let no other hold him, despite all the well wishes of these new relatives. It was within this parental wisdom that life began in a new home for Jonathan.

A Counselor Perspective

Here before us is the common experience of so many adoptees who have engaged in a struggle for survival-- physical and emotional and spiritual—prior to placement in an adoptive family. In observing Jonathan, we see the evidence that not attending to the difficulties of relinquishment leaves all of us only partially understanding the heart and soul of this little boy.

Acting "as if" these third parents are Jonathan's first parents leaves the first chapters out of the book of the life story of the adoptee. And, because those first chapters are so foundational and so primary, doing so translates into only partial connection to the adoptee, for that is as much as he or she can tolerate. Put differently, when the painful and powerful dynamics around relinquishment and foster care are ignored, then, sad to say, the most important part of this child's history stays hidden in avoidance, secrecy, and denial.

Well, back to Jonathan. Raising him became much more of a challenge than his adoptive parents ever expected it to be. If, indeed, one size does fit all, then certainly loving this child, as parents of course wish to do, should have done the job. But loving Jonathan was challenging because as much as his new parents tried, they could not find a way to his heart.

This is the central challenge in this entire book, namely seeking a pathway to the heart of the child so that more substantial bonding occurs. In Jonathan's case, love was not enough--it did not change behaviors which were so troubling.

For example, one day in preschool, 3-year-old Jonathan got in a squabble with another little boy and proceeded to throw a wooden block at his adversary. Suddenly there were tears and screams and a bloodied forehead needing immediate attention, comfort, and an adhesive bandage. Jonathan faced instruction: "Jonathan, you must use words. You must not throw blocks to tell us that you are angry."

Of course, Jonathan's primary concern was not learning a lesson; his immediate concern was his own survival in this anxiety-ridden moment. The impulse to withdraw was extreme, and so with a blank face he pulled back toward a corner in the room with his preschool attendant following and sitting at his side.

But the preschool staff could tell that Jonathan felt no remorse for his actions against his classmate. He did not seem bothered by the other child's tears of pain and fright. It was as if there were some kind of disconnect between Jonathan and the injury toward this other boy. He knew that he was in trouble, but he did not seem to be concerned about the suffering that he had caused.

A Counselor Perspective

Empathy is born out of suffering. Let me explain. As we defined empathy in Chapter One, it means entering the emotional experience of another person, wondering what it is like to be that other person. One ought never to assume in a story like Jonathan's that any of us can fully know and appreciate the experience of another. **At best, we can only approximate the life experience of someone else.** Of necessity, there must be the ability to imagine and identify with what another person is experiencing. Together with suffering, these lay the foundation for the capacity to be empathic.

When he pitched wooden blocks, clocking another boy in the forehead, Jonathan had the opportunity to recall a moment of his own suffering, perhaps when he was hit in the head by something, and then to identify with the suffering and begin to wonder what hurt the other boy may be experiencing. This is getting out of one's own skin and fitting into the skin of another as best one can. In this way, a healthy child can leave himself and enter the life experience of others

Jonathan is to some degree disconnected from his own heart and consequently disconnected from the hearts of others. Put differently, **when we cannot find our own deeper emotions, it is usually also the case that we cannot relate to the deeper emotions of others**. With this understanding, it should be obvious that love would not be enough to turn the tide of Jonathan's emotional life. His relationships with others are usually "thin." Whereas Sonja Joy was very much bonded to her parents, Jonathan was much less so and needed a different kind of parental response.

He needed parenting that would be much more cognitively oriented because careful thinking about his options would be the most helpful in terms of helping him see a better way to behave. He would need to be convinced.

Now what might that kind of response look like? Maybe "firm persuasion" is a useful tool to build a case for good behavior. For example, he needs to understand the consequences for his behavior. (More on rewards and consequences in a moment.)

Explaining the choices that a child may have is a cognitive enterprise. Helping him understand and then appreciate why behaving a certain way is unhelpful is a cognitive enterprise. Thinking about what follows unacceptable behavior is, of course, a cognitive enterprise. By this method, adoptive parents can engage in a conversation with the child, thought by thought.

So engaged, children learn to think about behavior a bit differently, and parents are enabled to manage their children. That tantrum in the grocery store, when it is correctly ignored (a behavioral parental response discussed in a moment), is a battle for power. A wise parent chooses an appropriate cognitive–oriented response depending upon the thinking ability of the child, appropriate for his age.

Let's look closer at that example. Mother might respond, "When you have a tantrum on the floor of the grocery store, you will never get what you want there. If you learn to use kind words, like the word please as in saying, 'Mom, may I please have that box of Cracker Jacks?' you might get what you are asking for."

This mother is simply stating reality and, most importantly, she is not hooked by his behavior. She speaks calmly. She is naming the truth about this moment of tantrum and inviting her child to think about his behavior. And she backs this up by stating the reality that this little boy may succeed when he learns appropriate behavior and words.

A Counselor Perspective

This adoptive mother is adjusting her parental response "down" somewhat from appealing to the child's heart, saying "Honey, we love you. Please don't do that." Instead, a more cognitively oriented response, like the one given in the above example, simply states reality as in "When you are screaming on the floor it is very difficult for me to talk with you." Here again is an invitation for the child to think about something. And in so doing, this informed adoptive mother matches her parenting method with the assessment of her child's ability to access his own heart as well as the heart of his mother.

This mother has learned that simply loving and offering a hug and being kind is not a sufficient foundation for a helpful relationship with this child. Instead, because the child's bonding is less than it really needs to be, a more fitting parental response will be cognitive in nature. We might say that this way of parenting is firm but gentle persuasion.

We need two important qualifiers here. **The first is the challenge of speaking age-appropriate truth.** This goes sometimes too high and sometimes too low. Going too high means talking to a child almost as if the child were an adult or a teenager or a nine-year-old when she is five years old. I often see this in public when parents desire a change in behavior but speak to a six-year-old as if he were 16. That young boy is not "tracking" the parent's request, hardly noticing what she is saying. He stands there simply trying to figure out how to get out of the fix that he may be in. He wants to move away from that moment of conflict and just get out of trouble. The opposite is to go to low, meaning talking down as if to a less mature child. This is demeaning and communicates lack of respect to children, as it does to adults.

The second challenge is that of staying calm. We'll return later to the so-called "white coat" parental posture that wise parents need to employ for successful communication. This challenge is really a big deal. Staying calm during that trauma in the grocery store requires personal discipline. "Putting on a white coat,"[10] so to speak, the kind that physicians wear when they speak to their patients, is an important reminder when using a cognitively oriented parental response. This is about calm in the midst of the storm, in which truth is spoken; **reality is explained without emotion.** This is a very difficult thing to do when we have been "hooked" by our children, but not impossible.

Our third category of adoptees, the more difficult to parent, are in a group that we might kindly call behavior-oriented. The relationship between parent and child in this case is usually very conflicted and on a daily basis plays out as a battle for the control of the child's behavior. These children push back and fight. Sadly, even at a young age they have learned from experience that their world is not a safe place to be, to live in, to

---

[10] There is something called "white coat syndrome" whereby the sight of a physician's white coat stirs anxiety in a person. This is not that of which I write. Here I mean to borrow from the objectivity with which a physician speaks with a patient, saying for example, "The test reveals that there is cancer". She says this objectively, without emotion. This capacity to be dispassionate, without emotion, is sometimes a necessary skill for adoptive parents who must simply speak the truth of the moment to their children.

cooperate with, or much less to enjoy. **Sadly, these children live within a significant disconnect from their adoptive parents.**

This is usually heartbreaking for new parents who want so badly to relate to their children, to the hearts of little boys and girls. But sadly, these hearts have hardened as a necessary defense against earlier suffering, even abuse, and so these children come to adoption for food and for bread and for a roof over their heads.

Remember the conversation about the primal wound in the introduction to this book? What if we add this variable into our discussion of hurt that adoptees carry from early life experience? Is relinquishment itself an injury? Is it a painful experience of its own that sets up a defense against accessing the very love that would restore them?

Some adoptive parents must face the reality that their children are not able, at least not yet, to open up, to tolerate vulnerability, and to love back. Closeness, as described and experienced in that intimate, warm spot on the parents' neck where bonding should be happening, where a child should be taking in the "oxygen" of deep connection to both mother and father, may be frightening in a way that few of us can ever appreciate or learn to understand.

Mother and father are looking for love, for the warmth of affection; their relinquished and adopted child is not looking for warmth, but instead is looking for safety. So, understandably, they "miss" each other in tragic fashion, as two ships passing in the night.

It is time for another example. Little Tommy was not so little now, ten years after joining his adoptive family. At two years, old, he was taken from an orphanage, one of many in Moldova where orphans live in very difficult circumstances. In those first two years, Tommy was neglected much of the time and the victim of some form of abuse, which may or may not have been sexual. His new parents did not know for sure.

Their response to this information, given to them at the time of the adoption, was that love and prayer would be sufficient to move Tommy towards a healthy emotional and spiritual life. Missionaries in Moldova, they spoke about trusting that God would get the job done one way or another. They believed that their love towards Tommy supported by their prayers for him would be sufficient.

They were quite wrong, uninformed about the challenges before them. Tommy was more than a handful. He never connected at that soft spot in his new mother's neck. When he was held, he squirmed and, to use this phrase once again, regularly "bit the hands that fed him." His parents were surprised and very disappointed that they could not find a way to the heart of their new son. Instead, his heart seemed sealed, unavailable for review or relation. In his early years with this family, there was no crack in his armor.

Tommy lived in a world of his own where he carefully managed and quickly learned the skill of manipulation. To get what he thought he needed, he would sometimes just take it. Even though there were only nine students in his missionary school class and so the truth could easily be found out, he stole a shirt from his classmate. When his teacher reprimanded him, he would simply look the other way without any sense of guilt for what he did or shame for who he was.

Like many adoptees who have been relinquished to an orphanage and adopted sometime later, Tommy's primary value was survival. Understandably, Tommy learned that at times he needed to lie or steal, as he did with his classmate's shirt.

Two important markers signaled the beginning of this disorder of his character. The first was his **poor eye contact**. His eyes stayed away from other people's, especially when he was in trouble. The second marker was that of having **little conscience about doing wrong**. Again, we all know what the word remorse means. When a child shows little remorse for troublesome destructive behavior, sadly that is another indication of a problem with character.

Tommy was a child who regularly pressed against the edges of the limits that his parents gave him, to see how far he could go. In the classroom, he sometimes drew attention to himself simply by being noisy and disruptive. Quite often he was found in conflict with classmates and had only one serious friendship with a boy in the fifth grade while he was in the sixth.

He and his teacher worked out a plan whereby Tommy could go to another room when he became disruptive and simply return to the classroom when he thought he could handle himself, that is, be obedient and attentive and quiet. The plan was useful because Tommy did not like being alone. As with many adoptees, being punished by being alone is especially difficult and draws the relinquished child back toward very painful primitive memories of rejection. So, in this story of troubles at school, the teacher could identify an effective consequence for troublesome behavior.

Let us be clear that Tommy did not alter his behavior because he loved his sixth-grade teacher. The relationship had no real warmth at all. Tommy did not alter his behavior because he was persuaded, that is, cognitively convinced that he should work on being quiet. No, Tommy altered his behavior because of the consequence imposed for troublesome behavior. In the economy of emotions, behaving was a better deal than being put in another room all alone.

One other especially troublesome problem was quite difficult for his adoptive parents to address: properly wiping himself after having a bowel movement. Fellow students noticed that Tommy smelled bad. At first Tommy simply denied this to himself and to others. But the smell kept smelling. Yet he did not notice the odor as objectionable. Tommy was rather oblivious.

There is a disorder that has to do with sensory integration. This challenge has to do with our brain's taking in the different sensory experiences within our environment and collecting and organizing them in such a way that we can focus on one at a time and integrate it and others to prioritize what may be the most important thing to deal with, or perhaps to enjoy. And that kind of focus, or lack thereof, may explain Tommy's difficulty in smelling himself and managing his bathroom wiping skill so that the smell would go away. How surprising to most of us that such a thing would happen.

A Counselor Perspective

For many adoptees who have been significantly neglected, sensory integration is a challenge. This phenomenon has to do with the way the brain processes and organizes all the data that comes to the brain from one's body and one's environment. Think about sight, smell, sound, touch, taste, and then wonder how the human brain deals with this multi-sensory experience.

Sometimes there's just too much going on in terms of sounds, for example. Little Lily, who was adopted at 18 months from Russia, always covers her ears when the fire truck goes by her home, the siren blazing. Sounds like this with all their intensity are too much for her to take in, to integrate into that moment of her life experience.

On the other hand, again in reference to significant neglect, it becomes understandable that a child would literally create pain in order to feel something. When little Lily came from Russia, her new parents noticed right away that she would sometimes bang her head against the wall. Not something any of us would think to do, but for Lily it served the purpose of organizing her momentary experience, helping her feel something to stay as integrated as she could be.

Now, in this conversation, we are reaching into the depths of the suffering that adoptees sometimes experience well before they are ever placed in families who want to love them but struggle to find a way to successfully do so.

So, what about Tommy? How could his adoptive family–including children by birth and other relinquished and adopted siblings--help Tommy, now 10 years old, change his behaviors and find a way to be a more normal member of the community? So many adoptive parents keep guessing at how to answer such a question. And guessing is so frustrating because the results are so unpredictable. How difficult it is not to know what to do.

Tommy's connection to his new parents and new siblings was, for the most part, superficial. He could relate to them and even be playful at times. but there was always this scanning behavior, as if something could go wrong. The world was not yet to be trusted. The bonding that he could do was minimal. The attachment that parents offered him was overwhelming and frightening. Unfortunately, the relationships that he had within his adoptive family could not carry the weight of helping Tommy feel safe.

So now we must "dial down" to wonder together what kind of a thinker Tommy could be. Could he make the cognitive connection between wiping himself and the behavior of his classmates toward him, especially when they made fun of his smell? Could he make that connection without the helpful interpretation of his parents and his siblings?

Adoptive parents must regularly ask questions like these.

Rather quickly, it became clear to Tommy's parents that it didn't work to talk with him--that is, to seek to convince him of the truth that wiping himself is a very important thing to do because it relates to having friends or not having friends at school. Tommy couldn't seem to see the connections between these two variables. For the most part he remained rather oblivious and the not-wiping problem continued.

This conversation now brings us to the challenge of a helpful response to children whom we may call behavior-oriented. When the door is shut to the powerful dynamics of what a relationship can be and do, when the door is shut to all the creative ideas that adoptive parents may have about arranging life in a way that is successful, when all such efforts at persuasion fall empty to the ground, what do we do?

Here, the answer has to do with methods that are developed that simply manage behavior, paying little attention to distinct feelings or to possible thoughts or ideas. By this way of parenting, mothers and fathers come to serve as cheerleaders and wardens.

But before we explain these parental roles, we must speak again about the critical importance of "wearing a white coat."[11] As a counselor to adoptive families, this is one of the parental challenges that I speak to the most because it demands insight, discipline, and restraint on the part of the parents.

Most of us know well that trip that we occasionally take to the doctor's office or to the hospital for a variety of medical needs and interventions. Of course, getting healthy is the goal of such an adventure when we are the patients. And we know rather well that we may face the physician when he speaks directly to us or to family members about medical challenges or bad news.

---

[11] See previous footnote.

The doctor speaks dispassionately. She addresses Mr. Smith: "Sir, the test results have come back, and I am sorry to tell you that unfortunately, after this exploratory surgery, we have learned that you have cancer, and this cancer has spread significantly throughout your body. We will immediately begin an aggressive treatment of both radiation and chemotherapy, and we hope to push back this cancer as best we can."

Aside from the overwhelming disappointment of such a report, notice that the doctor has a white coat as her professional uniform in the hospital setting. It is a symbol of professional demeanor. She does not weep, although there may be a tinge of sadness in her voice. She is respectful of the personal sorrow in the room. She takes her time in this conversation, and she speaks with great objectivity about the nature of this newly discovered medical reality.

Putting on a white coat is the number one critical thing to do as parents, adoptive or otherwise, seek to be effective in changing a child's behavior. The "white coat" does several things. First, it has the intent of speaking authoritatively about the truth of a person's condition. Quite naturally, we respect the authority of the doctor or law enforcement officer or airplane pilot, and the uniform–in this case the white coat–serves to establish clear boundaries that give us relief. If the physician mentioned above came out in sweats and a T-shirt picturing her favorite rock group, we would likely be less respectful of the news that she brings. It would be much easier to doubt her words.

The white coat, secondly, protects the physician by helping her manage her emotions by reminding her to keep them in check. Her job is to tell the truth objectively.

Likewise, parents who have children who are behaviorally oriented must learn to speak objectively in precisely the same manner, "wearing a white coat" when they speak to their children. Emotions are "out the window" and further thinking about difficulties to be addressed must fall away.

An example here would be useful. One of the most telling markers for how a young boy or girl is doing in life is the report card that comes home several times a year. Usually a child doing well in school is an important positive to celebrate and reinforce. It indicates an ability to organize, study, be responsible, and stay focused on a given task. Good grades are good indicators of children who can accept authority and live within the boundaries that parents and parental institutions put upon them.

On the other hand, when the report card has D's and F's, the parent does not explode. Instead, in a thoughtful, nonjudgmental, rather objective "white coat" voice he announces, "Well, Tommy, these are not good grades. This report card is not OK; it looks like you need more time to study, so maybe you must begin working on your homework 30 minutes after you come home from school."

His father's lack of harshness is a great relief to Tommy. He anticipated something very different like the harsh abusive responses from adults in his past. This objective statement of reality stands as the truth about the report card. No one can argue. And this calm, thoughtful response back to the child makes very clear that he is responsible, that he is the person who must own the reality of these bad grades. Nothing about love or the lack thereof, and nothing about thinking poorly and deciding to make a poor choice--only an objective "white coat" statement of reality.

This is the kind of response that is needed from parents of a child who is oppositional and struggling to adopt them. Remembering the white coat metaphor always helps parents who are guessing as to how they might respond to their children. And now, moving forward, these adoptive parents can begin to think about rewards and consequences and realistic goals for future academic behavior.

When adoptive parents employ a reward-and-consequence method as the primary approach to their children, they must consider many variables. Let's review some of the basics to see what happens and what does not happen when we adjust parental responses based on a careful assessment of how behavior-oriented a child may be.

First let's consider some things about rewards.

Tommy's mother began to see that all her efforts expressing love to him or trying to convince him that he should change his behavior both at home and at school were really getting her nowhere. She had a now 12-year-old son who was getting taller than she and was continuously angry and reactive to her parental expectations. Her prayers had not been answered, at least not yet, for a healthier, happier son.

99

In our beginning discussions together, we began to explore rewards and consequences for Tommy that would restore parental authority to her and press for more accountability from Tommy. My first suggestion was about money as a useful reward.

For every day that Tommy could behave both at school and at home, he would be rewarded with a one-dollar bill. I suggested that this cash reward be presented to Tommy at the end of every day when he did well. Further, we separated the dollar reward so that he could receive $.50 for not being disruptive at school and $.50 for not being disruptive at home. When there was no school, the dollar bill would rest on behavior at home or out at play. His mother thought she could easily give him seven dollars at the end of the week.

He received this cash reward at the end of every day because Tommy was not in a place to manage delayed gratification. **Usually, rewards should be immediate in order to reinforce good behavior.** Tommy's immediate 12-year-old response was sheer delight at the idea of being paid to behave.

(Please remember the earlier comment that paying children for good grades really depends upon an assessment of the child. Well attached children would have no need for the money and may experience it as somewhat insulting and disappointing, as if a parent did not understand and appreciate that, for them, good behavior is an act of love.)

The first few weeks of this regiment of reward were quite successful in terms of Tommy's interest to earn the money. Weeks on as this continued, his mother grew tired of the plan and allowed it to slip away, even after Tommy's ongoing request that it continue. (Sometimes supporting and firming up the parents of these difficult-to-raise children is just as important as noticing the needs of the child.)

And, of course, there were consequences as well in being a parent to Tommy. You may remember the report that he stole one of his classmate's shirts from his locker. How foolish, by the way. How did he ever think he would not get caught with nine students in his class? He simply sought the reward of being cool, wearing the cool shirt that other classmates admired. Evidently, he did not think beyond this wish.

Well, what happened was what we call **the natural consequence of negative behavior.** Wise parents will always make use of these consequences and not protect their children from them. For example, hiring an attorney to assist a teen to get out of the natural consequence for a speeding ticket is almost always a parental mistake. For Tommy, he had to return the shirt to its owner and apologize for taking it. An additional consequence for the poor choice that Tommy made was that he was grounded from all Internet use for one week.

The consequence given to a son like Tommy should never be especially harsh. I sometimes say to parents, **"Even if your son robs a bank, never ground him for more than one week."** When the consequence becomes harsh, too big to get over or get through, a subtle hopelessness creeps into the experience of the child.

Consequences from parents who are angry, with no "white coat" to wear, are messages that communicate

101

anger and rejection. And, of course, **judgment that is outside of a caring relationship is always experienced as condemnation.** Adoptees are especially sensitive to rejections because their lives began with such.

While essential, the "white coat" becomes an incredible challenge when adoptive parents are called upon to manage children in this third category of behavior–oriented children. **It is very difficult to sort out one's anger and put it on the back shelf of one's mind and speak objectively to a troublesome child**.

Before proceeding further, let's consider the helpful yet subtle distinction between a consequence and a punishment. We often use the words interchangeably, which is unfortunate. The difference has to do with the nature of the relationship within which the consequence occurs. As a child like Tommy experiences a consequence, he also experiences the care and lack of condemnation from his parents.

One example makes the point in a very striking way. At a conference I attended, one of the speakers was Warden Burl Cain of Angola State Penitentiary, 30 miles north of Baton Rouge, Louisiana. He explained to us the prison's policy that all of the mostly lifetime 5000 inmates need not wear orange prison garb jumpsuits. Instead, they are invited to wear the normal street clothes that all the rest of us wear. When asked why this policy was in place, Warden Cain answered with this very telling response: "These men are here in prison, most for the rest of their lives, *for their sentence, not for their punishment.*"

Hopefully, you the reader, can sense the difference between a sentence and a punishment. A prison sentence has to do with paying back the price for behavior against society in some way. Sentence, as it is used by Cain, signals a much more humane and respectful attitude toward the offending prisoner. By way of contrast, the term punishment comes along with anger, judgment, and rejection. It does not hold a respectful attitude toward the prisoner who is now in a state penitentiary for years and years and for many, the rest of their lives. What a difference a word makes.

Tommy responded well to both the rewards and the consequences for his daily behavior--so much so that he kept his mother in line, making sure that she took note of the money that was owed at the end of the day–an immediate gratification for getting through the day without acting out the anger or the melancholy that resided in his heart. This regimen of response began to turn things forward in Tommy's daily life.

The most interesting change in his behavior was that he began to wipe himself more carefully in the bathroom. He did not smell so bad anymore. That problematic behavior was extinguished, not so much because he thought it through socially or because he smelled it–or integrated the sensation of smell itself. Tommy wanted the money.

Despite the initiating reason, good behavior has its own reward, its own natural positive reinforcement as it is noticed and elicits a positive response from others. And this may boost Tommy's self-esteem to a somewhat higher level where self-care begins to matter to him.

Finally, Tommy may want to present himself in a better light.

Another group within the behavior-oriented category certainly needs to be noticed within this conversation about rewards and consequences. Sad to say, this is the child most difficult to parent, most heartbreaking to manage, because the balance of power begins to shift with children who hold their adoptive families hostage.

As soon as I use this term, *hostage*, some adoptive parents will know exactly what I mean. These children are extremely exasperating to parents. They change the lives of all family members and especially parents.

We must take note of the fact that in all the examples presented so far in this discussion, the parents have more power to correct behavior than the children do. The mom and the dad are in charge and they make the daily determinations of how things are going to be in their family life as they parent their children. Troublesome children really press the limits, but nonetheless when we ask who has the most power in this family, clearly the answer is still that the parents do.

Well, what about adoptive families where one single child has more power than anyone else in the family?

Hostage–holding a family hostage–what power a child can have! In such an adoptive family, the balance of power has clearly shifted and the family's adoptee is pretty much in charge. Going out to eat now depends on the mood of this child.

Homeschooling, as useful as it may indeed be, becomes the only option for education because this little boy is so disruptive and out-of-control in the classroom. Family vacations may be put off or canceled because the "power child," if we might call him that, is running the show in his adoptive family. And, of course, this power dynamic is nothing that these well-intended parents ever anticipated.

This adoptee has learned, of necessity, to stay away from everyone, emotionally speaking. This adoption story is parental love unrequited. Following the order of our adoption triage, first, his heart is very much sealed off from both himself and all his family members. In the second tier of review, there is no successful persuasion, no cognitive making sense of things.

And, in this third tier of review, this "power child" has been able to push back successfully against all the consequences that have come toward him from parents seeking to be parents. They regularly cave to his wishes. They set parameters on his behavior but cannot enforce the consequences that they have arranged. These adoptive parents cannot see a path forward as this child adoptee continues to grow up and become even stronger. What are they to do?

With regard to this battle for control that adoptive parents often engage, especially as this relates to consequences for negative behavior, it should be clear that ultimately, they will never win this contest for power. Unless, some form of bonding occurs, the battle will go on indeterminately. Usual methods of parenting will often fall short. Positive reinforcement, ongoing rewards for doing things well, needs to be primary in the responses of adoptive parents.

Stephanie was a child that was holding her adoptive family hostage. This 10-year-old young lady had clearly won the power struggle with her adoptive parents. The tantrums that she would throw in her earlier days, around ages 7 to 9, were spectacular shows of drama and power. She just would never give in in a way whereby her parents could be her parents; she did not accept their authority in her life.

One of the things her parents fought over with Stephanie was the requirement that she brush her teeth before she went to bed. She did not want to do it and simply refused to do it. (Remember problems with sensory integration?) Stephanie saw no need for brushing her teeth and, in terms of integrating all the sensations around her, she did not notice the unrefreshing tastes in her mouth. And, of course, this is a clue that in her earlier orphanage life she was unable to manage all the sensations that came her way. Accordingly, from some of those sensations she simply disconnected. But again, what were her parents to do?

Probably **the most important agenda in such a story is to figure out a method whereby the parents can be empowered to once again "call the shots" in family** life. With an obstinate child like Stephanie, it is a significant challenge to be clever enough and strong enough to change the balance of power. Let's remember that in our parenting approach we need to adjust our parental responses to our assessment of the bonding or lack of bonding on the side of the adoptee.

Certainly, in Stephanie's case, she was at the lower end of the behavior-oriented section in the spectrum of different kinds of children. So, she probably needs to be paid one dollar for brushing her teeth. With such a reward, if she agrees to it, everybody wins. But you can see that the way in which she presents herself has to do with her own survival and with little interest in the lives of other people, especially her new parents.

Sad to say, getting one's power back as an adoptive parent, which is critically important for successful parenting, is increasingly difficult as this kind of child grows older and gets stronger. This power struggle which creates constant tension within adoptive parents and such difficult children is a battle that ultimately children will win as they become older, stronger. Parents have a window of opportunity to love, to form, to direct, to influence and to discipline such a growing up adoptee.

Angry children, and especially angry adoptees, may put on a fight the whole way towards adult life. Understandably, it is difficult to keep in mind that closeness to parents is just too frightening.

So, in such a story, as parents painfully lower their expectations of their oppositional child, it is challenging to stay neutral–to wear the "white coat" of objective parenting. But this is pretty much all that is left for them to utilize. Unless they get that power back, the entire family will live in an atmosphere that is charged with anxiety and ongoing irritation. The cohesiveness and strength of the family breaks down.

It is wise to take note of how siblings of this troublesome child will begin to resent the power that the adoptee will have. The other siblings will get less attention. They will resent the existence of this new sibling stranger. And soon they will "act out" to present their anger, or they will "act in" by withdrawing from the entire family.

So, we see that unless the balance of power changes, the family that wants to go on a vacation, and the family as individuals who want positive space to live and grow within—these family members will be paying a significant price for the presence of this stranger-adoptee.

As taxing and as challenging as such behavior-oriented parenting may be, several things should be noted about its value for both the family and the oppositional adoptee. First, we should take care to see that a regimen of rewards and consequences is, in fact, an empathic gift to the child. The child cannot create structure in her own life that works positively for her. And the structure that is offered, that is possible, with a strict regimen of do's and don'ts with corresponding rewards and consequences is a structure that makes the adoptee feel safe.

As much as it may not look this way, to really grow up, some children need a given structure for their daily lives. The structure itself is empathic because it responds to the inherent difficulties of being that little person, of being frightened by closeness with others, of being chronically angry and scared. A firm structure in which the parents have sufficient power brings inner relief to the troublesome adoptee.

In this kind of story, without the benefit of a good relationship or the helpfulness of critical thinking, creating structure in the life of the child is one way to forge a connection that the child can both relate to and appreciate. Such a message may be very important when adoptive parents experience despair and a beginning sense of hopelessness about changing things for both the adoptive family and for the adoptee.

A Counselor Perspective

The cleverness that adoptive parents may need to successfully manage and parent troubled adoptees who are giving them so much difficulty, who are not able to be obedient, who are not able to really join the family in a way that is pleasing and gratifying, may seem out of reach. This task may appear to be nearly impossible when the adoptee's resistance is so intense. These parents may feel worn down and exhausted from their efforts to find the hearts of their children.

At this point it is very wise to get help. Professional therapists, especially those who are family-oriented in their method, are usually available for assistance in this challenging story.

Better, though, if they are relinquishment-and-adoption-informed therapists. The problem here is that few therapists are informed about the dynamics of relinquishment and adoption, with useful training in managing life in an adoptive family. Therefore, asking questions about such knowledge is recommended. Nevertheless, finding a good family therapist who can assist in restoring power to parents and guiding adoptees towards healthy personal development is a wise thing to do.

*It is important to point out that **all three orientations of adoptive parenting--relationship-oriented, thinking-oriented, and behavior-oriented methods-- are always operating all the time.** They are dynamic,*

109

and adoptive parents are called upon to emphasize one or another depending on their all-important assessment of how a child relates to them. Each has its own challenges.

We have teased all three apart in order to understand and identify the parenting method that is best matched with discernment of the different capacities of the adoptee. As there is no one kind of child, here we identify different parenting methods because there is no one kind of parenting style that would always work the best. Allow me to offer an example of each.

In the case of the well-bonded and happily attached adoptee, certainly the primary parenting method would be that of trading on the relationship between parent and child and enjoying the love. Remember Sonja Joy as an example of such. Her parents need not pay her to get good grades. But there are rewards and consequences in one's environment with people all the time. The smile on the face of her parents and the warmth of physical expressions of affection reinforce good behavior.

Sonja Joy's parents would also participate in thoughtful conversation about her behavior. From a thinking-oriented perspective she would be challenged to take notice in a very cognitive way that brushing her teeth would prevent tooth decay and an unwanted trip to the dentist. She would understand that brushing our teeth matters in a way that Stephanie could not compute.

Further, in this instance with the kind of child that Sonja Joy is, rewards and consequences also inform and sometimes impact her behavior. All three methods of influence are always working in some way, but in Sonja

Joy's case the primary parenting method is a delight with warmth coming from both directions.

In the case of the cognitive-oriented child, wise parenting has a very different point of emphasis. Remember Jonathan? He was a boy who needed a primary emphasis on thinking through the wisdom of his behavior. And so, his parents were challenged day after day to be helpful by persuading him to behave in a certain fashion because the outcome of such behavior could be positive.

It was difficult for him to access the feelings of his heart, so he kept making sense of his life by thinking. His capacity to think things through was a strength for him. Although his parents certainly wanted more in terms of warmth from him and sometimes more appreciation from him, they quietly lowered their expectations of warmth returned and did the best they could with an ongoing conversation with a bright little boy who was oriented toward thinking more than feeling.

Although the primary parenting method was cognitively oriented, the blessings that these parents offered to little Jonathan were acts of care presented in the context of their love for their son. Put simply, good hard thinking was an empathic experience for a little boy who struggled to find his feelings.

And, certainly reward and consequence also was present in the Jonathan's world. It was always part of his daily reality, but it was not primary in terms of how his parents approached him. They did some good hard thinking together.

Finally, as all three different methods are engaging the child all the time, we might notice **that sometimes structuring a child's life and creating a daily experience of rewards for good behavior and consequences for bad behavior is empathic to the child.** Why? Because this reward and consequence method engages him and takes him seriously and does not ask for an emotional response along the lines of relationship nor does it seek to convince someone like Stephanie to think through the consequences of her behavior. It meets the child where the child is. The structure becomes empathic and the schedule of rewards and consequences is an act of love because it once again captures what is needed in the life of this child.

So once again, all three methods are always operating all the time. Our option is to choose the one that matches the needs of the child and emphasize that way of being with that son or that daughter.

This chapter closes with an observation that is hopefully now obvious. **Given all that we have reviewed in terms of the difficulties that relinquished and adopted children sometimes face, adoptive parents too often get a "bum rap" in terms of being blamed for the struggles of their children.**

In my 25 years of counseling experience with all the members within the circle of adoption, so often I hear testimonies of shame and embarrassment on the part of adoptive parents as they review the behavior of their children. They are judged. They are thought to be not so good at being parents and sometimes told that, yes, adopted children have problems but these children should grow up okay. Well, sometimes they do and sometimes they don't.

Adoptive parents are most often judged without understanding. The resulting shame and sense of embarrassment is so unfortunate, so unhelpful, so unfair. Much better would it be if those in judgment would instead salute the commitment that these adopting parents are making to continue on with children who really struggle to let them be their new parents.

4

Family Roles That Adoptees Play

The internal workings that go on inside as a child grows up are not the only factors that influence the development of an adoptee's personality. So far we have set up the somewhat fluid overlapping categories of relationship building, cognitive persuasion, and behavior influence as ways to understand the adoptee's experience as well as the most effective parental responses. We have teased these apart in order to carefully understand how each informs adoptive difficulties. Each is useful in understanding how and why adoptees sometimes struggle deeply with adopting their parents.

We think of these as internal theories, each focusing in different ways upon the inner life of the adoptee as an individual who is discerning how to live his or her life. Notice that when interpreting behavior in conjunction with these categories, no mention has been made of the way in which adoptees live within the networks of their family relationships.

Perhaps the behavior influence category captures some of a child's external environment in terms of rewards and consequences received within family life, but it does so while still focusing on the individual. **So far, we have thought about children only as individuals. There is so much more to see and to say!**

In this chapter, I will explain the basics of systems theory so that we have a working understanding of how one person in a family is formed in part by that family. This view of personality development focuses on the various roles that family members play.

I will also explain the psychological concepts of both *projection* and *projective identification*. Understanding these terms helps us to appreciate just what happens between parents and children in an adoptive family.

Next, we'll examine seven different roles that adoptees sometimes play in their families along with counselor-type reflections on each case presented. They are included so that you'll have some insight into how a counselor might approach them and help you choose wisely for your family.

Finally, I will make some suggestions about engaging the family system for positive change in the adoptee's life.

What Are Family Roles?

Let's wonder first about the different roles that family members play. It is never just one role. Marriage, for example, is a system of two. When couples join up, they make decisions about who is in charge of the finances and who is in charge of housecleaning and who is in charge of "bringing in the bacon," so to speak. In the past, these roles were determined by gender, but today these domestic roles are often shared; somebody's got to do each of them in one way or another.

From another perspective, our family perspective, there are other questions. We might wonder about why some children shine in happy obedience to their parents and get great grades, while other children in the same family, for some reason, need to do the opposite. They play contradictory roles.

It is as if, to fit into a family, different roles are assigned to different family members. Not consciously, of course, but nevertheless clearly assigned. As we continue to wonder "Why does he or she have to act that way?" we question why the system of the family is arranged the way it is so as to facilitate such roles and accompanying behavior.

In some cultures, for example, fathers may be assigned the role of protector, perhaps because of their physical strength. Mothers may be the maternal providers who pay attention to emotional signals and attend to the emotional exchanges within the home. A child can be seen and not heard, or labeled "our pride and joy," the future of our family, the fulfillment of dreams, an emotional drain or a financial burden.

When we acknowledge that this assignment of roles has purpose or intentions that may not be carried out consciously, we are now open to wondering how some of our ways of experiencing and relating to one another in a family are more ambiguous, complex, and multi-dimensional than we might at first have ever expected.

Our goal in this chapter is to see the relinquished and adopted child as part of something bigger than simply an individual self. This method opens the door to understanding the roles that parents and family unconsciously ask an adoptee to play. Quickly, we will see how useful this systems way of thinking is to help us understand the adoptee as a person-in-relationship, within a network of relationships.

An oft-quoted statement, familiar to professionals trained to provide care for families is this: "When one person enters a family, the entire family changes, and, when one person leaves a family, the entire family changes." Also, from the perspective of the children, "Each child in a family has different parents," referencing the reality that parents continue to evolve, to have different life experiences, especially with other siblings of the adoptee, that might inform how they parent each child as the years go by. These statements come from a systems way of thinking.

Adoptees Within Family Systems

Let's now consider the roles that adoptees sometimes play within the context of relationships in their adoptive families. Now we are no longer thinking about the adoptee as an individual, but instead moving to a different way of noticing how children grow up, a perspective that helps us see something new about adoptive development. We are seeing the adoptee as part of the web of relationships or the system of the adoptive family

This very different way of theorizing is quite helpful in getting at basic issues that adoptees face because of the way they are connected to each and every member of their adoptive families.

I'll begin with a very useful example of roles within a family. Almost all of us have probably heard about how

118

birth order informs our development as persons. Kevin Leman, author of The *New Birth Order Book: Why You Are the Way You Are*[12], captures this perspective very well. Certainly, generalizations only go so far, but his description of how birth order influences one's personality development is remarkably accurate for many of us.

For example, firstborn children are usually attentive to adults and work at pleasing them and internalizing their values. Though the parents and child are obviously not peers, these are the only folks in the system, and the child has only the parents with whom to relate until a sibling or two or more come along--if they do. As said earlier, every oldest child is at first an only child in the formation of a family (except in the case of firstborn multiple births).

"Perfectionist, reliable, conscientious, list-maker, well-organized, self-driving, natural leader, critical, serious, scholarly, logical, doesn't like surprises, and loves computers"[13]– all of these are said to describe the usual firstborn children. And these descriptors are usually quite accurate. We do not have to look very far to notice how firstborns usually play many leadership roles as they are trained by their early environment to do so. These roles are sometimes disliked and even resented by their younger siblings.

---

[12] Kevin Leman, *The New Birth Order Book: why you are the way you are*, New York: Fleming H Revell, 1998, see pages 14 – 17 for the little quiz that Lehman uses to introduce his descriptions of different birth ordering as formative.

[13] See page 15 for descriptors of firstborns, middle children, youngest child, and only children.

Similarly, Leman's descriptions of middle-born children, last-born children, and only children are rather accurate as well. This systems understanding of family relationships is useful in explaining the different roles that children then play within a family.

If birth order plays accurately as one of the influences on a child's development, **could it be that relinquishment and adoption, in a similar way, set the stage for certain roles that adoptees are to play in family life?** In this chapter we will review several possibilities, some more a blessing and, sad to say, some less a blessing and quite challenging to carry. Certainly, adoptive parents and adoptive grandparents as well as others in the extended family system also play different roles. For now, we will keep our focus on the roles that adoptees play.

These roles will sometimes overlap and look very similar to one another. Our effort here is to tease them apart as carefully as we can so that we can grasp the unique way in which the family system sometimes puts a "trip" on the adoptee. A kinder word for this manipulation would be influence.

In some sense that's what parenting is often about. We do desire to influence our children for positive outcomes in the process of their growing up, their maturation. But remember that in this chapter we think systemically, and we wonder about family members not so much as individuals with unique inner lives, but also as part of a network of connections, something bigger that forms them by setting up unique family life expectations for each family member.

We should also understand the psychological processes called projection and projective identification. Sometimes, these dynamics play in adoptive family relationships.

Projection is a psychological phenomenon whereby primitive feelings and more undeveloped emotions of parents are sometimes projected onto our children. We may see these emotions in our children, having put them there unconsciously as a defensive way of not seeing these emotions in ourselves.

We do not recognize our own anxiety, for example, but sometimes we mistakenly see that anxiety projected onto our mates or our children within our family stories. Even though that anxiety was never there in the first place, we may come home and ask, "Why are you so anxious?" when really we are the anxious ones.

When children receive such a projection from the outside, from a parent usually, and take on that assignment, taking it in as part of themselves, this we call *projective identification.*

Within this dynamic, when "you put something on me that is not me," this we call projection. When "I accept that projection--of being sorrowful, for example--and experience it as my own experience," this is projective identification. "What was not part of me but projected onto me, this I now take as part of me. I then become that which was put upon me."

Looking through a systems lens, we see quickly that the relationships between parents and children in any family may be complex and challenging to understand. Hopefully, reviewing these role-playing narratives will help us once again to appreciate and understand the challenges that the adoptees face as a significant part of the adoptive family.

An important disclaimer is critical as we move into examining these seven narratives of adoptees' family roles. Each role may sound simplistic and thereby easy to dismiss. There are many roles that we play with each other in our families. Lifting up these particular narratives for review needs to be seen amidst the reality of the many complex ways in which children relate to each other and to their parents.

Seven Family Roles Adoptees May Play

1. Carriers of Joy

The girls were always smiling, so much so that their adoptive parents, their second parents, could hardly contain their joy as they brought them over the Pacific Ocean and home to their new life in Wisconsin. Hanoek and Sera were Korean-born twins who had been left by their birth father in an alley behind the large home of well-to-do people.

Sad to say, in places like Seoul, Korea, this is a common practice. You'll read about another such child in a later chapter. First parents often reason that in such a place, plenty of money and other resources will be available to help see that these just-born little children are cared for.

From there, the girls were taken to a local police station. Then, after a foster care stay of only three months through Holts Children's Services, they were adopted by their second parents and flown with them to

America for a new and very different life. The first few nights at home all four members of this new family slept on mats on the floor because that's what people in Korea do. It was just a straw mat, but it carried each of them and their various feelings into the relief of sleep.

Eventually each of the girls found that special warm spot on their adoptive mother's and father's necks where they could feel safe and be comforted. This is so important: Skin-to-skin is a great communicator of parental affection.

When Hanoek's and Sera's adoptive parents looked at these two girls, what did they see? What did they presume these girls to be? What expectations came along on that trip across the Pacific Ocean? And what did they believe about how these twin girls would fit into their new family?

No longer a childless couple, they had immediately become a two-child family. Joy! Joy--This word best describes the fullness of heart that these parents felt as they flew back to what would become home for all four of them.

These relinquished and adopted girls grew up, keeping those smiles on their faces. As their adoptive parents observed them, they saw lots of happiness. These daughters openly expressed their curiosity about their own birth history and birth story and whatever was Korean on the bookshelves brought back from Seoul. And at times, in the midst of their questions there was real sorrow, an understandable sadness about the painful story of being left in that alley in Seoul. So, they had some grieving to do, but usually grieving takes time.

Of course, they related to each other in many ways, as family relationships are usually complex. But one dynamic was of specific importance. The twins' role in family life became that of reflecting and then carrying the joy that this family had as it came together. Adopting these girls was a real solution to the emptiness that their parents had experienced in their first eight years of marriage.

Hanoek and Sera slowly got the message that they were always supposed to be carrying the family joy as some sort of mantle set upon their shoulders. Among the many interactions between parents and children, this seemed to be the one unconscious rule for the girls to obey. There was a subtle responsibility on their part, as they experienced it, to present themselves as always joyful.

Usually they handled this challenge well, but sometimes less so. Their new parents were done being sad; the girls had hardly begun. At times, carrying such joy came to be a burden, a joyless experience for both of them.

From the perspectives of Hanoek and Sera, they had limited freedom to really be themselves. They carried their disappointments and their personal emotional injuries quietly in their bedrooms. They were greatly blessed to have each other and to express the truths of their mixed experience to each other.

Put simply, of course they were not always happy. Who is? These girls were well bonded to their parents and did not want to disappoint them. Usually, they took pleasure in pleasing them. Their achievements were many: excellent grades in school, musical talent (one playing an oboe and the other a violin), pleasant appearances, and real friendships with good peers.

All of this sounds rather wonderful, but then those troubling questions showed up every now and then: "What happened in that alley in Seoul? Could we ever find out more about our birth parents?" So, for whom was this adoption, really? How were they growing up in reference to their new family?

At times they tired of their role to carry joy. And they found that real joy for them became more and more an issue, as did defining themselves both with and without reference to the happiness that their parents nearly always expected and needed to see.

Conflict developed in their adolescent years as they each sought to define themselves as unique individuals. Less and less did they do the dance of joy to somehow fulfill the wishes of their parents. Their parents struggled to understand or accept these changes, but as they listened more carefully, they began to appreciate the feelings of their daughters. They began to see how their girls had been living so much to please them that they had had little room to become themselves, to be both joyful and sad, and to be in relationships and to be separate from relationships.

In managing this conflict, the girls slowly released themselves from the expected role that they had learned to play, and their parents were insightful of their daughter's needs. As anxiety about the girls' futures subsided, this family system was able to lift the ban on joylessness and give this story a happy ending.

It took time, but how ironic that real joy began to fill their hearts when the expectation to be joyful subsided.

A Counselor Perspective

Sometimes we are only barely aware of why we behave as we do because our complex intentions are deeply embedded. Let's notice that it took years for these girls to become aware of the role that they were expected to play in their adoptive family. In their early adolescence they needed to give themselves permission to move away from playing this role and move forward to become more authentic, more honest with themselves about the constellation of many emotions, especially sadness, that each of them carried.

In part because their parents were sensitive to the hearts of their daughters, these girls were able to move away from the role they felt expected to play and achieve a significant degree of emotional health and spiritual well-being.

Relinquishment and adoption within a family may inadvertently add a layer of learning in order to know each other as parent and child.

2. Carriers of Sadness

Usually the experience of sadness is woven into the processes of relinquishment and adoption. This is rather easy to understand but rather difficult to engage.

Managing sadness within the adoptive family system is a very important task for both parents and children. It's one of the many challenges that adoptive parents face. For adoptees who are well-connected to their hearts, sadness is part of their lives. As one adoptee put it, "Adoption is formed out of loss. Everybody loses in one way or another when it comes to adoption."

The first parents of an adoptee lose their child, relinquished or legally transferred to the new parents and to an unknown future. Usually, this is a never-ending grief for birth mothers especially. Getting over it are impossible words for healthy birth mothers who usually grieve for the rest of their lives. Birth mothers nearly always have a place in their hearts for the children whom they lost or relinquished. As one birth mother said, "There is never a day in my life that I do not think about the baby that I gave up."

The very words getting over such sadness fail to appreciate the depth of the wound that many birth parents, especially birth mothers, live with every day. They are spoken by people who do not understand, or do not want to understand, the challenges of grieving that birth parents face.

And what about the sadness of adoptive parents? They look like the winners here because they receive a child and take the child in and become the needed second parents. Because of them, these children are no longer orphans, at least on the outside. This appears to be a life-giving attachment from and for adoptive parents. So what might they be sad about?

First, some couples adopt because of struggles with infertility. In this case, these parents experience the loss of the "wished-for child." Often, they have a fantasy about what that child might have looked like because their children by adoption usually do not look like them.

Losing the so-called bloodline in one's family has its own sting of disappointment.

Grieving the wished-for child is so necessary to the emotional health of both parents and children. Unless this emotional "homework" of grieving is sufficiently accomplished, they may project this onto their children, seeing sadness in them even when it is not there.

As childhood proceeds, parents sometimes revisit sadness from their own childhood because of the way in which their children are treated on the playground. When their children are humiliated, parents feel the hurt as much as the children do.

So we see, adoptive parents do have a share in mourning the losses that come with relinquishment and adoption.

The adoptee is the one who loses the most, and, of course, has no voice in the transaction. No matter how inadequate first parents may be in terms of keeping their children and managing their lives, adoptees still lose their first parents. And when adoptees are well-connected to their own hearts, sorrow is there, even if left unexpressed.

Sometimes we can see sadness in the eyes of the orphan who is becoming son or daughter, if we look carefully. It's there because this is such a lifelong injury that adoptees must manage. Remember the moment at the airport when friends and family first met the newly adopted child? Everyone was smiling, except the child.

Consider, too, the losses of their birth story and birth family history. International relinquishment and adoption stories usually come with very little, if any, identifying information about the names and/or the whereabouts of a child's first parents. Living without access to such vital information because the record is sealed or it does not exist leaves an adoptee feeling like a partial self. This is a significant loss for adoptees to mourn. Pieces of their identity puzzle are forever missing.

Domestically, more open adoptions, usually now insisted on by birth parents, may mean that adoptees lose less because there is greater access to their birth parents, birth stories, and birth parents' family histories as well as their original birth certificates. Yet even in these circumstances, there is still a loss, even in wondering about why they were relinquished in the first place.

Usually, around the second or third grade, adoptees really figure out cognitively that they have real but ghost parents out there, "Somewhere. Over the Rainbow," as the song suggests. Like the little girl described earlier, they may be found on the playground all alone looking through that chain-link fence and wondering where these other real but ghost parents really are.

Further, when it registers with them that all is not well in the match between themselves and their newly adopted adoptive parents, this realization may be depressing. They see that their own fantasies about who their adoptive parents might be do not match up with their day-to-day reality of living with them. It becomes quite understandable that they might want to protest their adoption.

Liam's was a story often played out where systemic expectations are put upon the adoptee for the sake of the family. His role became that of carrying sadness.

Prior to his adoption, Nancy, his second mother, had gone through a series of four miscarriages, each of which was met with increasing sadness as well as anger about her inability to have a child of "her own" (a very harsh comment for any adoptee to hear--are relinquished and adopted children not their "own" as well?). Nancy's sorrow continued to pile up in all the corners of her heart.

Disheartened, Nancy and her husband, Tom, signed up with a local agency to begin the process of adopting. It is important to notice that they thought that adoption would cure their sadness and anger about their losses and infertility. These adoptive parents never really did their grieving homework around their losses by way of the miscarriages.

A plan for adoption is not a solution to the grieving around infertility. So many people think that it is, and in so doing they start out on the wrong foot, trying to skip the necessary sadness. Their hope is that the adoptive child will fill that space and fit the face, so to speak, of the child that cannot be born to them. But it doesn't work that way.

This personal suffering does not go away without getting the "infertility homework" done. By this I mean actively engaging the grief that lies in the hearts of adoptive parents who have wished--sometimes desperately--to have a child by birth.

Unfortunately, with Liam's arrival in their home, Nancy and Tom were still very sad people. Liam came to remind them of their painful struggles with infertility that they thought would go away. Alongside the usual delight of receiving a child, melancholy lay in the hearts of these adoptive parents. But how did it come about that Liam became the carrier of more sadness?

Consider Liam's experience, even as an infant, when he looked into the face of his new mother and father and did not see or experience the returning parental smile that draws our children toward us. Their offering of attachment was quite insufficient. He began his adoptive life looking at unhappy faces. He could not return his own smile. Nancy and Tom, in fact, spread the problem of carrying sorrow like a virus by now including Liam in that task. Without words or awareness, they projected their sadness and grief upon him.

Well, off to the family counselor they traveled where they explained the troubling reality that their son was so very sad. Certainly, these puzzled parents wanted their son to have a good life filled with real joy. As their family story unfolded, their insightful family therapist asked them to say more about the experience of dealing with their four miscarriages prior to Liam's adoption.

As they did so, the flood of sorrow broke and swept them back to the homework never done, the sadness never grieved. Finally, they could mourn appropriately and begin to enjoy Liam, that is, to smile at him.

By returning to the scene of the injury, they were able to do some significant mourning, weeping for the loss of those four neonates. As part of their recovery, they gave names to each of the four little persons who were never born to live. As Nancy and Tom's own personal miscarriage grief subsided, they themselves began to smile, discovering joy in their family life with Liam. Finally, they could see him without the overlay of sadness.

And funny thing, Liam's struggle with sadness, his projective identification whereby he came to own the parental projections of sorrow, began to subside as well. His role had been to carry sadness for this family and in fact lighten the load for his parents who were deeply distressed by so much sorrow in their hearts. In a way, Liam had been asked to mirror their own suffering back to them--too much for any child to do. But now the parents could manage their family sadness without putting a "trip" on Liam to carry a similar load.

With the help of the relinquishment-and-adoption-informed family therapist, this couple could now delight in the handsome face of their little boy. Now the dance could go back and forth, smiling and counter-smiling and smiling and counter-smiling in a way that began to heal the deeper sadness that had kept Liam so far away. No longer did the system of the family need Liam to be another sad person. Liam was now free to begin enjoying his life--just what his parents quite consciously wanted for him. The clock of growing up now began to tick in a different direction.

A Counselor Perspective

Within the ongoing processes of relinquishment and adoption, people are sad for so many reasons. Loss touches everyone within the circle of adoption in one way or another. And, of course, for the adoptee, the loss is the greatest. It is understandable that we seek to push sorrow away or cover it up, making believe that things don't hurt us as much as they do. When things become more painful than we can handle, it would make sense to push back from the intensity of the emotional experience of our painful reality.

But consider the difficulties that the adoptee faces without the psychological tools that are needed to notice, name, and express such loss. Infants, especially, are looking for a much needed sense of security. When they begin to mature and make sense of things cognitively around ages four or five, of course, they ask lots of honest and important questions.

But to the degree that these questions raise anxiety of some sort within adoptive parents who may wish to believe that things are just fine, such anxiety will be quickly noticed by the child. The child may learn then to bury that sorrow just as her adoptive parents do. It is no wonder that even years down the road there is loss left to be grieved.

When adoptive parents have done their "grieving homework," there will be no need to pass on such unacknowledged sorrow to their children. They will be able to identify the adoptee's real sadness, name it as such, and share it in a manner that takes the sting away, at least to some degree. Being sad with the child, joining him or her in sorrow--this is good adoptive parenting.

3. Carriers of Guilt

How would an adoptee come to be the representation of guilt, and then become a child who feels guilty (again, his projective identification) about his own life experience?

A few introductory remarks are in order here. First, we must distinguish guilt from shame. So often these words are spoken together--guilt and shame–and have come to mean almost the same thing, namely feeling badly about ourselves. But distinguishing them is important, in part because without defining them carefully, we may miss seeing something important.

Guilt, carefully defined, is the experience of feeling poorly about ourselves because of what we have done.

Put differently, guilt comes from an examination of personal behavior. Formally, guilt is a status before a law. Guilt has to do with managing right and wrong and noticing when we have crossed the line away from good behavior and, instead, acted in disobedience to our own moral code. Sometimes such behavior is simply called sin.

Shame is very different as we will see it described in our next narrative. But now let's consider the family role of carrying guilt that adoptees sometimes play.

Rena found herself pregnant at 17 and frightened by the prospect of having a fatherless child whom she was so unprepared to parent.

To begin with, she was angry at herself for the unprotected intercourse that led to this pregnancy. As well, she was angry with the young man who had fathered a child and then quickly disappeared. So it was not without struggle that she finally decided to have an abortion to solve her personal dilemma.

She thought that she would be fine, but she remembers experiencing a profound sense of guilt about the abortion. She also remembers experiencing fear and anxiety around the possibility of giving birth and becoming a parent, feelings that drove her decision. It was a very difficult choice for her to make—"the lesser of two evils," she remembers--but she made it and struggled to live with it.

After several years, Rena married with the great expectation of becoming a mother and starting her family. But such was not to be the case. She found herself unable to become pregnant. She remembers, "Once again, more guilt, as I felt punished by God for that abortion years ago. Now no one can talk me out of it." After nearly two years of infertility treatment, she and her husband made the decision to adopt as the needed way to create their family.

Guilt about her abortion years ago hung as a cloud over her life, and no matter how much delight she and her husband took in receiving their newborn adoptee, David, she knew quite well that her "abortion guilt" was not yet a thing of the past. She struggled to admit this, first of all, to herself.

Unfortunately, the role that David was eventually asked to play within this family story was that of joining Rena in the unresolved heartbreak of her ongoing guiltiness and the darkness of remorse. David became a very self-critical child who judged his own mistakes and waywardness harshly (his projective identification). He saw his own shortcomings as examples of doing things wrong all the time.

It was only with the help of an informed family therapist that self-forgiveness came along to heal Rena's guilt.

And, of course, then David no longer needed to play that role in his new family. Rena could withdraw the projection of self-critical guilt, making room for David to begin the work of becoming himself. Of course, this takes time. But finally, this family was relieved of the weight of carrying the satchel of guilt. David, the heavy-laden adoptee, could now begin to release himself from this powerful identification with his mother's guilt.

A Counselor Perspective

Guilt has been called "the gift that keeps on giving." It does have the capacity to nag as a memory of a regrettable choice, even on the back burner of our consciousness. But it is still there, and it may work in a powerful way to bring a person down to a state of ongoing depression. In such a case, the depression serves as a "lid" that may keep guilt from becoming very conscious.

The story of Rena serves as an example of a mother struggling with ongoing guilt for a choice that she made years ago. The only real solution to guilt is forgiving oneself and, on some occasions, being forgiven by others.

With David, however, she noticed that he carried a sense of guiltiness about himself even though there was no great iniquity from which he needed somehow to recover. He declared himself as guilty, yet without any real sin of which to speak. His guilt was borrowed from Rena by way of this unconscious process of projective identification.

And the only way to personal freedom for him was to withdraw that projection and become a person who was able to live within his own voice. As a child, of course, he had no choice but to live within the struggle that Rena continued to face. When she was able to forgive herself, she was able to withdraw the projection of her guilt that she had unconsciously put upon David. Of course, this takes time, sometimes even years.

This illustrates how tricky these projections can be and how susceptible adoptees may especially be to their projective identification, given the complexity of all the emotions that surround relinquishment and adoption. Parents and children play many roles in family life. Adoptees are at risk as they come to an adoptive family and become aware of their own pain and suffering around their own losses. These difficult negative feelings can be mixed up with the unfortunate projections that adoptive parents sometimes make. The informed family therapist who understands the dynamics around relinquishment and adoption can help a family sort out these difficulties and bring these struggles to rest.

4. Carriers of Shame

Shame is a significant issue in relinquishment and adoption. It is sinister. Whereas guilt has to do with the examination of personal behavior, **shame has to do with the value of one's personal being**. Guilt entails that I did bad; shame entails that I **am** bad. Guilt often leads to shame, but they are different!

Shame takes us to the core of our own self-esteem. For whatever reason, self-negation, feeling very low, believing that we do not matter or do not deserve to live, and the need to erase our personal worth--all of these are part of the painful experience of carrying shame, even to the point of becoming suicidal.

We've already seen that historically shame was such a significant variable in stories of relinquishment and adoption that often birth mothers would hide the reality of their pregnancy, often at the insistence of their families, churches, and society at large.

Many mothers who gave birth decades ago and relinquished their children (some would say "surrendered" their children) have lived on for years and years with significant regrets about allowing the fear of shame to drive their decisions and separate them from their babies. Shame was an enemy so strong that years ago, the price for unplanned, unmarried pregnancy in middle-class America was the demand by both Church and Society that birth parents should surrender their children.

Today, open adoptions are prevalent and demanded by most birth mothers, and shame plays much less a role in relinquishment and adoptive planning for all involved. For this, we can be thankful.

But still, many moments of personal shame and shaming occur in adoptive living. Shame about becoming pregnant and the social embarrassment that may come along with a surprise pregnancy depends upon how much Church and Society become more understanding and more accepting. For some, there is seldom-spoken shame about infertility. Often, for first-time adoptive parents, who sense both personal and family embarrassment, shame still lies in the background of everyday life in some stories of adopting.

Here is a story where shame became destructive, bringing suffering to all the players in the circle of adoption. This is not so much a story about projection or projective identification as it is a child's shameful birth story that accompanied her to her adoptive family home.

Karina was adopted at 18 months of age. That first year and a half of her life was spent in a children's home in Calcutta. The story given was that the children there were treated well, meaning that the facility was clean and there was food every day for Karina. But the all-important skin-to-skin contact was nearly nonexistent. She learned to live without touch as best she could, but not without great difficulty.

Like Sally Anne in our introduction, Karina immediately protested her adoption. Her experience of her new world in America was very different from her first experiences in India. Throughout her early years in her adoptive family, she struggled to feel safe near anyone because of the insecurity that filled her heart. So early in life, closeness to anyone seemed impossible for Karina.

Rather than drawing close to family members, seeking out skin contact, she would squirm and free herself from any attempt at a loving embrace. Her adoptive parents and older siblings by birth worked very hard to connect with her. But she fought them off.

When Karina was about four and a half, her adoptive parents told her the tragic story of her beginning: Several days after her birth, her first mother brought her to a river intending to take Karina's life under the waters of her shame. Just in time, Karina's birth father stopped her and took Karina to the safety of that Calcutta orphanage. Unfortunately, but understandably, Karina took that story to heart in a painful self-defeating way. Think of it: What is it like to learn that your mother's first impulse upon your birth was to bring you to the waters of your death? Should they have ever told her? Well, truth matters.

In her ongoing years of development, Karina carried painful and powerful images of her birth mother preparing to take Karina's life and probably her own life as a shamed young woman. These mental images stayed with her well into her adoptive life in America.

They formed her negatively in such a way that the very basis of her personal self-esteem was wanting--we might say under the water of Karina's self-judgment. Sometimes her negative behavior invited her adoptive parents to reinforce her negative self-belief. She would interpret their irritation and their anger at her behavior as more "truth" that shame should be her middle name.

Ultimately, this was a story about shame in living, about her divided heart towards her own life and her own death. Recalling that image of her birth mother's story was a very significant challenge for Karina.

In her adolescence, she continued her fight, ultimately against herself, acting out within her adoptive family. She refused to obey any curfew. She arranged conflict, with fight after fight, in order to successfully stay away from everyone. In misbehaving, she would actually press her parents once again to confirm this tragic truth about her beginnings, that she was a child without value, not worthy to live.

It was only years later, when she gave birth to her own first child, that Katrina could begin to release that painful birth mother image and find positive meaning in the experience of attaching to her own little girl. All of this, of course, was a great and wonderful surprise, a blessing for Karina.

Shame is the sense of not mattering to anyone, it comes with the inherent abandonment of the orphan. Karina was the carrier of the shame put upon her, in this case, not by projection from this family, but lent to her by her birth mother and the story of her moment by the river. Her arrival in this family at 18 months of age was an experience of considerable chaos and difficulty; at times Karina fought hard against the very care that could restore her.

She would disallow and push back against the very arms and hands that sought to hold her. Her difficult behavior may have been one way to convince them of her lack of worth.

The role that Karina played in her adoptive family was certainly that of the family troublemaker. Yet at deeper level, she played the role of recipient of her family's extended care. This family wanted to care beyond its usual biological family boundaries. And they did so well, absorbing her anger and struggling to help her manage her life. Then came her pregnancy, an experience that moved her deeply, as she finally learned to love as well as to begin hesitantly to trust the love of her adoptive family members.

A Counselor Perspective

Whenever one person enters a family or one person leaves a family, there is a significant shift in the way in which the family "retunes" itself. When Karina joined her adoptive family, she brought with her deep shame about her own existence. When she learned her story, of course, it was a very painful narrative for her to "hold" within herself. In those early years, she struggled with her reality that on the day she was born she was dispensable to her birth mother. However, within this family, Karina could be real about her story, her own narrative about her painful beginning in life. Over her developing years, this served as an important corrective for her view of herself.

Besides being a carrier of family shame, the role that Karina brought to play within her adoptive family might also be called that of a family challenge and a redeeming project of sorts. This family was able to deliver the consistent touch, the attentive care that Karina needed, so that she could begin to move beyond feeling shame for her very existence.

Then, after years and years and as troubled as she still was, when Karina gave birth to a little girl, she could finally begin to release her negative identity, her personal experience of shame, and move beyond it. She has found meaning in her life as a parent. Now she matters as both person and mother, and the demon of shame has been relinquished to some degree, pushed away and held at a greater distance. Finally, Karina can cry not only tears of sorrow but also tears of joy.

A sense of shame is usually part of an adoptee's self-experience.

142

In the early years of the 20th century the birth certificate of a so-called "illegitimate child" was sometimes stamped with that title, or, even the word "bastard", and when an amended birth certificate was presented at adoption, the words illegitimate or bastard were taken away. It should be remembered that **there is no such thing as an illegitimate child.**

We notice how shame was projected onto the innocent child, labeled with this pejorative term (a ready-made projection), in an insensitive and unjust fashion. It seems contradictory that at a time when adoption practice supposedly centered on minimizing the shame for all the members of the adoption circle, both Church and Society reinforced powerful condemnations of unwed mothers and so-called "bastard" children.

5. Carriers of Fear and Anxiety

Relinquishment and adoption usually, understandably, precipitate significant changes in family life, and change always creates anxiety.

Young Silas has a story of fear. He remembers with good detail what it was like for him and his younger sister, who was also relinquished and adopted, to walk through the airport during their childhood family excursions. Silas recalls the way in which his adoptive mother was holding his hand, sometimes so tightly that it was on the edge of pain. Silas would say, "Ouch!" and his mother would immediately soften her grip. He wondered about why that always happened in airports.

This specific adoptive mother, Caroline, with her husband, Dan, had gone through a good deal of difficulty prior to adopting Silas and his sister, Maria. In their case, raising nearly $30,000 for adoption expenses was a considerable hardship as she and her husband saved up to make these adoptions possible. And the two of them, as a married couple, had had differences about the decision to adopt these two relinquished children. Caroline was more interested in adoption than her husband was.

As often was the case in years gone by, this was a closed adoption meaning that there would be no communication, no interaction at all between adopted children and their individual birth mothers. (Birth fathers weren't mentioned then.) These agreements called "one-way ratchet" provisions meant that the birth parents promised to never interfere with the adoptive family; the adoptive parents promised nothing in return to the birth parents.

This kind of legal silence and secrecy quickly becomes the seed bed of fear and anxiety around adoption. Caroline had lived with both excitement and apprehension prior to the adoptions of their two children. She found herself worried day after day about the possibility of never having children by birth. Even when considering that reality, tears came to her eyes. And then, what would these adoptive children be like? Could she love them "as if they were her own"?–again, a very difficult thing for any adoptee to hear. These words should never be spoken. Nevertheless, this becomes a real question to be addressed. And Caroline was no different.

She had often heard that "adopted children have problems." (A correction here would be to say that "relinquished children have problems". And why wouldn't they, given the developmental challenges before them?) This societal assessment of adoptees increased her nervousness about her children's mental health. So, lots to think about.

All these issues raised her anxiety especially while walking through the airport. It was then that her greatest fear surfaced, hardly conscious, that the birth parents of her children might return and take them back. She feared losing these children whom she loved so much.

Caroline's fantasy about the birth parents "stealing her children back" is not uncommon, especially in closed adoptions. It is only when adoptive parents are able to know the birth parents as real people that such fear and anxieties subside.

So now we have a sense about why Caroline held on to those hands so tightly as they strolled through the airport terminal. She was fearful that someone in that crowd of people might take her children, and they would be lost to her forever.

What an incredibly painful way for this adoptive mother to live, feeling insufficiently entitled to her own children. She did not fully "own" them as a mother. Somehow the connection with her children always felt partial.

When adoptive parents struggle to feel fully entitled to their sons and daughters, they may become overprotective and anxious in ways that are seldom conscious, and never helpful.

Because of projective identification with his mother, Silas himself saw the world as a frightening, dangerous place to inhabit. Silas and his sister developed their own difficulties with separation and the challenges of becoming independent.

The anxiety that they faced, labeled "separation anxieties" by most everybody, is not that uncommon for adoptees. From their side of this dynamic of managing anxiety, adoptees often struggle with leaving home, going to college, separating from their adoptive family and being on their own. The losses that adoptees have already incurred stack up along with the fear of the possible loss of these, their second parents.

Adoptees never like losing people or saying goodbye. In this story, the role that both adoptees played was to join their adoptive family and also join their mother especially in carrying the heavy weight of the fear and the anxiety that sometimes come along with the experience of adopting and of being adopted. Years later, when Silas understood what his mother was experiencing and became empathic with her deeply embedded fears and anxieties, he could gently differentiate himself from Mom and Dad.

A Counselor Perspective

In different ways adoptees are set up to take on the roles that they play in their new adoptive families. Depending on their age at adoption, in one way or another, they have known their own fears and sorrows and anxieties. Contrary to the wishes of many adoptive parents, adoptees come to their homes with narratives already written that carry significant personal negatives about change. We might wonder how many little "nerves" have been cut between their heads and their hearts, so to speak.

To survive emotionally, sometimes children will "disconnect from their own hearts" when the challenges they face are overwhelming to manage at an early age. Yet these connections of the heart are essential for children to grow up and become emotionally healthy adults. Otherwise, and this is our great fear, if too many nerves are cut, their hearts may turn to stone.

6. Replacement Children

In years past it was not uncommon for a child to be named after a deceased sibling or a deceased close relative. Few of us need to look very far back to grandparents and generations of ancestors to hear how certain names were carried forward to babies. These children had an invisible "in memory of" pasted on their foreheads as part of their personal identity.

This practice may have been a way to honor the memory of those deceased who had meant much within the family circle, especially if that person were a deceased brother or sister. However, some people who learned the history of their names felt ambivalent about being given a name to replace someone else.

With relinquishment and adoption, **adoptees at times have become aware that in some way they are replacing someone else, perhaps another child never to be born.** That child, of course, was the wished-for baby that would have come to this family by way of genetic line through pregnancy and birth. As a

147

replacement they would be seen under the long shadow of someone else.

As odd as it may sound, **sometimes adoptees feel like they are supposed to be that somebody else, that wished-for child by birth. T**his adoptive experience would disavow them of the opportunity to be discovered for who they really are. Instead, they find themselves being formed by their parents in the image of another.

Sergei and Gina were so delighted when news came that a newborn girl would soon become part of their family by way of adoption. The baby room had been painted in pink and white. The chest of drawers stood ready, carefully bolted to the wall, filled with little outfits that brought smiles to many faces at the baby shower several weeks earlier.

Now all the excitement and pleasure that comes with receiving that child took focus as they packed up and drove to the local adoption agency where both birth parents sat with their little girl. One baby, four parents. Both moms were weeping.

The first parents sat quietly, she 15, he 17. She looked so sad, appropriately so; he was expressionless, barely in the room and staring out the window. Because this was to be a relatively open adoption, these first parents knew that they would see their baby every now and then and stay connected in some way. It made the decision to relinquish at least a bit more tolerable.

In an effort of kindness, Sergei and Gina restrained themselves as best they could from expressing their incredible delight about finally becoming parents. This task was difficult and awkward, but they were well aware of the struggle that especially the young mother had with letting go of this just three-days-old little girl. They held back their joy, speaking appreciation and saying that they would keep in touch and mail pictures every now and then.

They promised that come Thanksgiving, they would all meet so that this young couple could see their relinquished child. They could watch and take notice as this little girl grew up. This was one of the conditions that both birth parents required in exchange for their child, and Sergei and Gina were quite happy to agree.

Now, after months had gone by, both adoptive parents found themselves talking about how their "own" child would have been. They wondered what she, their fantasy daughter by birth, would have looked like, especially as their new daughter, Sylvia, looked quite different from them. She was pretty, but she was certainly someone else.

They began to see, as mentioned before, that adoption does not solve the problems of infertility. Loss, sadness, and disappointment are inevitable. Gina especially was surprised with her sadness and saw that the challenge of mourning the loss of that fantasy daughter was still before them.

The delight of adopting a child can be so powerful that the parents overlook or ignore the grieving that sometimes needs to be done. Wishes die hard. Sometimes adoptive parents try to skip their sadness as well as their deep-seated disappointments, but that never really works. One major point of this chapter is that whatever we do not acknowledge in ourselves, we may ask our children to carry. This is the projection of unresolved distress that adoptive parents may sometimes put upon their children.

A Counselor Perspective

We parents know quite well how important it is for us to participate in the formation of our children. We think about "instilling values" as a primary parental challenge. We seek to manipulate with rewards and consequences so that certain good behaviors result. In many ways we would like them to be like us, carrying our own world views, and behaving in ways that make family life enjoyable. But this challenge of personal formation may sometimes hit a rocky road when an adoptee feels like he or she should be somebody else.

This quandary understandably leads to confusion on the part of the child. "Who am I?" is the first question, and it is held in tension with the second question "Who was I supposed to be?"

Identity formation can be very complicated for an adoptee. Just as Simon struggled to become himself, so it is with many adoptees who are challenged to figure out their own identities, often with some of the pieces to the puzzle simply missing. Knowing their own stories, especially the why of relinquishment stories, is very helpful in this process of personal formation.

Adoptive parents do well to work at discovering their children as much as forming them. Discovery has to do with learning all those details about birth story and birth family history. Discovery means sorting out skills, athletic abilities, musical talent, areas of interest, and whatever else relinquished and adopted children bring to the family table. Discovery means adoptive parents see and affirm who their children are in terms of the genetic blueprint that gives them many unique qualities, even when they may not fit into the intended family design.

7. Carriers of Perfection

For some people an A-minus is just not good enough. This is true across sectors of a community, but our focus here is on trying to understand why and how this drive to perfection might haunt adoptees.

Rather than protest and argue and spend so much energy in creating and managing family conflict, some children go the opposite route and become carefully focused on never making a single mistake. This kind of behavior is at the extreme end of the "good adoptee" that Betty Jean Lifton describes in her book, *Lost and Found*.[14] This child is very invested in the role of carrying perfection for her family.

Although it is certainly impossible, nevertheless, some adoptees become compulsive about perfect performance. Their own voice, their true voice, is perceptibly absent, carefully hidden. Striving to be perfect is one way to control one's environment, but it may mean the loss of soul in the life of a child.

Sometimes perfection in everything, being "the good adoptee," becomes the role played within the adoptive

---

[14] See Chapter 9 of the book, "Good Adoptee- Bad Adoptee," in which Lifton explains how either position may be a carefully constructed defense against the vulnerability of being the "real adoptee" or the real self of the child. For our purposes, from a systems perspective, being the good adoptee serves a role within the system of the adoptive family whereby the family makes the unconscious request for this role to be played.

family. Sometimes perfectionism is shown in how one dresses and presents himself. "Looking good" offers an attractive outward appearance, but there is so much more going on that is covered over by a stylish presentation. An A or A-plus is usually the only acceptable grade. Remember that, within relinquishment and adoption, carrying the load of perfection serves to express the hope of a guarantee against ever being relinquished again.

Autumn serves as an example. She was relinquished to the local social service authorities and adopted by a couple that was very excited to receive her. Autumn was coming to her adoptive family from a tragically broken inner-city family where abuse and neglect were part of her story. Her way of finding security in this second family was to "be perfect in every way." Autumn was so very good, never a problem in her relations, which were for the most part superficial, and, of course, she acted like a child who never needed much attention.

From a very young age she was "on her own." But children should never be "on their own." **All of us need parents, people that are older and stronger than children, in order to grow up.**

Autumn was never a problem for anyone. This served as an easy way for her to be in this family. Never a problem. She did not appear to be needy in terms of friendships. It was almost as if a glass wall were around her whereby she could be seen and noticed, but never close-up. She was certainly guaranteeing that she would not once again be taken away.

Even as a teenager, Autumn's room was perfectly clean and thoughtfully organized. Never dirty clothing on the floor. Never a piece of pizza left on a paper plate. Not even a smudge on the neatly dressed window. All her clothes were carefully organized and hung in her closet by order of color and size on white plastic clothes hangers. Her world was so ordered that, in her room, she knew that she was in charge.

Understandably, although her parents were puzzled by her perfectionistic tendencies, they took great delight and were proud around her successes. Autumn stood out as a stellar student, a winning athlete, and an accomplished pianist. This was very satisfying to these parents who had felt so defective when their own infertility became clear. Her adoptive parents experienced great relief in the success of their daughter and saw this as a wonderful blessing.

In Autumn's story, there was no clear sign of distress. **But, the real genuine Autumn hardly ever saw the light of day**. Only in her diary did words hint at her real truth. She never felt safe with people, but she did not know why. She could not deal with living in a sloppy world, but she did not know why. She could not really trust her friends, much less her parents, but she did not know why. All Autumn knew was that she had to play it safe, keeping her own environment as perfect as it could be.

Unfortunately, in a story like Autumn's, an explanation of her behavior does little to change her behavior. (Insight on its own is not curative.) She would continue to "work out her salvation" by carrying her load of perfectionism. Of course, this turns out to be a tragic story if no intervention is sufficient to let her true voice be heard, to open that space in herself where she carefully protects her fears and anxieties.

In contrast, her younger relinquished and adopted brother, Sam, paved the way for ongoing conflict with their adoptive parents. He was quite conscious of how different he looked from his parents as well as his sister, Autumn. His parents sometimes were exhausted, emotionally spent, by their efforts to not only manage Sam's oppositional behavior, but also seek as best they could to appreciate the struggles of his relinquished heart. Sam was certainly hurting but not able to admit it. He played the role of the "bad adoptee" in such a way that he embarrassed his parents and was unable to let them come close. Keeping his distance worked for Sam.

Autumn played the role of the "good adoptee" in such a fashion that they had a child of whom they truly could be proud. Her parents felt relief from their worries. Sam taught them difficult things about the behavior of relinquished and adopted children. So, for Autumn to be so perfect worked, not only as a defense against her fear of another relinquishment but also as a "family solution" to the need of the family system to have a stellar family member, the pride of mother and father and the quarreling sibling partner, Sam.

Certainly, informed professional help may be important here. But for our purposes, we can see how parents' issues around relinquishment and adoption sometimes set the stage for the pursuit of perfection in ways that may derail adoptees like Autumn from living the nourishing life that would have been available to her.

A Counselor Perspective

When people find themselves compulsive about making all things perfect, there is little room for them to breathe fresh air and enjoy their lives. Living with the compulsion to "be perfect in every way" leaves a person anxious and even fearful about the messiness of living in relationship to others. We might imagine what it is like to look in every direction, vigilantly scanning the room to make sure that things are in order as best they can be. Perfectionism becomes a prison and one's heart is squeezed so much that the vulnerability that comes with healthy relationships is unavailable.

Precisely here, with stories like those of Autumn, adoptive parents are often at a loss as to how they might attach to a child who pushes them away. The compulsion to be perfect stands in the way of any healthy relationship. Usually professional help is needed to break through the rather thick walls that stand around someone like Autumn.

An insightful family therapist could assist in helping adoptive parents to frame their expectations differently, learning that the true person of the child can be hidden behind good behavior to the extent that she is not known. Equally important is to assist the child to learn that she need not worry about once again being relinquished. Stating this and reinforcing the idea of permanence, taking on the elephant in the room, so to speak, could be the beginning of a healthier family life.

A wiser family life would cohere because of the care that comes along with personal vulnerability. This is a significant challenge for adoptive parents, but, nevertheless, speaking to the issue is the way to begin.

Engaging the Adoptive Family for Change

Without doubt, the most important initiative that adoptive parents can take is to ask themselves the hard questions around the relinquishment and adoption of their children.

They may have grieving to do. Historically, adoption was seen as a last chance to have a family. The possible anger and the possible sadness around infertility is a profound challenge to many would-be adoptive parents who choose to adopt in order to create a family. Mourning our losses is so painful that sometimes it is just too hard to face, and we keep it away. This is understandable; however, it sets up a troublesome adoption.

Many adoptive parents think that somehow adoption is a solution. What a dangerous thing to think! Not at all. Making believe that adopting a child takes away the grief of losing the child by birth never born is an end run around the necessary grieving that needs to be done. Grief ungrieved is always a barrier to a healthy relationship and is always acted out in one way or another. And it is always the case that, in one way or another, the adoptee pays the price.

Remember the tragic family role of being the "replacement child". That dynamic is first set in motion when an adoptive parent fails to grieve the loss of that phantom child-by-birth and attempts to create the adoptee in the image of the baby never born.

Obviously, it would be much better for these adoptive parents to be sad for a while and to be angry for a while, facing the losses of their dreams about having the usual nuclear family before proceeding with adopting. Seeing an informed family therapist is probably the best way to facilitate this hardball grieving homework. The main reason I recommend this is that much of our personal turmoil as parents is not quite conscious. We can't quite see ourselves in the mirror of objectivity.

Accordingly, adoptive parents need to be persistently mindful of the fact that they will naturally and inevitably enact those dimensions of themselves that remain unresolved. They must be thoughtful about how histories repeat themselves, how things are carried forward unconsciously, how people sometimes enlist others to carry emotions and to play roles.

The work involves a deepening appreciation of the complexity of emotional life, of relationships, of how we convey thoughts and feelings and "truths" unconsciously as well as consciously. Becoming aware, being able to see ourselves more honestly, and doing the hard work of experiencing that anger and sadness that may hook us is sometimes impossible to do by ourselves. We all have blind spots.

Remember that shame-based parental narrative wherein the child is called to represent the shame of premarital pregnancy or infertility? It is so unfair to the child born of other parents to now live in the shadow of the unresolved struggles of his or her new parents. For any adoptee to be tagged with the destructive label of "family shame" is tragic.

157

All of us have demons that we must wrestle to the ground and defeat; otherwise, in one way or another, we are held hostage by them. It would be wonderful if we could somehow quickly remove the often less than conscious "trips" that we place on our children. But changes happen slowly, over time, with concerted effort. None of us works through our past completely, and so our task is not to re-enact it, but to develop habits and practices that contribute to revising it.

In the midst of these revisions, in the midst of parenting, adoptive fathers and mothers do well to seek to understand unconscious communication and patterns of relating with their children. We become more alert to their recurrence, to our chagrin, and then learn to address them as soon as we possibly can.

A second recommendation that assists in creating change in family narratives is that of simply asking the question. And the question is always, first of all, "What roles do each of us play in our family systems?" A system is a network of relationships and interactions in which different roles are unconsciously assigned to different family members, depending on what the system needs in order to function. Simply asking the role-play question may be the beginning of a vital awareness of how adoptees may be seen and managed in unfair, destructive ways.

Just as oldest children usually adapt in a primary way to the wishes of their parents and other adults, relinquished and adopted children may serve certain roles in the adoptive family that help families function, but in less than healthy ways. For example, being asked to join one's parents in carrying sadness so that these parents have partners in pain is unhealthy and, also, unjust.

Being asked to serve as a replacement for another child is unfair, leaving no room for that adoptee to become his or her real self. Being put upon to display the family symbol of perfection robs the adoptee of the freedom to make mistakes.

Parenting in general is challenging. In the case of relinquishment and adoption, things become more complex and messy in ways that adoptive parents are seldom prepared to address.

It is often said that we want to "lift the spirits of our children" so that they live their lives in a positive, successful way. Lifting those spirits entails taking away whatever depresses those spirits destructively, including family roles.

One thing to notice here is that in so doing, adoptive parents may be more involved in discovering their children–who they are, how they operate, what they think, how they feel–than forming them in the image of others. An adoptive parent cannot say that his or her child "looks like mom" or "has his father's eyes" or "is athletic like Uncle George." All the usual genetic connectors are missing in the adoptive narrative, so adoptees do indeed need to be discovered in a way that parents by birth seldom consider.

Once again, simply asking the question of what roles adoptees may be asked to play in adoptive families may serve as the beginning of that pathway of discovery.

A third consideration regarding effective parenting from a systems perspective has to do with a shift in emphasis from empathy to power as the most useful tool of change. This might sound contradictory to what you'd think, but please stay with me. Let's consider the story of Simon, who was the victim of the termination of rights of his parents by birth. Both his mother and father were drug addicted and unable to parent. Because these legal matters took up so much time, as they usually do, Simon spent his first four months in substandard foster care after which he was adopted by his new parents.

Simon was a guarded and distant infant. He did not find that warm skin-to-skin spot on his adoptive mother's neck. Fear stops closeness. And it appeared that Simon was fearful in one way or another of being close to his new parents. To use empathy as our primary tool of change now that Simon is ten, we would open an individual conversation with Simon, as well as with his parents about how difficult it was to get along.

We briefly discussed empathy earlier. To review, it means entering the life of another in such a way that we begin to understand what it is like to be that other person. Empathy, in a sense, has to do with leaving ourselves and struggling to appreciate what different family members are experiencing as they relate to each other. The underlying theory is that when a person is understood, deeply understood, transformation happens. An emotional bond is formed and healthier life experience results.

From a systems perspective, transformation occurs not so much because of any individual in a family being understood, but because power is used differently. We might think of empathy in the broader sense of being empathic with the entire family and asking the questions around what this family needs so that this family understands itself more enough to change. And that takes time.

For our purposes, power might be thought about as the capacity to significantly influence another person by way of strength in the family system. Within a given family system, there is usually one person who has the most power over the others. When this person is the adoptee, the entire family is held hostage by the strength of his or her behavior. Adoptive parents may choose not to go out to eat at a restaurant because Simon will yell and scream and create a fuss if he does not get whatever he wants. Everyone else suffers because Simon is the strongest person in the family, even at age ten.

In this case the family is best assisted by taking Simon's power away. For example, Simon and his father head off to a nearby outdoor hot dog stand where Simon can act out in the parking lot if he needs to do so. The rest of the family goes to the restaurant for the food that they enjoy, relaxing in peace and in quiet. Simon would then have lost some of his destructive power. Limiting Simon's power to manipulate his family is empathic to the family as a whole.

This suggestion of managing power within the family in a more empathic manner intends to empower parents to become stronger than their ten-year-old son. Once adoptive parents are empowered, they can use that strength to positively manipulate the adoptee. As is often said, children need parents to grow up well. And in this discussion, they need parents who are stronger than they are in terms of guiding the family process of relating to each other. These parents become able to enforce both rewards and consequences for the behavior of children who may be deeply protesting their adoptions.

To rephrase: **sometimes it is may not be empathic to the family as a whole if we are only empathic to one individual within the family.** As we explored in chapter three, listening reflectively and offering emotional care and support to children who are cut off emotionally from their adoptive families will do little good if the child is not able to engage such an attempt at attachment. Instead, what is important is seeing the needs of the family in terms of the need for change among family members. And this change often comes from changes in the power structures of the family.

One simple example serves to make this point. In his teen years, Simon got into daily conflict with his mother, whose efforts to make sure his homework got done were overbearing. Simon and his mother became enemies, each intent on getting his or her way. This family deadlock seemed unresolvable. Empathic responses to each were of little use in terms of resolving this conflict. However, what roles were family members playing? This was the most important question as it looked in a different direction for the help that was needed.

It became clear that Simon's father was only passively involved in managing him. He seemed to be most comfortable sitting on the sidelines, leaving Simon's mother to run this family's daily life. The informed family therapist asked that for the next week, before they met again, Simon's mother was to act only as Simon's friend–

as an interested, supportive family member. Understandably, taking away her effort to control what was going on made her quite uncomfortable.

On the other hand, Simon's father was asked to do all the disciplining as well as all the supervision of Simon's homework. Of course, this made him quite uncomfortable, too, as now he was front and center, the agent of accountability with his son. Simon was to call him at work throughout the day whenever he needed permission for something or help with homework. Simon's dad was now in charge and, with a lump in his throat, he accepted his assignment.

The role change for both parents was significant and incongruous with their given personalities. But they each made the attempt. They did marginally well. Simon's conflict with his mother subsided as he now looked to his father, the easier-going parent, for his direction.

When one person enters a family, an adoptee for example, the entire family changes in some way. Authority and responsibility shift. Examining the roles that family members play, especially in adoptive families, brings to light both the useful as well as the problematic ways in which these members relate to each other. For this reason, shifting the power balance in a family is usually the most effective way to change a child's negative behavior. As family roles change and children adapt to new variables, new opportunities occur for them to find a way to relate and to live more successfully.

Fourth and finally, adoptive parents must challenge themselves to "see" their children differently. With new eyes, not shielded or distorted by preconceived expectations, adoptive parents can look again and wonder what's different from what they may have planned that child to be. They can see with different eyes the significant contrasts that may exist between their wish and the reality of each little boy and girl. To minimize these differences or to even deny them is to not "see" the child for who the child really is.

Loving the child in fantasy is so "off" and loving the real child is so "on" in terms of facilitating a strong attachment to that child. Despite his passive style, Simon's father could better understand his son's struggles as he could relate to Simon's struggles with his anxious wife.

Simon's father could see Simon more accurately as a struggling boy in contrast to his mother's view of him as simply stubborn and unwilling to comply. When Simon realized that his father understood him better, some of his protest began to subside.

This family had shifted enough of its power balances that Simon gained room to become the young man that he truly wanted and needed to be. He was able to "speak more from inside his own voice." Such is the power of the family for good.

5

It's Time to Talk More about Empathy

When adoptive parents sit back for moment and wonder what might be the most important variable in the care of their children, the answer still has to do with empathy. Even in rather extreme circumstances where bonding from the side of the child seems nearly nonexistent, **understanding the child's inner life experience becomes critical to some success in both bonding to a parent and attachment to that daughter or son.**

To be perfectly clear, the usual methods of parenting, as described in chapter 3, even where the emphasis is on the structure of rewards and consequences, may sometimes nevertheless fail.

Adoptees who appear unable to bond sufficiently with their parents need to be parented differently. This chapter intends to demonstrate how empathy alongside the more usual parenting methods become critically important in establishing some form of relational health with the heart of the frightened child.

Accordingly, in this chapter let's spend more time in conversation about the nature of empathy, especially relating to the challenges that adoptive parents sometimes face.

We begin with the story about one of those very difficult adoptees who presently has enough power to turn living upside down in the adoptive home. We will then use the story as a springboard for discussion in our attempt to deepen adoptive parents' understanding of empathy and its power to facilitate healing between child and parent.

Hopefully, at the chapter's end, adoptive parents will have a deeper understanding of what it means to be empathic with their children.

Abigail, running out of the house, found a brick and threw it right through the kitchen window of the family's new home. Although she was only ten years old, she had the muscle to throw it hard. It crashed onto the kitchen floor with shards of glass all around.

She was just so angry, so tired of being pushed to do her fourth-grade math lessons, so tired that out to the backyard she ran in a fit of rage, yelling back over her shoulder, "I hate math. I hate my math teacher. And I hate you!"

All the best efforts to be a good parent, all the energy and attention that Jean, her adoptive mother, had offered to Abigail daily, all the prayers that she sent sky high asking God to soften the heart of her daughter–all this felt as if it were for naught.

The neighbors next door saw the whole thing happen. They shook their heads, without much understanding, of course, and quietly whispered to each other that Abigail was more than a handful.

The $50 that it cost to replace the glass and repair the window frame came right out of Abigail's piggy bank, money from friends and grandparents for her recent birthday. And she was angry about that too. Why should she have to pay? Her mother was the one that made her so angry. No self-blame for Abigail; obviously, her mother was at fault for insisting that she sit at the kitchen table until the math homework was done. As usual, she was projecting blame onto somebody else.

Once again, her adoptive mother took it on the chin. Jean was getting tired, too, of Abigail's ongoing opposition to whatever her mom would request. The teachers at school, however, reported that Abigail generally behaved well in class. Although rather controlling of other girls, Abigail played pretty well at recess. Her grades were inconsistent, but she had no problems in her classroom. And so, the report of such disruptive yelling and screaming and throwing a brick really surprised her fourth-grade teacher. What could her parents, Johnny and Jean, make of this puzzling contrast?

No one seemed to have the answers, and the battle at home went on and on, making everyone else in the family irritated and tired. Her two siblings, children by birth to this family, were Matthew, age 14, and Julie, age 12. Matthew maintained simple disinterest in Abigail's behavior. He experienced her as a nuisance and just stayed out of her way.

But Julie, only two years older, experienced an ongoing battle of sibling rivalry. Julie did her best to be gracious to her new younger sister. She stretched a long way to be tolerant of the ways Abigail bugged her. For instance, Abigail would take her makeup, then lie about lifting it off the dresser in Julie's room. If Julie had something missing, she would walk to Abigail's room and retrieve her stuff because that's where it usually was. And, of course, Abigail felt no guilt about lying.

At school she made up stories about Julie that put Julie in a bad light, if only for a moment, so that Abigail could become queen for the day. Abigail's defiant behavior wore on Julie, and so she became increasingly ambivalent about relating to her younger sister. Sometimes she wished that Abigail were gone.

This family of four initially never expected these kinds of struggles with Abigail. Quite naïvely, Johnny and Jean had anticipated the opposite. They thought that this little girl, adopted at two years of age, would be happy to have a home of her own. As they went through the process of adoption, they looked forward to the pleasure of loving and being loved by another child.

And so, as Abigail grew up, seemingly filled with internal struggles, they, along with Matthew and Julie, were surprised and disappointed. In eight years, the family had changed so much. The peace and calm that the four of them had come to know was a long-ago memory.

Instead, Abigail had become the central focus of the family. Each family member responded in different ways to the push/pull dynamic as they sought to build a relationship with her. Sometimes she was quite friendly and playful. But really, she was only happy when she got her way.

She had learned some powerful maneuvers, especially screaming, that gave her power and prominence in whatever the family might wish to be or do. In the summer time, when Abigail wanted to go to the nearby playground, usually Jean or Julie went along. If, for some reason, neither was available, Abigail would take them on by having a fit, throwing things and screaming whatever negative thought she might have in their direction.

Remembering that classic story of Humpty Dumpty, well, "All the king's horses and all the king's men could not put Abigail together again." **Johnny and Jean were at a loss in terms of what to do.**

Abigail's birth history is important to know. She was one of many babies adopted from Guatemala before that country shut down international adoptions because of its graft and corruption. Women at that time were having babies in order to relinquish them for money.

The adoption agency that Johnny and Jean employed gave them the name of both the birth mother and the village where Abigail began her life. For reasons unknown, Abigail had been quickly placed, at about three months of age, in an orphanage that arranged international adoptions. Johnny and Jean were told that her orphanage was a good one, meaning there was food every day and good orphanage workers who regularly bathed the children.

But one thing stuck out in the orphanage report. **Orphanage workers were instructed not to respond to crying babies so as to "toughen them up for life."** This was a painful thing for Johnny and Jean to hear. Under this philosophy of such non-care, children would not get the skin contact so necessary to feel truly alive. Of course, these children began life with a significant disadvantage in their relational capacities. Sad to say, this way of thinking is common with international adoptions.

Simply put, Johnny and Jean had no idea what was coming because of such a difficult developmental history. **No map existed for such parenting challenges.**

Abigail's resistance to closeness changed very little between ages two and ten. In fact, her protest against letting Johnny and Jean be her parents seemed to grow stronger as each year went by. They felt like they were going it alone without sufficient education in matters of attachment or sufficient support from others who might not only care but also help them to think through best parenting practices.

These parents had often heard that talking and listening with the child may be most successful when speaking back to the feelings of the child. This is active listening, attending to a child as carefully as possible by noticing the emotions between the words and reflecting those emotions back to that child. Over and over they made use of this practice, but with very limited success.

They would tell Abigail that they understood how frustrated or angry or sad she might feel. This effort at being empathic one-to-one with Abigail is an example of empathy in the narrow sense. It had limited success because Abigail had so carefully pushed away such difficult and hurtful emotions that she herself could not tap them or discuss them as she related to her adoptive parents.

In the wider sense of empathy, Johnny and Jean paid attention to the outside turmoil of Abigail's life by noticing her struggles with her siblings by adoption as well as her controlling behaviors with other students and superficial friends. Noticing and reflecting the setting for her life would help them understand some of her frustrations.

She would never be a child--by--birth in this family. She needed her anger to keep people away as intimate relationships were so frightening to her. For Abigail, survival meant keeping up her guard and carefully keeping her distance.

Thinking more globally about empathy, we might notice the ways in which neither Church nor Society have been empathic with the suffering of relinquished and adopted children like Abigail. As we discussed in Chapter 2, even in recent decades little attention was given to the developmental challenges that adoptees face. For one, being told that birth parents were out of the picture, whether or not it were true, cut adoptees off from the emotional resource of learning about and coming to own one's birth story and birth history.

Johnny and Jean had endless days of conversation with Abigail during which they worked hard to point out how her behavior continued to get her into deeper trouble. With every argument imaginable they sought to persuade her that behaving differently would make her life so much easier. But, of course, the wisdom they sought to offer fell on deaf ears. Abigail was thinking only about how she might stay out of trouble in the present moment and, at that time, was not able to listen to the good counsel of her parents.

Her parents at first resisted a regimen of rewards and consequences for Abigail's troublesome behavior. They hoped that she would begin to behave because they loved her, and further, they hoped that she would begin to love them back and become a better person. **But this wish was unrealistic; they did not understand Abigail's survival-oriented way of life.**

Parenting with immediate rewards and consequences did bring some success to managing ten-year-old Abigail. When she was paid money, as little as it might be, for a certain act of good behavior, things began to improve. But helping her find her way was an ongoing challenge for these parents.

In this story of Abigail, empathy took various forms. The attempts at empathy in one-to-one reflective conversations about her inner struggles as well as her "outside of herself" challenges had little success. Nevertheless, they were sincere attempts to help Abigail understand herself and become more aware of the world around her in a limited way.

Johnny might have said to her: "Abigail, I can see that there are times you are so angry that you feel you HAVE to do something like this. You want to make sure people know how angry you are and pay attention to what you feel so intensely and deeply."

And maybe at another time: "I imagine that when you threw that brick you were doing what needed to be done, and it felt right and good to do. I wonder, though, if at other moments you wished you could convey what you felt and needed without having to destroy something."

Abigail might have ignored such an attempt by Johnny to be empathic in the narrow sense with her. She might have pushed it off. But perhaps, time after time, at some point, it might hit home. She might come to admit that her dad understands, at least a little bit, what it is like to be Abigail. And even if his comment is brushed off, still the intent is empathic itself. Such intent communicates that someone is trying to care.

Here was a little girl who so needed care and understanding but did so much to stop this from happening. Again, the Catch-22 of adoptive development made the relationship so much more complex. Jean and Johnny saw her need for empathy, but they also saw how strong her defenses were against the fulfillment of that need.

As odd as it may sound, the structure of rewards and consequences was perhaps more empathic with Abigail's challenge to behave well. This regimen somehow "understood" her as someone needing very clear boundaries and rewards for good behavior within her adoptive family. Knowing exactly where she stood was part of feeling safe. This may be the most empathic response possible with someone like her.

So now we close this story of an adoptive family's struggle with little Abigail, who was so frightened of being close to them, perhaps fearing that once again she might be hurt, thrown away, just like that brick she threw. She did not want to be lying on the floor in shards of hurt and sorrow, again facing the pain of being alone. Maybe Abby was so afraid for her life itself that she found no one whom she could trust. That is what it may be like to be an orphan.

Ways to Think about Empathy

As we proceed in this conversation, we will keep young Abigail in mind as she faces the challenges that come with forming and trusting good relationships.

Today, the term empathy is used in so many ways. There are what we might call "soft" differences between the ways in which words are used in our everyday conversations. By soft I mean that uses of the word sometimes overlap and even begin to blend together in what we might call caring conversations.

First, as we mentioned before, **being empathic is different from being sympathetic.** Both terms are used to communicate care in sharing the pain and sorrow of another person, someone like Abigail. But sympathy and empathy originate from different places.

Sympathy, which means "feeling with," is the expression of our own emotional reaction to someone else's experience. It's what happens to us as we consider the plight of someone like Abigail. We might say, "Abigail, I am so sorry that you are having such a difficult time doing your homework."

Again, when I express my sympathy to you, I am telling you my emotional experience. For example, when I am sympathetic, when I say, "I am sorry for your loss," I am joining you in some way by telling you how I felt as I walked before the casket of your friend or family member. Sympathy is about how I feel and it may get close to how you feel. It may bring me into the "vicinity" of understanding your personal suffering, but it is different.

We are usually rather quick to offer sympathy, thereby telling another, a suffering person like Abigail, how his or her experience has affected us, in hopes that that person will experience our care.

In my own work as a therapist, I regularly notice how sympathy is kind and well-intended. It is certainly a personal attempt to relieve the heavy heart of another person, but sympathy may also miss understanding and reflecting the experience of the suffering person.

In Abigail's case again, we might say, "I'm sorry you are having such a difficult time. It makes me sad to see that you are so frustrated these days."

And her angry thought might be, "Bug off! You have no idea what it's like to be me!"

So the dilemma with personal sympathy is that though we may be well intended, we are speaking about ourselves in the context of the life of another different and unique human being.

Second, being empathic is not the same as identifying with someone in distress. This difference is often overlooked, and therefore it is important to point it out. **Identification with someone is noticing similarities between our own experience and that of another, suffering person.** It goes this way: The one

177

suffering, Abigail, for example, begins to tell her story and quickly her narrative reminds us of our own similar experience.

Then comes the misstep when we assume that she feels the way that we felt when we had our supposedly similar experiences, when we struggled with our homework. So now we believe that we know how she feels because we think that we were there at one time in our life as well.

This unfortunate assumption, though well intended, usually leads to a misfiring of sorts. Because we were never relinquished as Abigail was. Differences usually outweigh similarities, and then our effort to demonstrate our care falls short.

With some professional embarrassment, I give this example: I remember talking with a five-year-old whose grandmother had just died. I sat with him and his older brother and recalled, I thought for their benefit, my own memory of losing my grandmother. I mentioned to them that it was okay to cry. Patiently, they allowed me the time to tell my story. How surprised I was when, after a moment of silence, the five-year-old blurted out, "Well, I am glad she's dead!" **Truth from a child**. My identification with this little boy clearly had very little to do with his experience.

My good intentions were a colossal misfire of intended care. His was the grandmother who forced oatmeal down the throats of these boys and who regularly scolded them for bad manners. Both boys were relieved when Grandma went away. My grandmother was so very different; her blueberry muffins were wonderful.

So, resisting this kind of identifying is important because no two stories are ever the same. As we are noticing in this book, the adoptee's narrative is especially unique and cannot be compared with other experiences of loss.

Another example makes this point even more. People often say to adoptees that they understand how the adoptee feels because they too lost their parents in a similar way, perhaps through divorce. This comment is, of course, intended to be a helpful way of connecting with the difficulties of the adoptee. But it too is a misfire; dealing with one's relinquishment is qualitatively different from dealing with the divorce of one's parents.

The experience of relinquishment is unique and categorically different from the experience of children of divorce. Children of divorce usually grow up for an extended period of time with their divorcing parents. They know them. They usually have ongoing access to each of them, even during troublesome custody battles. They do lose the attention of their parents to some extent, but this is a much more modified injury than that of the adoptee.

Certainly, the children of divorce suffer, but using this experience as a way of identifying with the adoptee may be an unfortunate mis-step in a well-intended attempt to connect. It is always a guess whether explaining our identification with another's suffering will fall within the vicinity of the life experience of an adoptee.

Adoptees suffer differently. Their experience is one of losing first parents, even at birth, and enduring challenges of grieving deeply, of creating a different identity, often with pieces of the puzzle missing, of struggling with trust in close relationships (hopefully beginning with adoptive parents), and of dissolving their fantasies into reality as they learn more and more about their own birth story[15]. These challenges certainly make the life of an adoptee like Abigail unique.

Any comparisons of this experience to others, for example children of divorce, will certainly reduce one story significantly in order to fit it into proximity with another story. Simply put, identifying with other experiences of loss runs short of truly understanding what first parent loss is like for the adoptee.

Third, being empathic is different from extending emotional warmth to a person, though at times they may look the same. These ideas are often used interchangeably, and once again the unique character of empathy may get lost in the conversation.

Seeking to be helpful to a suffering person usually generates a caring response toward him. His deeply felt sorrow may stir in us a certain warmth towards him. Expressing that warmth is often called being empathic, and it may fall within the vicinity of empathy, but it may miss the mark of what the term really intends. Empathy is still something different.

Samuel is a 14-year-old adoptee from Ethiopia. He came to the United States along with his brother, Marcos, five years ago, when Sam was nine and Marcos was seven. We should note that at these later ages of

---

[15] For an extended description of these normal developmental challenges of adoptees, consider my *Adoptees Come of Age: living within two families*. Louisville, Kentucky: Westminster/John Knox Press, 1999.

adoption, so much has happened in the first years of their life that much of their personalities and life attitudes are clearly in place.

These boys, whose mother and father had both died from AIDS, had significant history of physical and emotional neglect as well as sexual abuse in the orphanages that had kept them. Samuel came with angry eyes and Marcos came with sad eyes, both having lost so much and become so confused about the future.

Even this short description of their story stirs something within us. It may be pity, a certain kind of sympathy that feels badly about another's circumstances in life. Truly, there may be tears in our eyes about the plight of these orphans from a land far away. And we may be drawn toward these boys wanting to express real warmth and care to them. But still, this is not quite empathy. Being empathic is still different.

The Practice of Becoming Empathic

Learning and practicing the skill of empathy is a difficult task. One reason for this is that so many things get in the way of our simple curiosity. We may quickly gravitate toward needing to help more than simply listening in an open-ended way. We want to know enough, just enough, to spring into action and offer a good solution to the dilemma presented. And this impulse sometimes gets in the way.

Emptying ourselves of our own solutions or our own biases and assumptions about people is always challenging and somewhat unnerving. Or, we may have our own anxiety about being a good friend, so much so that our responses misfire because our concerns, once again, get in the way of listening. Even more problematic, we sometimes come to the conversation with an agenda. We have something in mind to be accomplished and so we may try to manipulate the conversation to a certain goal that may be in our best interest much more than that of the other person.

For all these reasons, being empathic is not an easily acquired parenting skill. Well, what then happens when we become empathic to someone else? Empathy with another person begins differently, not from the positions of self-reference that are part of sympathy or identification or warmth and care. **It usually begins with curiosity.** Being empathic begins with our ordinary curiosity about what it is like to be that other person. But first we must sort out and bracket our own assumptions, the ways in which we think we know well ahead of really knowing.

The most useful perspective is to be aware of our own ignorance about the other person. We must know that we do not know and that the experience of that other person is unique and true only to that person. Comparisons are always reductionistic; they immediately reduce that person's life experience into categories that are familiar to us. Again, we must remember that we don't know.

We find ourselves wondering without knowing. However, if that ignorance is eclipsed by quick comparisons, then almost immediately we have shut off the very curiosity that is necessary for the development of a truly empathic response. Our unfortunate need to know quickly may sabotage our efforts to become empathic with someone else.

Becoming empathic also has to do with imagination. Empathy will begin by asking this simple question: "What is it like to be you?" It is within our awareness of not knowing the answer to this question that empathy may come to life within us as we imagine what life is like for that someone else, that suffering person before us, that orphaned child like Abigail who is struggling to allow the love of her parents into her life.

Because the answers to this question lie within the mind and heart of the other person, only that person can determine whether a response from us is truly empathic. If it is, if our reflection of another's experience is accurate, that person will experience being understood. And if that person, that suffering orphan if you will, experiences you or me as understanding the plight of her life experience, the groundwork for an emotional relationship may have begun. An empathic moment has occurred.

Achieving that emotional/empathic response happens over time. We misunderstand, and we misunderstand, and then we misunderstand again until, finally, we begin to understand. In each attempt to correctly mirror the emotional experience of another, we may be drawing closer and closer, getting warmer and warmer, to an accurate reflection of his or her experience.

Listening carefully is different from only hearing what is said. Empathic listening, born out of being curious and not knowing and imagining, attends to the music between the lines. As we work to sidestep our own preconceived ideas, bracket our own assumptions about the life of another, and wonder about the biases within us, only then do we enter that sacred space where two people begin to connect in a helpful, sometimes healing way.

Again, **practicing being empathic is tricky.** We sometimes hear it said that empathy is "walking in someone else's moccasins." As good as it sounds, this analogy is, nevertheless, problematic. If it is I walking in another's shoes, then it is still I, reflecting on my own experience, as I project myself into another's life. We would think, "If I were you and I experienced what you experienced, then I would feel this way." Notice that the reference is still more a reference to me than it is to the lived experience of the other.

Really, the other person's experience evaporates, getting lost in the conversation. Getting close to human suffering is usually counter-intuitive, and so it takes disciplined intent to listen to the story of a wounded child such as Abigail. We struggle to truly notice the other person whose experience is unique and complex and certainly different from our own.

Examples of Differing Responses

Suppose that as an adoptive parent you are faced in the kitchen with the sneer of your young adoptee who yells at you, "You are not my father!" or "You are not my mother!" This aggressive retort is not unusual in the ongoing struggles that some parents face with angry adoptees. Obviously, it is intended to hurt the adoptive parent. After long, drawn-out verbal battles with relinquished and adopted children, tolerance may be in short supply. So, one might easily be hooked by such an attack.

First, that adoptive father might say, "I'm sorry that you feel that way." His intent would be a good first step toward conversation. We would consider this a form of being sympathetic, whereby he describes his experience in response to this verbal attack: "When I think about your troublesome experience, this is how I feel."

Or, second, that adoptive mother might respond, "When I was a little girl, I remember times when I didn't want my mother to be my mother either." Such a response certainly intends to show interest and care as a first step in a conversation. But this attempt at connecting by identifying would probably gain little traction in the mind and heart of the adoptee who would secretly be thinking, "You have no idea what you are talking about. You still have your real mother." Understandably, this good intention might also miss the mark of appreciating the adoptee's emotional dilemma.

Now obviously, such a glass-on-the-kitchen-floor drama would not facilitate warm feelings towards this child. As parents, we might feel frustration, hurt, and anger, quite understandably. However, reaching beyond the moment and wondering how frightened this child might be could move a parent towards, "I know you're angry right now, but I still love you." Warmth and care, anyway.

But imagine this adoptive mother, probably after pausing to catch her breath, responding to this attack with the words, "I can tell that you're really angry with me. Really angry. And you're using words that hurt me because you really need to let me know how upset you are." **This would be the gold of being empathic, coming very much within the vicinity of another's**

pain. She carefully reflects the personal experience of that angry, most likely very frightened, young son or daughter. Just remember Abigail.

This adoptive mother does not get hooked by the harsh retort of her relinquished and adopted child. Here again is that "white coat," objective response that keeps the power of this interchange in the hands of the parent. Most likely, both parts of her response would register with her child as accurate reflections of his current emotional state. He is angry. He is seeking to inflict an emotional wound. His words are like arrows aimed at his mother's heart. But rather than taking this verbal attack personally, she is able to shield herself, deflect the arrows, and remain thoughtful and sensitive to the deeper issues of this little boy's heart.

Being empathic, as an adoptive parent, might be understood as intentionally and personally reflecting the emotional struggle of an adoptee to that son or daughter in a way that captures his or her lived experience in that moment. Neither person gets lost in the interchange. Instead, in this case, both mother and child "stay present," at least for a moment, within the conversation.

Here, this adoptive mother accurately mirrors what she sees and hears from the heart of her son. This is the unique parenting method most helpful. Usually consequences for negative behavior, though necessary, have little traction, whereas speaking to the moment, as carefully as an adoptive parent can, may be the most helpful response to a child like Abigail.

Experiencing the empathy of another, as a relinquished and adopted child, means sensing that

"Mom or Dad or someone else is trying to understand me and get what my life is like."

Within this experience, the child described above would most likely agree with his mom's reflection of his anger and perhaps become more aware of his own emotional experience at that moment. The experience of being understood might possibly calm things down, unless of course the child now feels the strength and the freedom to express more about that anger.

Further conversation about her reasons for being angry could possibly deepen the connection between parent and child. This adoptee might then be "getting through" to his mother or father with the nature of his struggles, bringing a new and deeper understanding of how hard it is to be relinquished and adopted, to be someone like Abigail. Receiving empathy might then help her to develop a deeper understanding of herself. Being empathic, then, facilitates that understanding.

So far in this chapter we have been using the term empathy in its narrow sense as the communication of understanding the plight of another, both cognitively and emotionally. This specific definition has to do with the one-to-one relationship whereby an adoptive parent, for example, communicates understanding and care to a child by reflecting that child's emotional experience. It describes a listening skill used not only by therapists and other trained caregivers, but, hopefully, by most all of us at some time in our daily conversations with others.

Being empathic facilitates connection in the webs of our familial and social existence. By way of empathy, we listen and we reflect the music between the lines of another's life in everyday conversation. This, once again, is empathy in its narrow sense.

A wider understanding of empathy relates directly to the daily household experience of adoptive families. Empathy in this sense pays attention differently, noticing not only what may be evident in a one-to-one conversation about a person's inner life, but attending also to that person's experience of what is outside, in the larger web of relationships in a family or neighborhood or school or church or tribe or beyond.

Both the internal struggles of an individual and the external familial or political or social settings within which that person may live are important. To attend only to one of these obviously misses a great deal of information about what is going on in the life of the adoptee.

In fact, **to be empathic in the narrow sense with any single individual in a family may actually be unempathic with the adoptive family**. Empathy in the wider sense is critical to a positive experience of therapeutic care for that child and that family. In most instances of adoptive family therapy, an approach of "both/and" is wisest.

Certainly, individuals within the family who are suffering may need a narrower experience of empathic understanding, but a care provider should also be aware of and attend to the family that needs to be understood and appreciated. Adoptive parents can develop the art of balancing between these two objectives.

Take the example of Leon, whom we will meet again in Chapter 8. He is an only child who was adopted at birth.

For much of his life within his adoptive family, he has been oppositional and increasingly defiant. Leon, at age 17, now uses marijuana to medicate his chronic anxiety, an emotional state of mind that has made it quite difficult for him to manage himself. His ongoing anger, especially with his adoptive mother, has been the focus of one-to-one therapeutic conversations.

The power struggle between Leon and his mother has increased over the last several years as he has become older and stronger. The current goal of counseling is to assist him in managing his side of this ongoing struggle. Giving voice to his complaints has been useful to some degree in helping his parents adjust their approach to him.

However, hearing Leon's voice about himself is one thing; hearing his experience of the voices of his parents is another. These are the voices that Leon must also attend to in addition to his own inner struggles.

We may look again and notice how this family, as a family, functions, and see the way an over-functioning mother and under-functioning father play significant roles, leading to the very important question of what it means to be empathic to the family as family. This is an example of empathy in the wider sense. It includes the challenge of holding Leon accountable for his misbehavior and restoring a sense of authority and power to Leon's adoptive parents and to this family as a whole.

Listening only to Leon about his internal struggles is quite insufficient and ultimately unhelpful to him and to his family as a whole. A key change-up here is to bring

Leon's adoptive father into more prominence in dealing with Leon in the day-to-day negotiations. It also means assisting his adoptive mother to back away from so strenuously seeking to hold Leon accountable and shifting that responsibility to his father.

Obviously, these shifts would create some discomfort for each and appear to be less than empathic with the mother and father. But such interventions would certainly be empathic with the family as a family.

So once again, we see how it may be unempathic with a family, in the wider sense, if we seek to be empathic only with the individual person, usually the adoptee, within that family.

A third, more global way to consider the focus of empathy, involves understanding a larger group of people. In this case empathy can come not only from one person, but also from one group and then be experienced by another group.

For example, Native Americans protesting a pipeline through their sacred grounds compose a group of people who must be understood if the process of political resolution is to be healthy and just. Society needs to be empathic with their struggle to honor and protect their holy land. Undocumented immigrants facing deportation who may hide in the basements of churches need understanding in order to be managed wisely by the powers that be.

And back to our adoptive families, they need to be understood as part of the system, that web of relationships within which their relinquished and adopted children face the challenges of growing up. But

190

few non-adoptive families or groups in church or in society can appreciate the struggles of adoptive families. So, in this case, empathy with adoptive parents seldom happens.

Other Experiences of Empathy

Being empathic takes on so many different forms. A **book** can be empathic with the life experience of people. Certainly, I hope that this book will be experienced as empathic with adoptive parents who are in the midst of struggles with children who are too fearful to trust them and to love them back. If the readers of this text find themselves feeling understood, then empathy is happening, not simply to individuals (in the narrow or wider senses), but also to the larger community of people involved with relinquishment and adoption (in the global sense).

A **speech** can be empathic with the life experience of people. When hearers of a certain presentation find themselves listening to someone who "gets" their life experience, especially the suffering involved, then this is a moment of empathic appreciation.

Creating structure for a child who struggles to manage himself can be empathic. Even when it is significantly resisted, a daily routine that structures the life of a struggling child may be a very useful experience for the boy or girl who needs to feel safe. When we know what is coming toward us day after day, usually a sense of security develops.

Certainly, a **gift** can be empathic. When we are opening a present and noticing how much the giver understands us, we experience our wishes as being known and understood.

Being Empathic Has the Power to Change Enemies into Friends.

Let's notice that as we forgive someone for the hurt that we may have experienced, the dynamics of letting go of an injury begin to shift when we become empathic with the personal suffering of the person who caused us injury. This is a collateral gain of being empathic to another. By this I mean when we find our way to become empathic with our so-called enemies, seeking to understand the troublesome experiences in their lives, we usually discover the freedom to truly forgive and release ourselves from vengeful wishes.

And this takes us full circle to the challenge of forgiving our own children for the injuries that we sustain, the kicks in the shins that hurt both body and soul. This is about loving our enemies, especially when our enemies happen to be our own children.

We then stretch ourselves to look beyond the hurts that we receive and begin to listen for the many reasons why our relinquished and adopted children may strike out against us, and we become more able to grieve the personal injury, absorb their anger, and stay present with the realities that challenge them. Offering an empathic response such as "It must be hard to be so angry" may soften the hardened heart of a wounded girl or boy.

But we still have a dilemma about empathy. With many children who struggle with adoptive parents, empathy in the narrow sense of communicating emotional understanding may fall upon ears that are deafened by the loud inner noises of past neglect and painful abuse. Many of these children have learned not to feel and not to trust and not to open themselves up to any form of emotional vulnerability.

Such boys and girls with hardened hearts may not be able to experience empathy. Proverbially, they may bite the hand that feeds them. Empathy's invitation for closeness may move healthier children, but deeply wounded adoptees may shy away from the loving hearts of their parents.

This resistance to empathy is protective; they may experience empathy as dangerous, threatening, or painful for many reasons. Better, it is thought, to avoid the possibility of being hurt, wounded once again. You may recall the Catch-22 of adoptive development presented earlier. This is a vivid example.

We must always seek to be empathic, to understand, and to appreciate the ways in which relinquished and adopted children fear vulnerability. This open-ended empathic invitation needs always to be in place.

We may then move to the wider question of serving the adoptive family by being empathic in that wider sense and wondering about ways in which such a family can be helped to heal of its hurts and disappointments. In so doing, the adoptive family can become the place where children become healed of the wounds in their hearts.

We know well that relinquishment and adoption tamper with the most important and intimate relationship in human experience, the connection between a parent and child. Something that should never have happened has happened when children lose parents, especially when they lose a mother.

Understandably, repair of this most primitive and profound relationship is an incredibly difficult challenge. Being empathic translates into joining this painful experience in the life of someone like Abigail. It means taking on the challenge of entering into her experience of fear and absorbing her anger and joining in her sadness in the deep frustration of wondering how to make her life work.

Some pathways in life are too frightening to walk alone. And we learn once again that all of us as humans, but especially these children, grow so much more in the presence of another.

As we close this chapter on empathy, the final question becomes what to do when you do not know what to do. What do you say when it seems that there is nothing left to say?

The final answer is this – "Join them!" Use words that demonstrate that you are in the struggle with your son or your daughter, seeking to understand the heart of the issue. Communicating to the deeply wounded adoptee that he or she is not alone, that the cry of the orphan is being heard--this is the message that empathy can bring!

6

Appreciating, Engaging First Parents

Whenever I hear about adoptive parents who have chosen to proceed with an international plan in their pursuit for a child in order to avoid having to deal with the first parents of their children, I am quite concerned. And then, immediately, I find myself wondering how that child, growing up relinquished and adopted, will face this disengagement from birth parents in the years to come.

With recent more open domestic adoptions, birth parents in America are more available for relationship. In fact, sometimes they insist upon ongoing contact as a condition for the placement of their child. As adoptive parents face these new pressures in one way or another, they sometimes see birth parents as people to be put away, forgotten, or somehow erased, people who in some way threaten the construction of an adoptive family.

This may be an understandable protective response; however, **this impulse to push birth parents out of the adoptive family picture sets up troublesome dynamics in the relation between adoptive parent and adoptee.**

Remember our most important question, "For whom is the adoption?" Adoption must, first of all, be for the child. It is a way to create a family where the adoptive family becomes a resource for the development of the child. Otherwise, that child would be left an orphan, unable to mature on the inside because he or she matters to no one on the outside. This is the "hell" of not belonging to someone.

But if the birth parents of an adoptee are seen in a negative light, if they are blocked out of the adoptee's story, the adoptee may grow up experiencing even more difficulty in relation to his or her first parents who are still there in fantasy, if not in reality. The adoptee must then face another challenge that seems like it cannot be the subject of open conversation with their primary source of emotional and spiritual support, their adoptive parents.

In everyday life at home, of course, things are more complex. On the one hand, adoptive parents may want to more or less "bury" the birth parents, but on the other hand they may also hold an ongoing curiosity about who these people are and how their lives after relinquishment have turned out.

Adoptees as well may hold conflicting attitudes about their birth parents. They, too, may wish to place their first parents outside of their own day-to-day consciousness. But they may also want to maintain the image of the birth parents they hold, even in secrecy or in denial.

Ambivalence, then, describes the experience of both adoptive parents and adoptees. **Each is of two minds.**

Understandably, sorting out these contradictory attitudes and feelings and coming to terms with them in a gracious fashion may be difficult for them both.

Adoptive parents may think that by disposing of all the traces of birth parents, as if they are to be ghosts with whom there is no contact in real life, then one complication need never be addressed. But both the adoptee and the adoptive parents have placed these birth parents somewhere. An image of these birth parents remains in mind and in heart that needs to be managed in some way, even by denial.

When the reality of the birth parents and the birth family story is not addressed in the adoptive home, that reality is usually managed by the adoptee's imagination and the development of an adoptee's rich fantasy world.

But you cannot build a sense of self out of fantasy.

Adoptive parents are called to assist the adoptee in grieving the loss of her real but "ghost" parents by birth. But children quickly learn what is acceptable to discuss with their parents. These boys and girls are always carefully interpreting the words and the behavior of their second parents. They quickly learn, mostly by the tone of their parent's voices, what they may or may not discuss. And sadly, too often adoptees figure out that they cannot bring up the subject of the parents who created them, their first parents in life.

When an adoptee senses this lack of permission to bring the subject up for conversation, he has to grow up being quietly instructed that he ought not think about his first parents, and of course, that he ought not feel anything about them. He then learns that his first parents need to be "gone," and his grief remains in the shadows.

Our primary concern in this book is to empathically listen to the challenges of children who struggle to adopt their parents, and then to assist adoptive parents in helping them with struggles. The more we understand the child, the wiser our parenting can be. In this chapter, we will spend some time noticing the importance of appreciating an adoptee's parents by birth, and then we will consider the challenges of engaging these first parents, when that is possible.

Many in North America who have experienced international adoptions from South Korea or China, South America or Eastern Europe may have no information at all, including, of course, no contact information for these first parents. Understandably but sadly, many adoptive parents prefer it this way.

The challenge of appreciating and then engaging the forever unknown parents by birth is nevertheless very much of concern for the adoptee. For example, one young Chinese adoptee confessed to me that she thinks about her Chinese birth mother every day--this important connection is that important in her thought life.

In local and domestic adoptions, birth parents may be nearby and available for engagement, especially as the legal impingements of the closed adoption system in North America become something of the past. Thankfully, open adoption has become today's method in adoption practice because placing a child in an adoptive family in America is now driven by the choice of the birth parents, usually by the birth mother.

Arrangements for engagement with the birth parents become quite possible for adoptive parents to consider. And many times, children in these adoptive homes may have more success in their emotional development. They may struggle less to bond with their second parents, in part because less has been lost from their first parents.

Earlier I explained how, between 1856 and 1929, so-called Orphan Trains took children from the back alleys and abandoned buildings of New York City, and headed to the rural spaces of the West where "good Christian people" were thought to provide better homes for these children. Unfortunately, they were stripped of all identifying information about their roots.

Any piece of paper with the name or address that might help a child contact a mother or a father or an uncle somewhere in New York was taken away and destroyed. The thinking at that time was that these children were of "bad seed" and the less known about their origins the better in terms of giving them a chance and a new life on a farm or ranch. There they could be given a new identity, separate from the reality of their first parents.

This happened to about 150,000 children until the last orphan train rolled into Clarksville, Texas, in 1929.The problem with this way of thinking about the parents of these children is that no matter how much second parents out West may have attempted to deny reality and "make-believe" that this new environment would solve the problems of these children, these young boys and girls, usually about ages 5 to 12, had considerable difficulty adopting these parents.

Many of them were seen as "good hands" for the farm chores or ranch work that needed to be done. And, of course, they resented this arrangement and grieved not being allowed to know anything about members of their families back home in New York City. Accordingly, many ran away and either tried to find a way back home or, once again, lived as orphans in the streets and alleys of the towns and cities nearby.

These children usually had important memories of their parents and friends back home who could not provide for their basic needs. Their personal identities could not be simply stripped away and forgotten. Even the children who were well cared for on farms and ranches had to process memories, images, and the sad stories of their first parents. Any effort to dispose of the record or blacklist these first parents in difficult circumstances usually failed.

These children had, of course, taken into their minds and hearts the first parents with whom their lives began. No matter the distance of thousands of miles, and no matter the tragedy of broken families, the social experiment of the orphan trains could not succeed. First parents still mattered to these children as part of their personal identities. If the parents were "bad seed," then the children were of "bad seed."

Certainly, these very difficult informal adoptions in the American West's history are extreme examples of parent loss. But this story makes the point that certain realities that these orphans had internalized could not be simply wiped away. Their early life stories, initially with their first parents, could not somehow be erased or blended into being the children of second parents out West. They had taken in memories, images, and then the fantasies of these people back East, and such representations of their first parents were in their minds and hearts to stay.

All of this is to say, with this historical example, that in one way or another first parents always matter; whether dead or alive, in fantasy or in reality, they have undeniable meaning for both adoptive parents and child.

Pro-First-Parent Considerations

But why is this so? I believe adoptive parents need to consider ten different concerns as they form their opinions about these first parents and then make decisions about how they will respond to them and manage the question of engagement or non-engagement, whatever the case may be. These considerations intertwine understanding the significance of birth parents from the perspective of the child as well as from the perspective of the adoptive parent.

Understanding how parents see things and understanding how the adoptee sees things are both important points of reference. Often one informs the other; they weave together forming the matrix of the parent-child relationship. In each case, I will offer recommendations for adoptive parent choices while also writing on behalf of adoptees who may someday read these words.

First, the adoptive parents' representations of the birth mother and birth father will directly inform the

attitudes and the responses of adoptees to these people. In the classic scenario of a childless couple adopting a baby, very predictable dynamics usually occur. With all the effort, all the expense, and all the shame that accompanies the infertility that couples sometimes face, the adoptive mother may be envious, and even angry, as the initial reaction to an adoptee's first mother who became pregnant so easily.

Similarly, adoptive fathers who may have insufficient sperm counts. This classic scenario is less and less the case today in domestic adoptions, but nevertheless, initial reactions such as this set the stage for a distance from birth parents that may compromise healthy adoptive development for the child.

Adoptive parents seeing a child's first parents as threats may be further understood in terms of a deep-seated fear that these first parents might change their minds, return, and reclaim the child that was "given away." Adoptees may experience this fear in such a way that their image of their birth parents becomes suspect-- of people not to be trusted, of bad people. Still then, they remain children of "bad seed," like the orphan train children.

Obviously, this threatening view that adoptive parents may have of birth parents sets the stage wherein they come to be seen in a negative light by both adoptive parents and by adoptees. Here then, the negative birth parent representations in the minds of the adoptive parents result in similar negative birth parent representations in the minds of the adoptee. The first informs the second.

First impressions are so important. Looking at adoptive parents, it is challenging to notice how much we may project our own fears and anxieties onto that first impression. In terms of learning to appreciate birth parents, much is at stake. It is not simply about the adoptive parent's perception; it is most importantly about the adoptee's perception. The first creates the second. Our children know quite well how we as parents see other people.

Of course, our own fantasies of others are always different from the realities of these people as we learn to know them. Adoptive parents have representations, or shall we say images, of birth parents whether or not these first parents ever become known or ever become real in the narrative of the adoptive family.

When these images are painted in positive, respectful colors, whether known or not, adoptees can then internalize a positive view of their beginnings. Conversely, of course, when birth parents are described in dark and negative ways, then adoptees are challenged to manage negative voices about who they are because of the people who gave them life.

Accordingly, one counter-intuitive recommendation is that adoptive parents spend some time wondering about their personal attitudes towards those other parents who partnered with them, in early life or even in death, to form their adoptive families. Therefore, adoptive parent homework needs to begin with introspection.

This challenge of reflecting on such attitudes and feelings is, of course, more difficult than it sounds because, as human beings, we both know and do not know at the same time. We are conscious of some things but carefully not conscious of other things that we might be thinking about birth parents. And usually, difficulty results whenever we are unable to allow our deepest truths to become conscious. Conversation about these concerns is still the beginning of the road towards more conscious life.

Second, the interior world of the adoptee usually consists of two very important relationships, one with one's first parents and one with one's second parents. They live alongside each other.[16]

So many times over the years the television screen has shown people "finding each other" after 40 years or so of separation of birth parents, usually birth mothers, from their relinquished, or they would sometimes say "surrendered," children. Stepping off the runway from the airplane, in days gone by when visitors could wait in the concourses, broadcast cameras would capture that moment, that camera flash of awareness, when these people would meet each other--hugs and hugs and hugs and kisses on the cheek and smiles, broad smiles, and strong, lengthy embraces and then, tears.

Why this flood of emotion? Why these buckets of tears that just kept coming? It is important, first of all, to notice that these adults were most often quite functional people, living their lives in stable family stories where success had come their way in terms of friendships and careers and their own families. Usually, these were not broken people in need of repair in order to

---

[16] Therefore, the title of my first book, *Adoptees Come of Age: living within two families*. Westminster/John Knox Press, 1999.

live a productive, relatively happy life. They were ordinary people and they were incredibly emotional. So, what might have been the source of these deep wells of joy overflowing at the end of the airplane walkway?

Once again, the interior world of the adoptee can never be reduced to only the adoptive parent relationship, and so let's look at the birth parent relationship. Some speak of it as a spiritual connection, as if to say that in some way in the record of the universe, mother and father and child are forever connected and forever in relationship. Whether these first parents are dead or alive, a mystical connection, though difficult to articulate, is felt.

Others speak of it more psychologically and suggest that prenatal bonding and the experience of birthing itself begin a connection that is forever present in some way. After all, the first sound that each of us hears at 24 weeks of gestation is the sound of our mother's heartbeat. This is the beginning of a profoundly powerful primitive connection with a life of its own that may be suppressed but never erased.

And still other birth parents and adoptees might say that the history of the birth story, the birth family and the birth culture, as well as the many possible reasons for loss or relinquishment or termination of rights--all of these constitute sufficient historical reasons why part of each adoptee is always in relation to his or her first parents.

The challenge for adoptive parents in this regard is to acknowledge and understand this duality in the life of the adoptee. They may be tempted to minimize or even deny this reality in a manner that is destructive to the emotional and spiritual well-being of the child. When, for example, in response to an innocent inquiry by a young adoptee about her birth parents "out there somewhere," as it was explained to her, an adoptive mother sternly yells back, "I am your mother!" there is trouble in that moment as well as trouble ahead within the heart of that little girl.

In responding this way, that adoptive mother may be pushing away her own unresolved grief around her infertility or that of her husband so that the make-believe of non-reality can have its way. However, there will be more hell to pay, if by hell we mean the agony of isolation, the life experience of being an orphan.

Third, a high degree of respect from the adoptive parents for birth parents will translate into more self-esteem for the adoptee. This is the obvious result of what has been stated so far about adoptive parent representations and the duality of the adoptive experience itself. But it needs to be said so clearly: Adoptees will listen, first of all, to the tone of conversation and the attitude of adoptive parents.

Consider the fantasy world that adoptees might create as they form images in their minds of people that they may never see or, as in the case of more open adoption, might see only occasionally. Constructing such fantasies about birth parents may be one way by which adoptees seek and keep these secret connections with the parents whom they have lost.

Further, these fantasies may become the foundation for their views of these people as well as their views of

208

themselves. This is the point precisely; whatever is thought or felt about first parents will be part of the foundation for how adoptees see themselves.

The insensitive, judgmental, or disrespectful comment about a birth parent would certainly paint that child's birth parents fantasy with negative, dark colors. And then, of course, the connection so easy to ignore is simply this: "What you think about my first parents is what you think about me. What you say about my birth parents is probably what you say about me when I cannot hear you. So probably, you don't really like me either."

The developmental challenge for every child, adopted or otherwise, is to construct a positive view of himself or herself. A good bit of the "stuff" of that self-image, for adoptees, has to do with how that child's adoptive parents look upon his birth parents. Positive yet realistic comments, attitudes, and well-constructed opinions about a child's birth parents set the stage for that young adoptee to think well of himself or herself.

Consider these recommendations for referring to birth parents who have struggled with various difficulties.

For one, **using person-first language is always helpful.** For example, "When you were born, your birth mother *was a person* who was not able to care of you because she was sick. She had a disease that we sometimes call addiction."

It is always helpful as well to use explanatory language that is carefully nonjudgmental. "When you were born, your birth father *was a man* who did not have a job. He did not make enough money to help with your care. We are not sure why that was the case." Or, "When you were born, your birth mother in Thailand *was a woman* who had a sickness called AIDS and, sad to say, she was not able to live to be your mother. She was a good person in the middle of a sad story."

Simply put, pay attention to how a young child will hear the tone of our voices and the connotation of our words. This will have a great deal to do with how they see themselves, hopefully in a positive light.

Fourth, allowing the reality of first parents into the adoptee's narrative opens the door for the adoptee to grieve the loss of these people.

In contrast to all the joy that may surround adoption for adoptive parents, the transition to second parents always involves loss for the adoptee. Accordingly, one of the most important roles that adoptive parents play in the lives of their children is helping their children be sad.

Naming the reality of birth parents, expressing interest in their stories and their lives, dead or alive, far away in a Third World country or just across town, opens up the opportunity for adoptive parents to assist in the slow-moving project of grieving that each adoptee faces. **Joining the adoptee inside this sad but critically important challenge is a given in good adoptive parenting**. It is usually not possible to face parental loss without some help; the path is often too painful to walk alone. Here, adoptive parents matter so much.

Conversely, seeking to erase the reality of these important figures in the life of the child sets the stage for the denial of grief on the part of the adoptive parents in such a way that they cannot help their children precisely where these adoptees may need the most assistance. Where the family rule is that "we will make believe that the things that hurt do not hurt," the adoptee is trapped in a very private world where sadness is quietly carried in a way that impedes healthy development.

Even the capacity to feel sorrow may be compromised and result in the formation of a partial sense of self where something is somehow missing. It may be unnamed and unarticulated, but it is there and yet to be dealt with down the road--if that is even possible when a child learns early in life to shut down his emotional life.

Fifth, learning the story of birth, birth parents, and specific circumstances offers an adoptee a more complete identity.

I will never forget the joyful report I have heard more than once from relinquished adoptees who finally meet their birth parent(s) in reunion, often years after their birth. With an incredibly large smile, nearly always they exclaim, "I finally feel real!" This is such a powerful refrain. Each of us needs to define ourselves with clarity and confidence about our truth in such a way that we can get on with life and the usual challenges of day-to-day experience.

One adult adoptee flew from Denver all the way to Minneapolis to meet his birth mother and his seven half-siblings. He was well-prepared emotionally because he had done his "search-and-reunion homework" of spending time talking through his fears and his concerns in his search as well as his excitement about meeting these people. When, finally, he met this group of relatives, he enjoyed the reunion very much because these people became real to him. But, he also realized his own separate identity. "It was really a delight to meet them all," he remembers, "but they all listen to Rush Limbaugh! And that just doesn't work for me."

Remember, even bad news is good news for the adoptee because it is real news!

This is not to say that seeing one's birth parents is an automatic moment of repair. Much depends upon how either party might anticipate that moment of reunion after a lifetime of separation. The fantasy about who the other might be may create either a positive or negative anticipation. Nevertheless, grounding oneself in the reality of one's birth parents is especially useful for a more complete sense of identity.

And very often the stories of first parents are narratives of significant difficulty that have to do with the drama of relinquishment. Joy is most often mixed with sadness; even so, the truth of the adoptees' birth story becomes clearer and more focused. **It is both a gift and a civil human right for each adoptee to know that reality.**

Another adult adoptee has a much more tender story. After years of time and energy searching, he found his birth mother. However, she was a person who was mentally ill, living with chronic schizophrenia. She did not recall the story of his birth nor did she recognize him in any meaningful way. Nevertheless, upon reflection, he was able to say, "Now I know my truth. My birth mother is not able to know me or to love me. She will spend the rest of her life in a mental institution. I wish it were different, but at least now, I know who she is and where she is, and I know more about me. I know my story."

Simply put, personal identity can only be constructed out of pieces of reality, painful or not, complete or less so. Reality addressed and accepted is always the foundation for personal identity. Every adoptee, young or old, needs enough reality to feel real about himself.

Sixth, learning the child's birth family narrative offers the adoptive parents the opportunity to know and honor the cultural heritage of their child.

Part of family life is to sometimes be stretched by the experiences of our children. They may help us see a bigger world. Being positive and open about birth narratives and birth parent histories quite naturally translates into an appreciation for and learning about the cultural histories of adoptees.

For example, young children in a Korean orphanage spent every night sleeping on braided bamboo mats. They were not familiar with sleeping on what we might call an American bed. Accordingly, for the first few weeks of transition to a new home in America, adoptive parents in Michigan quite wisely joined their adopted twin sisters on braided bamboo mats on the living room floor.

This was not an easy place for these adults to spend the night. For sure, they felt aches and pains in the morning. That was the sacrifice they decided to make to facilitate their bonding with these girls--sleeping together does that. In the beginning moments of their life together, these thoughtful adoptive parents were committed to being fully with their children and noticing what might comfort them.

But in a secondary way, this also set the stage for welcoming a part of Korean culture into their American home. These parents sought out wall decorations and clothing for the girls as well as themselves that fit Korean culture. And, of course, their menu was no longer simply meat and potatoes, but now included kimchi and bugogi. These were comfort foods for these young Korean children in the adoptive home in which they were to grow up. In these and other ways, their family was quite welcoming to the culture and the people of South Korea.

The recommendation for adoptive parents becomes obvious. The stretch of creating an adoptive family becomes a very positive challenge when it works to include the cultural heritage and current cultural story of adoptees. The world of this family thus becomes a bigger place. Minimizing differences in food, clothing, sleeping, and thinking might be seen as an effort to become empathic to the profoundly difficult transition that adoptees must face head-on as they begin life, sometimes in another country, sometimes on another continent.

Aside from these obvious differences with international adoptions, it is important to notice that each adoptee comes from a family, a different family with its own family culture, even within the same city. And appreciation for the culture as well as knowledge of it are important challenges for adoptive parents to engage. Such an effort demands a high level of tolerance for difference and the capacity to truly honor the heritage of other people, not simply our own.

Conversely, we are wise to take note of the dynamics set in motion when adoptive parents work intensely to form children in their own image, strictly within their own cultural norms. The wish to make a child in our own image, like us, is understandable, and seeing a reflection of ourselves more clearly may be seen as one of the rewards of adopting children.

However, from the perspective of the adoptee, such an approach to adoptive parenting minimizes what any relinquished child would value, namely her first cultural experience of clothing, her first taste of different food, her first smell of city or country, her first sense of hearing her name called. All of these cultural variables are part of the adoptee narrative. Dismissing or minimizing them sets the stage for resistance to the acceptance and affection that every child needs in order to grow up well.

Seventh, knowing the birth parent story together as a family facilitates more connection, more attachment to a relinquished or abandoned adopted child. As obvious as this may appear, still it needs to be stated clearly: Placing a high value on birth parents as persons in a child's adoptive narrative and positively seeking out the adoptee's birth story and birth family history and culture as well as occasionally the birth parents themselves, all of these may open the door in a very significant way to the heart of the adoptee.

These people and these concerns matter to each adoptee, as we have said, in terms of both identity and self-esteem. When they also matter to a child's adoptive parents, that child experiences the empathy of his parents as people who want to truly know and value his personal narrative of origin.

For example, consider the naming of an adoptee. How might adoptive parents think about this? Ought a child by adoption be given a name that relates only to the name history of their family, after a grandmother or grandfather, a middle name after the mother or father? Or, would it be wise to keep a given name, whether domestic or foreign, as part of the identity given to a child? What is the wisest way for adoptive parents to think about this?

Put differently, in retaining or giving a name, how much do adoptive parents wish to keep cultural heritage and how much might they wish to push it away? What about the name, for example, of "Elizabeth Chin.... "or "Michael Kim...." for children from China or South Korea? Or consider "Henry Allen...." for an adoptee whose birth father had the name Allen? From these examples it is certainly clear that the manner in which children by adoption are named signals the manner in which their birth parents, birth stories, and birth culture are recognized and valued within adoptive families.

In America today, few adoptions of Native American children occur as different tribal groups disallow the export of these children to other ethnic group families in our land. But there are some. For our purposes here, let us suppose that such a child is from the Navajo Tribe of the Southwest United States. And further, let us assume that this little boy's adoptive family in Boston looks forward to its plan to visit the hogans of Arizona and New Mexico.

At a young age, this adoptee joins his parents on that voyage to visit the red earth and the hot sun of ancient dwellings that date back well before the town of Santa Fe began in 1610 or the pilgrims landed at Plymouth Rock in 1620. This rich sense of history would include visits to the turquoise jewelry shops to notice the fine skills of Navajo silversmiths.

How might that little boy feel? How would he experience this journey backwards in time and back to his people of origin? His dark black hair has always contrasted with the hair color of his classmates in Boston. His skin color has always been different from that of all those people on the beaches of Cape Cod. He has always known that he is different, and he has had to face the challenge of recognizing and accepting that in some ways he will never be "one" with other children in the neighborhood.

But now, on this vacation trip to the Southwest, he knows more deeply that his parents understand him. They understand the questions he has lived with ever since the dawning of awareness of his own strikingly unique appearance among the Caucasian crowds of New England. He is pleased that his parents "get him" and know quite well that it is not easy to be really relinquished and adopted.

It is a different developmental path that he must walk, and **he knows that his adoptive parents seek to walk that path with him**. Every step along the way, these adoptive parents wondered how they might be able creatively and imaginatively to be with their child, appreciating his perspective on his adoptive life. And this is a good thing!

Eighth, in open adoptions, with the reality of present day birth parents well in focus, adoptive

parents are able to set wise boundaries with these first parents when needed. Dealing with the known is so different from dealing with the unknown, and, as this relates to relinquishment and adoption, dealing with the known is always better. This partly has to do with the so-called representations of first parents that second parents may create, based upon fear of the loss of the adopted child. But such fantasy formation is usually quite off the mark of an accurate understanding of who birth parents turn out to be.

Appreciating and knowing the birth parents, if possible, offers adoptive parents the opportunity to form positive, relatively accurate impressions of who these people are, these people who partnered with them in the formation of their adoptive family. When first parents become friends, if that is possible, fear usually subsides and the real truth, the birth parent story, becomes understandable and helpful.

When setting boundaries with such first parents, an accurate read on the emotional stability, maturity, and personality of birth parents is critically important. Whatever the case may be, a realistic picture of someone else will certainly make for better decisions about whatever family fence may be necessary for the well-being of a child's adoptive family.

A reality-informed understanding of first parents would hopefully offer adoptees the opportunity to internalize, to take in, accurate and positive impressions of their birth parents. In so doing, reality serves the interests of the adoptive family in a very important and positive way. When accurate impressions form adoptive parent appreciation for birth parents, these other people usually settle into becoming partners who become friends.

No child has too many people who might love him or her. And the significance here is the fact that adoptive parent anxiety and fear about birth parents subsides. Even in such cases, of course, there needs to be healthy boundaries between birth parents and adoptive parents. These can be negotiated in a manner that usually works best for both parties.

However, there are times when the maturity of birth parents and their psychological health may be questioned for good reason. Birth parents who have been extremely ambivalent about the decision to relinquish a child may have difficulty relating in a positive way with that child's second parents.

Or, they may have more deeply seated psychological struggles with coping in life after releasing a child to adoption. Given difficulties in their own early life experience, especially the parenting they themselves received, they may be birth parents who need to be kept at some distance in the best interest of the adoptive family.

Even then, setting realistic boundaries is quite different from guessing about it out of nameless fear. Birth parents who struggle with different forms of disorder of character may sometimes need a strong, firm, high wall between them and the adoptive family of their relinquished children. Sometimes that is best.

But when it is based on well-thought-out, careful reasoning about wisdom for the day, it is qualitatively different from simply pushing them away for protective purposes.

Remember, even bad news is good news about birth parents because it is real news. **Reality creates a different, wiser relationship blueprint than fearful fantasy about a birth parent ever can.**

One such story will make the point. Ruthann, in spite of her ambivalence about releasing her child to adoption, had chosen an adoptive couple out of a portfolio of six couples. All of these couples, of course, presented themselves in a most positive and wonderful light. They looked so healthy and handsome that Ruthann found herself settling for the most honest and open couple of the group.

The second parents she chose, Paul and Phyllis, appeared to Ruthann to be unassuming and level-headed in their written comments about their deep desire to become parents by adoption. They were quite willing to participate in the informal negotiations that are part of open adoptions today. These arrangements are voluntary as the adoptive parents become in charge legally once papers are filed with the local magistrate. But Ruthann assumed that openness would continue, especially in the early years of little Brian's life. Things appeared to be set for a good outcome both for Ruthann and for Paul and Phyllis.

Ruthann turned to finish her schooling and complete her training to become a nurse. After several months of occasional conversation with Phyllis and Paul and a single visit to see her son, now their son, Ruthann began to experience some significant depression. Grieving the loss of that part of herself that became Brian was an overwhelming challenge that she could barely endure. This took her by surprise as she had thought she could "get on with her life" once her baby was placed in a good home.

Sometimes part of grieving is becoming and being angry. This was the case with Ruthann. She was angry at herself for the decision in the first place. She was angry at Brian's birth father who professed his commitment to knowing his son in an open adoptive arrangement, but then left the relationship almost immediately after Brian's birth.

Ruthann would drive by the home of Paul and Phyllis, wondering where Brian might be in their house, even in that moment. When Paul and Phyllis found out that Ruthann had investigated the location of the daycare center where Brian spent his weekday hours, they became increasingly anxious about how to manage their commitment to Ruthann within the open adoption arrangement they had promised.

After several consultations with a relinquishment-and-adoption- informed family counselor, they decided to talk directly with Ruthann and discuss with her what difficulties she might be having with the loss of her son. They offered financial assistance to cover the cost of personal counseling for Ruthann and hoped that she could then find her way through the grieving that had overtaken her. But rather than talk through some of her understandable anger and sadness, Ruthann continued to act out her anxieties by finding ways to keep a close eye on Brian's development.

Unfortunately, as she continued to search for moments of connection as her method of pushing back against the grief that she felt so deeply, she got in trouble with Brian's second parents. Paul and Phyllis, after further consultation, confronted Ruthann directly and asked that she no longer visit the day care center, even by parking her car on the street in front of the building. Again, they recommended her own personal therapy. But they stated clearly that should she continue this behavior, they would speak to an attorney about a restraining order of some sort. They believed that this was necessary to protect the development of their little boy.

They had to set a boundary, but they did so in a wise and reality-informed way. They knew of the struggles that challenged Ruthann and with firm boundaries in place, they were able to communicate directly with her with the hope that down the road, when she was more accepting of her relinquishment of Brian, they might lower the boundary bar in Brian's interest, first of all, so that he could know of his birth mother in a positive fashion.

Ruthann's well-being was a goal for everyone involved. A wise and necessary boundary was in place that was informed by the reality of her struggles. This was a good and wise way to do things.

Ninth, in open adoptions when birth parents are available, they become resources in the life of the adoptee and his or her family. Perhaps the simplest, most important way they serve as a family resource is by answering questions. To begin, the question of an adoptee's medical family history is a standard concern.

With nearly 4,000 genetically related health disorders now identified, knowledge of the child's medical family history is very important. If, for example, an adoptee's birth mother develops breast cancer, knowing this is important in terms of both diagnosis and prevention for the adoptee.

But other questions are closer to the heart of the matter in terms of relating to birth parents. These begin with simple inquiries from a child such as "What color is my hair? What color is the hair of my birth mother?" Or, "Was my birth father athletic?" And then come the answers that form the personal identity of the child. "Your hair is as red as can be! And, your birth mother's hair is also red." "No, your birth father was not very athletic. But he loved music. And he enjoys playing the violin these days."

When such question and answer sessions with the adoptee are calm, knowledgeable, and positive, some of the many building blocks of the identity of the child fall in place. Sigmund Freud famously said that "reality is the best defense." By that he meant that facing and knowing reality is the key to mental health. Our concern here is that the more reality adoptive parents can offer to their children with regard to their many curiosities about their birth parents, the more opportunity the adoptee will have to construct a more complete and positive view of himself.

Conversely, **the less an adoptee has answers to these many curiosities about his birth parents, the more he is driven to imagine fantasies about who these people might be**. If he has heard negative things, a negative fantasy will usually be the outcome.

223

So quite obviously, truth about birth parents always serves the adoptee well. And birth parents themselves are the most useful source of that truth.

Another adoptee question needs an answer for healthy development. It goes along with "Why was I relinquished, given up by my birth parents?" which is usually standard in the mind and heart of each adoptee. That next question has to do with "I wonder whether my birth parents care about me now?" Even if this curiosity is never verbally expressed, it is usually somewhere in the wondering of the relinquished child.

How important it is to know that we matter to people. And quite understandably adoptees are usually curious about this very tender question, "Do they ever think about me?" If it is possible to be in relation to the child's birth parents who occasionally express their care for their relinquished baby, this word of affection is another positive building block for that adoptee.

Sadly, in the case of many international adoptions as well as some North American domestic adoptions, birth parents may be never known. So, what is an adoptee to do with this shortage of information? No medical history, no information at all about birth parents, just nothing–only that she was left on the side of the road in the Chinese countryside.

A significant fantasy world, even like that of imaginary friends, may develop when reality about birth parents is so far out of reach. These fantasy birth parents can never be resources to assist the adoptee and her family. And, sad to say, this leaves the adoptee at a greater disadvantage in terms of developing a more positive personal sense of self.

The encouragement to adoptive parents is simple: Even if nothing is known about these birth parents, they still need to be talked about. Adoptive parents need to join their children in their collective curiosity, their wondering about the child's story of birth. These birth parents may be gone and unavailable, but they are nevertheless real, so very real and part of the life experience of the child.

And when the child listens to his second parents be openly curious about his first parents, then in his very young mind he has the awareness that there are four people in his story, all of whom have a part in who he is.

Positive, compassionate comments open up possibilities. As difficult as these family stories and history and cultural problems may be, they speak to the mind and the heart of the adoptee in a positive and affirming way: "In all of this you are talking about me."

Tenth, when birth parents are no longer seen as "enemies" who might somehow steal a child back, but instead as family partners who can be helpful, adoptive parents are able to parent more out of confidence and less out of fear.

Certainly, being fearful brings along its own baggage in terms of how birth parents might be perceived. So much of adoptive parenting, even today, is parenting by guessing. And guessing creates its own anxiety in not being sure of a parenting decision or of one's self as a parent.

Post-adoptive training for parents is usually in short supply. Little is written or understood in our American Society about the difficulties that may come along with the adoption of a wounded child. Make-believe at a societal level is powerfully negative, especially when it comes to appreciating the challenges that adoptive parents face. To whatever degree adoptive parents feel like they are on their own with the day-to day-challenges of bringing up a child with a wounded heart, parenting is usually parenting by guessing.

If first parents are seen as competitors for the affections of the relinquished and adopted child, quickly they may become adversaries to adoptive parents. However, for adoptive parents who are able to learn as much as possible about these first parents, their parenting choices will be less by guessing. Parenting by knowing is so qualitatively different because it has a different tone. That tone carries confidence about making a good choice for the development of a child. And that confidence offers a sense of security to both parent and child because parents then knows the best move to make.

For example, a young adoptee was in a usual tug-of-war with his adoptive mother about doing his fourth-grade homework. In a moment of his own irritation and aggression toward her, seeking to wound her, he lobbed over the table the missile of "Well, you are not my real mother, and she would not treat me like this." Surely there was a sting for his adoptive mother here, an injury intended to push her away.

Now was the moment for her to absorb that anger and not react, but to act. Wisely she responded, "Well, let's find out. Why don't you write her a short letter (not an email!) and ask her about that? Maybe she would be easier on you, as you say. Let's find out."

At this point, this boy realized that his missile had little effect. It hadn't knocked his mother off balance, and he was left with the challenge to check things out. With a short note and an envelope and a postage stamp, he delivered his inquiry to the mailbox. Only a few days later came his birth mother's response:

"Hello, Jeffrey. Thanks for your note and for thinking of me the other day. I understand that doing your homework was really bugging you. But you need to know for sure; of course, I would make you do your homework. That's what mothers do!"

Now certainly, a lot more is going on in this moment of parental conflict. At deeper levels for both adoptee and adoptive mother, there's a lot to consider in terms of the depth of bonding and attachment as well as the resistance to this connection. There is also much to consider in terms of resolving some of the grief that both persons carry around the arrangements of an adoptive family.

But in this brief vignette all the right things happened. The adoptee had the courage to express himself and give voice to his wonderings about his birth mother. He may have been missing her in words never spoken, but he brought her to the table in this push and pull with his adoptive mom. And she, so wisely, did not take the bait, but acknowledged the reality of his birth mother and asked that she be a resource in parenting her child.

So the letter went in the mail. What followed was so good, so healthy. His connection to his birth mother was reaffirmed. His adoptive mother's role was reinforced by the words of his birth mother. What could be better?

In Conclusion

For all of us, our progenitors have meaning. Ancestors are worshiped and even considered divine in some cultures. In others, especially where poverty and hardship may be the case, little may be thought of the people who came and went before.

Hopefully, this chapter serves as an important challenge to adoptive parents to review the manner in which they think about and respond to those people who brought their children to life. Shifting away from guessing toward knowing, and from fear toward confidence are important steps for adoptive parents.

Truthfully acknowledging the wonderings of adopted children about birth parents is necessary. Certainly, this is what relinquished and adopted young children would hope for if they could speak to this issue on the day that they were born.

7

How Adoptive Moms Take It on the Chin

Certainly, many dynamics are at play in the complex challenges of becoming an adoptive family. When one or two or three persons join a family, everyone makes a shift. The system of the family changes, as we noticed in Chapter 4, as the web of family relationships adapts to a new person – the adoptee. The family makes room for this new son or daughter, new brother or sister, and is challenged to redefine its family identity as well as re-establish the family goings-on of everyday life, now including this stranger-become-family member.

Of course, adoptive fathers are in the mix of these relationships, but our focus for now is on the unique challenges that adoptive mothers often face. Within this complex network, most often, **a significant and often troublesome relationship develops between the adoptee or adoptees and their adoptive mother**. In this chapter, by way of conversation and illustration, we will attend to this most important and problematic adoptive dynamic.

I often say that behavior always tells the truth and that the challenge is to understand an adoptee's behavior as well as our own behavior as parents. "Where is this behavior coming from? Why would my daughter need to steal her grandmother's curling iron?" Understandably, adoptive parents are often baffled by the odd choices that their children may make.

Of course, there are different ways to think about an adoptee's behavior and misbehavior in reference to his/her adoptive mother. Here we will consider an approach that seeks to interpret things from an empathic perspective, listening to the struggles of both mother and child as they demonstrate problematic patterns of behavior towards each other.

The first question to be addressed has to do with whom the adoptive mother represents to the adoptee. And, of course, to each child she represents many different things. Some of those representations are wonderfully positive. That warm spot on an adoptive mother's neck is the place where a relinquished and adopted child may find warmth and security in the early days and months and years of life. Access, however, to this important warm spot depends upon the capacity of the child to trust within a developing relationship with his/her adoptive mother. As we have seen in earlier examples, this may be a significant challenge for the adoptees who have experienced abuse and neglect; their capacity to trust may be seriously compromised.

We might wonder about ways the adoptive mother may come to bear the imprint of the adoptee's history prior to that adoptee's joining with her. In other words, how does the child's relinquishment experience evoke preparedness for, and need for, a mother of a certain

232

kind or color or nature or shape? Or more simply put, even at a very early age, what does the adoptee expect?

Many adoptees have a very different story from that of the relinquished child who has been able to bond well with his or her adoptive mother or primary caregiver. But we are wise to wonder about the impact of a perception the adoptee might be transferring to his or her next mother that may be a considerable distortion of who she really is.

Adoptees of all ages face challenges as they transition from parents by birth to possible orphanage workers or foster parents and then on to parents by adoption. And quite understandably, the older the child is at the time of adoption, the more early-on difficult experiences may have already occurred that make it increasingly challenging to trust–to leave the past behind and see the light of the present day. In these situations, no matter how much affection and concern adopted children may be offered, their ability to receive such care may be significantly compromised.

Older adoptees may have many negative memories already in place. The sheer number and range of such memory traces may become the boilerplate with which adoptees anticipate their futures. Over the years such memories have had time to form themes and then to reinforce their negative truth so that the adoptees then learn by heart what has been demonstrated more than once. They habitually anticipate more drama– troublesome behavior when these themes come together– setting the stage for significant conflict with the negatively imagined adoptive mom.

As adoptive parents become aware of these relational distortions and personal limitations, the difference between the wished-for child and the very real child sitting before them may precipitate real disappointment. Adoptive parents sometimes swallow hard as they begin to see before them the challenge of pursuing their new son or daughter, searching for ways to connect and develop a warm relationship, but sadly feeling irritated and pushed away in the process.

We should also be careful to notice that each adoptive mother has certain representations in her mind of her new child. That is, whom does the adoptee represent to the adoptive mother? For example, is the adoptee seen as that "replacement child" mentioned in Chapter 5? Or, again, does the adoptee represent her dreams and her wishes to somehow feel more "normal," not childless, not infertile, as if the adoptee is her redeemer from all these painful things?

If she has romanticized this new relationship with her child by adoption, changing her view toward a more realistic picture of the actual child could be considerably distressing.

Our greatest concern in this book is the adoptee who is fearful of closeness. These children may behave in many negative ways in order to protect themselves from anticipated dangers of which adoptive parents may be entirely unaware. Starting fights with siblings (especially younger ones), yelling back at parents, stealing things like money or clothing or make-up, lying about misbehaviors with a straight face, and putting blame on other people are all defensive behaviors that serve to keep others at a distance. And often, with little remorse.

Of course, they also set the stage for troublesome connecting.

Rather than enjoying the pleasure of the warmth on an adoptive mother's neck or, as the years go by, on her lap, this child may resist that closeness in a heart-breaking fashion. Love toward this adoptee is sometimes unrequited; it does not come back toward the adoptive parents. With some adoptees, it may come back ever so slowly and in indirect, even disguised ways, even years later.

Nevertheless, without this infant's smile, without this warmth in return, without the usual happy child responses, we can understand that continuing to love and offer care can become more challenging. **Sadly, adoptive parents may get worn out, deeply distressed by this chronic emotional drain wrapped up in the relationship with a new son or new daughter.**

And, of course, these stresses and strains have a significant negative effect on family life. Parents and siblings ask, "How do you get along with a child, a brother or a sister, who does not want to get along?"

What comes to the fore in a surprising way is the never anticipated challenge of absorbing the anger of such a frightened child. Adoptive parents who believe that "love conquers all" are usually quite unprepared for parenting the orphan. The wounded child may be frustrated, unresponsive, frightened, and angry for very good reasons. We can certainly understand this adoptee anger when we consider what neglect or abuse may have set the stage for this angry response directed at nearly everyone.

For this child, the experiences of the past are not over. Instead, they continue to inform this child that getting close to other people, especially adults, is dangerous. Being left alone in a crib for hours and hours without food and with a dirty diaper, or being whipped by an orphanage worker in a foreign land with very different understandings of raising children--these may be the early-on experiences of orphans who have learned not to trust adults, whoever those adults may be.

Orphanage workers in Thailand once told me that they'd best not respond to the crying infant in order to "toughen them up for life." With experiences like these, the self-defense of a protective shield on the adoptee's part makes sense. Further, and quite tragically, such negative experiences in early life set up the probability of significant disorders of character. This challenge leaves adoptive parents at a loss to discern the best way to respond, to seek connection with the child who fears connection.

In some orphanages in Eastern Europe, even the babies do not cry because they have already learned that no one will pick them up. (I was there. And I stood among the silent infants, *heartbroken*.) In such a case, it's no wonder that they would struggle with relationships, no wonder that they are frightened by closeness with others. Others are frightening. So far in life, others have hurt them and/or abandoned them. To survive such neglect, understandably, they seal themselves off from other people. And sometimes, the single value that they live by is personal survival,

236

enduring overwhelming abandonment or whatever else may turn a heart to stone.

Or consider the boy from Ethiopia who clearly remembers being whipped, beaten on his back by one of the orphanage workers. In his case, clearly the lesson is that no one is to be trusted, especially adults. It may be that just below the surface of this boy's story, an untold narrative of significant suffering is kept away, sometimes at great costs even at times outside of awareness.

So now we return to our first question: **Whom does the adoptive mom represent to the adoptee?** It may not be as one would wish. Some children see the adoptive mom as a woman to be feared. "When might she lose her temper again?" "When will the beatings start to happen again?" Or even more frightening, "When will I be taken away, once more abandoned?" and "Will I ever be placed in another family?" These unspoken fears may lie in the heart of the adoptee--again, sometimes outside of awareness. Nevertheless, powerful, painful frights like these may drive the behavior of a child in ways that are disruptive and destructive, often to the entire adoptive family.

By way of an unconscious psychological phenomenon we call transference, such a child would understandably anticipate being hurt once again in one way or another. **Transference has to do with present expectations that are based upon experiences in the past.** This means that what has happened in the past, so one thinks, will probably happen again. Accordingly, the next adult will most likely do what the last adult has done. In a troubling manner, this phenomenon of transference is most often outside of awareness.

What has the child learned to expect from adults, especially *female* adults? Through negative transferring from the past to the present, adoptees would interpret the behavior of their adoptive mother through the lens of harsh treatment in the past. So the adoptee believes, and so it is quite understandable for such a child to be defensive and push away the very hands that feed him or her physically and emotionally and spiritually.

As these children mature and become more cognitively aware of the meaning of relinquishment and adoption, the usual questions come up about the why of one's adoption. It is a dark journey for some adoptees to learn about and to accept the reality of their painful beginnings, of suffering abuse and troublesome abandonments.

Sooner or later, as they continue to mature, adoptees usually feel this "hole" in their birth history. Most want to know the reasons for their being "given up," with a plan for adoption. Formulating this question may take lots of time. Some adoptees may become consciously aware of their wondering and ask directly about the story of their abandonment.

One little girl, adopted at birth, now at age 4 ½, is asking an incessant stream of questions about her relinquishment and the story around the why question. Her parents are unsettled and guessing at how best to respond to her daily inquiries.

Other children may allow it to take shape in a disguised form, just asking about family history or a bit later in life, medical information. And others will never formulate the question, leaving it in the recesses of their minds.

Now, to whatever degree these unanswered questions are troublesome for the adoptee, we might wonder how much the adoptive mother comes to represent the person who made those difficult, negative choices. Most often, the adoptive mother does begin to remind the child of the birth mother who may have made a choice to leave the baby on the steps of the church, trusting that someone else would serve as his or her parents.

All of this is to notice that adoptive mothers sometimes come to represent people in the adoptee's past who have caused pain and that usually includes birth mothers and birth fathers as people who did, in fact, abandon them. Relinquishment may be a kinder word, but adoptees usually think that abandonment is more accurate.

It then becomes understandable that adoptive mothers usually take it on the chin because of the child's earlier experiences of relinquishment and neglect and abuse and now because of how they may come to represent an adoptee's mother by birth.

How then can adoptive mothers become successful at parenting their children? This becomes a very difficult question. They are set in place to become targets for the anger of a troubled adoptee. At some point this reality needs to be named and discussed in a caring, nonjudgmental fashion.

However, **naming something alone is not sufficient for the behavioral changes for which we hope.** That

239

change happens when adoptees live within the experience of parental care, overcoming the negative expectations that they may anticipate. Some may never name anything and yet change begins to happen because of the power of staying within the relationship.

Nevertheless, understandably, the usual response to such difficulties in this relationship is to ignore them because this is so difficult for both mother and child to face. When the expectation of the child is repeatedly disconfirmed by the adoptive mother's positive affirming behavior, the adoptee may begin to see things differently, more accurately, and then slowly begin to behave more positively, allowing love.

The Story of Jenny Who Took It on the Chin

Adoptive parents Jenny and Thomas had proved unable to have children. They had much to grieve in their attempts to become parents by birth. As is usually the case, struggles with infertility were profoundly disheartening, so they were grieving the loss of the baby never to be born to them.

They then turned to becoming parents by adoption. When one birth mother changed her mind about relinquishing her baby, once again they faced deep disappointment. How thankful they were when baby Lawrence came to them on the day of his birth. Now finally, there was the sound of an infant crying at home.

They may not have been aware that day, but this dear infant may have already experienced a wound before he ever came home with Jenny and Thomas. All that day the mother of the birth mother, Cindy, wept over losing little Larry and begged her daughter to keep her son--her first grandchild. Both sorrow and joy filled the hospital room as these two parties involved sorted out these most important decisions of relinquishment by Cindy and adoption by Jenny and Thomas.

That first day Cindy breastfed her baby boy. We may wonder forever what kind of initial bonding between the two of them had already occurred when little Larry was introduced to his new parents. We shall never know.

The first year of Larry's life was a most important time of bonding by Larry and attachment offered by Jenny and Thomas. As they recall this time in his life, they remember it as peaceful and joyful. This is the way it ought to be with such an infant. Jenny was quite careful to protect her attachment with Larry and remembers enjoying being a day-to-day mother who loved loving her son.

But when Larry was about 12 months old, a tragic break in her relationship with him happened when she left for four days to attend a training conference for her career. Her judgment at the time was that little Larry could manage this four-day stretch and, most certainly, would return to her arms with delight upon her return. However, so sad to say, that never happened.

Almost as if a switch was turned off, Larry became "Daddy's boy," insisting that Thomas tuck him in and that Thomas put him to bed. When he needed something special in those early years of his development, he would ask his daddy for a drink of water. He would sit in Thomas's lap. Jenny recalls the nighttime moment when she heard Larry crying out, "Mommy, Mommy!" Finally, she thought, Larry had shifted his affections back in her direction. But when she entered the room, this little boy looked at her and spoke such painful words, "Not you!" Could this be?

At such an early age, just over 12 months, little Larry seemed to be quite aware of the loss of his first mother. Might we think about the strength of prenatal bonding here? Or, a break from that initial day of breastfeeding with Cindy? However we might wonder about this, the arrows of Larry's rejection sank deep into Jenny's heart.

Remember, the word tragedy means that something happens that should not happen in someone's life. After age one, Larry's conflicted relationship with Jenny continued in such a way that both she and Thomas spent much of the next 17 years managing Larry's bouts of anger, even rage, as he grew up. Pushing back against the expectations of his parents, of his teachers, of administrators, or anyone else who sought to hold him accountable for his troublesome behavior, one way or another, **Larry often got his way.**

Consequences were of little effect. As Jenny remembers it, "We still had consequences, though. I felt that it would be a disservice to Larry not to have consequences–that he would grow up even more out of control."

One of the positives in Larry's personality was his strong social skills, especially with adults who were not his adoptive parents. Larry could be very gracious and respectful and very engaging as a person. (Remember Eddie Haskell in "Leave it to Beaver"? He was such a "schmoozer.") He had a very likable quality in his informal presentation to people. His constant comfort speaking with adults served him well socially and kept him out of trouble on many occasions. This was the Larry that people very much enjoyed. Still today, Larry is a very good conversation partner with older people.

Nevertheless, it did not take long for people around him to notice how much Larry struggled every day with his own anxiety. He appeared to be the kind of person who could never sit still and stay focused to get homework done. When Larry was younger, he was put on an anti-anxiety medication for nearly five years. But this medication created memory problems for Larry so that he found it even more difficult to do his homework. Stimulants that most often calm a patient only increased Larry's anxieties.

Unfortunately, Larry was in that small minority of children for whom such medical interventions yield no therapeutic benefit. Although Larry was under the care of a child psychiatrist for that period, the medication that he was on yielded little help with his struggles with impulse control as he sought to manage this high level of anxiety.

As it turned out, the use of medical marijuana as an anti-anxiety agent became Larry's best solution. Larry found that he could function better and feel more comfortable with people with the regular use of cannabis. Living in Colorado where such usage is legal, this seemed to be the best solution for his struggles. His parents, feeling quite uneasy about drugs in general, wisely went along with this decision.

Larry was easier to live with when he was using marijuana to manage himself. The medical marijuana use began to calm his anxiety-driven brain, and Larry became calmer and more capable of relating to people as a result.

As the years went by, both adoptive parents learned that the best approach to Larry's destructive behavior was to let Larry deal with the natural consequences of his behavior. There were moments when Larry's anger drove him to break down the door to his room or smash something against the wall or rip the cupboard doors off their hinges. Later, in a calmer moment, he was told that he would have to pay for the repairs.

On several occasions Larry struck his parents. On one occasion he kicked Jenny. Once, Larry began to hit his father with a keyboard while his dad was driving their car. He had said "No" to one of Larry's many demands. Thomas pulled over to the side of the road and patiently waited until Larry calmed down. It was so obvious that Larry really struggled to contain himself, to reign in his own impulses. These fits of anger when he did not get his way were frightening, probably to Larry as well.

When Larry was younger, he became very attached to his play therapist, but, unfortunately, she left her practice when she got pregnant. Here was another moment of abandonment, now by another mother with child.

It is important to notice that in these early years Larry was capable of forming some bond with these female therapists with whom he worked. We might wonder whom they represented – perhaps Cindy? When he was switched to another therapist, the transition did not go well and counseling ended.

At age 16, continuing to be quite curious about himself, he became an interested participant in counseling. But when it became clear that this therapy was no magic bullet to help him manage his angry outbursts, his willingness to continue therapy subsided. In this counseling as an adolescent, Larry worked to present a very positive image to his counselor. It was important to him that he be seen in a positive light.

Now he continues to rely on the CBD components of cannabis that demonstrate medical benefit. Again, this self-medication has proved to be Larry's most useful aid in managing himself.

Well, what might be the story behind this story? What might explain Larry's behavior and help us appreciate the ways in which he tried so hard to do battle with his mother and refused to adapt to the expectations of authority figures in his life?

As Jenny was the primary administrator of the home, she bent over backwards absorbing Larry's anger–taking in the insults, the disrespect, and the injuries. At times Jenny would take herself away, cry, be sad, question everything, and then talk with Thomas about their next move in helping Larry manage himself. (A time of respite would certainly have been in order in those days.) Nevertheless, Jenny stayed with the parenting and continued to be in conversation with her angry, sometimes even raging son. She simply would not give up on Larry.

At times Larry would seek to take advantage of Jenny's commitment to him, hoping to manipulate her with the fear of the next outburst and fighting with considerable strength to get his way. Usually Jenny stood her ground, but sometimes she was so fatigued that this became taxing, incredibly difficult. His pushing against her and Thomas was relentless; parenting Larry was exhausting.

At one point in the midst of conflict, Jenny suggested that she back up a step and that Thomas take a step forward in holding Larry accountable for his behavior. For example, Thomas began insisting that Larry pay for the damage sometimes done to their home, or that he get at least some of his homework done so that he would not fail in school.

Jenny took this as a gift of sorts and felt some relief because she had permission to back away from the intensity of Larry's angry attacks towards her.

In his junior year of high school Larry got in a considerable amount of trouble. With some of his friends, he would party hard and drink as well as smoke his usual dosage of marijuana. When Larry was drunk, he demanded that everybody leave him alone, that no one touch him, and that no one try to get close to him in some attempt at being supportive. He felt safest by himself, even if he would once again become an "orphan."

One activity that motivated Larry was his desire to play sports. He is very talented athletically. It's this that he loved. As a junior, he was set to play quarterback position for his high school football team, but early in the season he sustained a concussion that took him out of all the games. Losing football participation was a devastating blow to Larry; it denied him the opportunity to shine on the athletic field.

And then, more seriously, Larry and two of his friends decided to sneak into school one weekend and steal some of the coach's clothing. They were quickly found out and apprehended. Sadly, as a senior, Larry again lost his place on the high school football team.

At that point, going to another high school with other friends looked like the right thing to do. This, of course, was another hit for Jenny and Thomas. What to do next became an ongoing challenge for Larry and for his parents.

As an aside, it is interesting to wonder about the theft of the coach's clothing. As it turns out, Larry had nearly 50 unclaimed sweatshirts in his bedroom closet. He told his parents that they were given to him. And perhaps a few were. Often, he knew to whom they belonged. He certainly could have returned them to the rightful students, but Larry never did that. He just kept the sweatshirts.

Maybe this puzzling behavior had something to do with his desire to be connected to the friends and teammates that spent time with him in his high school years. Maybe this was Larry's way of not feeling entirely alone. Maybe he wanted some of what others were given. Maybe Larry wanted to feel like a member of the team, so he had the entire team's clothing in his closet.

Or maybe he wanted something concrete to symbolize that he was a part of something, and that he belonged– that he was one of the group. Or maybe he wanted to choose to whom he belonged and not have it chosen for him. Maybe it was worth getting in trouble for some of these reasons. Of course, these are just guesses, but they may help us better appreciate how Larry saw the world around him. It is certainly something about which to wonder.

Now off the football team, Larry decided it was time to leave home and not be pressured by his parents to adapt to their expectations, even when the bar was so low: "Please, just graduate from high school!" Off he went in his beater car to the home of a friend in another town where he was allowed to stay for the summer. Returning home to go to school, he said that he could not tolerate living with his parents any longer. So, the plan then became that he would attend a different high school in a different locality.

Although Jenny worked very hard to make arrangements for him to be successful in a different high school, it did not take long for Larry to once again fail the responsibilities of being a student. Larry would rather sleep or "hang" with his friends than attend class or do his homework.

Another semester of education was lost. This was quite difficult for his adoptive parents, but it was not a big deal for Larry. He did not care about going to school. He only seemed to care about being with his friends. Even if they treated him poorly, he saw them as his friends.

His final attempt to graduate from high school was that of attending an alternate learning program. The principal of this school was very kind and flexible, wanting to help Larry as much as possible. He could still see a way to offer Larry a high school diploma if he could stay with this program. But Larry did not do much of his homework, and, increasingly, failed to show up for class.

At age 18, Larry had exhausted all of the options put before him to earn his high school diploma. And, **wisely, his adoptive parents took the pressure off; they simply said to Larry that it was his choice about going to school.** No need for more conflict in the family that would be unproductive and that would be a battle for control, once again, that Larry would certainly win, at least in the short term. He could not let his parents be his parents in terms of submitting to their authority.

After ending the battle over attending an alternate high school, all on his own, Larry found a job at a local restaurant. When, finally, he had the real freedom to determine his own future, whatever that might be, Larry began to turn a corner in terms of being more grown up, more responsible, less in need of his negative acting-out behavior.

Now, with money in his pocket and fellow workers who became his friends, Larry was able to settle down to some degree. The angry rants about horrible Jenny lessened. Larry became more cooperative at home as the battle about high school and concerns about his future were over.

Now it was time for Larry to make his own choices and deal with whatever consequences they bring. Marijuana continues to be his agent of self-medication and that continues to be useful. But certainly, Larry is beginning to find his way. Maybe there will be a GED down the road if he desires to do so, but only if he desires to do so. As it stands, Larry could complete five classes online and receive a regular high school diploma.

This, then, is an overview of Larry's complex relinquishment and adoption narrative. His story is seen through the eyes of its participants, and what we really have is their interpretations of their experience with Larry. On Jenny's side of this conflicted relationship was a story of enduring chronic verbal abuse from her son.

She was regularly pummeled by Larry's verbal attacks on her. She could not win this battle, but she continued to stay with it until she could see that trying to rein in or control Larry's life would always be challenging. Neither she nor Larry could bring peace to the table. **The whole experience of raising Larry has been very painful for Jenny.**

Both Jenny and Thomas did what they could do to accommodate his wishes as much as possible. Nevertheless, no amount of adapting could resolve the intensity of the conflicted relationship between Larry and Jenny. From her side of this conflict, she experienced deep fatigue and sometimes tearful disappointment because her dreams of mothering a happy adoptee had crashed upon the rocks of reality. At times she backed away, totally exhausted. Becoming a family never fully happened.

Eventually Jenny was able to look for the benefits of allowing Larry to be exactly who he was. Allowing Larry more room to make choices, like going to school or not, gave him as well as her more freedom, greatly easing some of the personal suffering in this story.

Few adoptive parents have been challenged as much as Jenny and Thomas in terms of absorbing the anger of a relinquished and adopted child. From Jenny's perspective, she allowed Larry the space that he needed because of her undying hope that he could one day come around and become someone who could learn to love her back. Hopefully, it appears that this shift is beginning to happen.

At this writing, Larry is 18 years old, a legal adult, who is moving beyond the party scene to a better place in terms of living his life as more of a "grown-up". Larry is certainly happier now that he is more in control of himself and more in charge of his life.

But More to the Story

An important part of Larry's story has little to do with Jenny and Thomas, but rather has to do with Larry's relinquishment and his on-and-off relationship with his birth mother, Cindy. She was a freshman in college when she learned of her pregnancy. Her older boyfriend, Craig, a star soccer player, left her alone and pregnant. Even today, Cindy cries as she recalls and re-experiences the pain of relinquishing Larry.

Up until more recently, there has been little contact between Cindy and Larry's family. Open adoption contact information was available, but Cindy never took initiative to make much of this possible relationship. However, at a certain point, as part of a counseling conversation, Larry took new interest in seeking out Cindy as someone with whom he would enjoy spending some time.

Although initially hesitant, Cindy responded to Larry's wish to meet her and began an ongoing conversation, usually by texting Larry. He was excited about this and worked at putting his best foot forward, hopefully to impress her with his accomplishments, especially in sports. Cindy and her family attended several of Larry's lacrosse games. On one occasion, they met for lunch at a local restaurant and Cindy, now married with three other children, was pleased to see him and to hear good things about him that they could both enjoy, even celebrate.

It appeared that Larry needed to impress her and did not want her to know anything about the struggles of his life. Larry spoke positively to Cindy about his adoptive parents and gave her the impression that things were going well. Together they took a walk in the parking lot outside the restaurant, with a baby half-brother in a stroller, to continue their conversation about how things were going in Larry's life. "I just wanted you to know that I am doing okay and that you made the right decision to let go of me"–so said Larry to Cindy. This comment brought tears to Cindy's eyes as she responded with "Thank you for telling me that."

After this meeting, they texted each other more consistently, and Larry found this to be a supportive benefit for him, at least for a while. "You cannot have too many people who care about you"–so he was told and so, at that time, he thought.

As time went on, it became quite clear that, in Larry's eyes, Cindy was quite special to him and he was very invested in having her see him in a good light. He did not want her to know more than that. He kept his struggles with school, with his parents, and with the police out of the conversation. It began to look like Cindy could do no wrong. On the other side of this, despite what Larry had said, Jenny could do nothing right in his eyes.

This behavior is called *splitting,* seeing things in such a way that one person can do no wrong and another person, a mom or a dad, a brother or a sister, an adoptive mother or a birth mother, can do no right. Instead of (more maturely) being able to see the strengths and weaknesses of different people and developing the capacity to carry ambivalence toward different people, **Larry was a person who needed to put Cindy in a totally wonderful light and to see Jenny in only a terrible light.**

When Larry got in more trouble, as he continued to do, conversations with Cindy subsided. He did not want Cindy to know the nature of his conflicted relationships. In Cindy's eyes he wanted to appear to be the "good adoptee" who had put himself together. He wished only to impress her.

So now in this scenario Larry's birth mother is being glorified and Larry's adoptive mother is being demonized, the target of his scorn. For the purposes of this chapter, it becomes clear that Jenny came to represent the rejecting side of his birth mother as well as all of herself as the abandoning mother when he was 12 months old. Evidently, that four-day break was more than he could manage in his fragile infantile emotional state.

What about all that anger that Larry so often failed to manage? We recall our earlier comments about the adoptive mom taking it on the chin because she becomes the target the adoptee's rage, in part, by unconsciously reminding him of the pain and of the many losses that come along with being relinquished and then further abandoned. Larry's anger was part of his life, almost from the beginning.

After Larry met Cindy, his birth mother, he pushed much of that anger away, at least for a time. And he may have kept his anger safely tucked away in the darker corners of his heart. But it's not a surprise that his anger continues.

If we cannot put our feelings and our emotions into words, we will inevitably act them out. Sometimes, even if we do name our struggles with some accuracy, we may still act out those troublesome feelings and emotions. No wonder Larry's angry outbursts would continue; his anger must go somewhere. Jenny was his target.

As stated earlier, **Jenny became the representation of the earliest rejections in Larry's life**. While Cindy came to be the loving birth mother, Jenny came to represent the rejecting birth mother and then the rejecting mother. The warmth of her care could not penetrate; she saw only glimpses of his concern for her, only brief moments of calm and affection.

Things are more peaceful now for Larry's family. Jenny and Thomas can see the wisdom of not pressuring Larry to do what they want him to do, especially as it relates to going to school. Instead, now Larry is more accountable for his own behavior to his employer, and that seems to be going well. Sometimes letting go is the right choice. And now the relationship between adoptive mother and adopted son is characterized by more care and less conflict, more thoughtful consideration and less angry responding.

In truth, this could have become a failed adoption, if the attacks from Larry became so overwhelming that something had to end. But Jenny persevered and Thomas learned how to be more involved with Larry's discipline, which pleased Jenny a great deal.

So, as these adoptive parents persevere--"we will never abandon you"- things are turning toward the good. That does not always happen, but in this story it has happened to a good and hopeful degree—finally and thankfully.

Larry has become less demanding. He takes pride in his full-time employment, earning his own money, having his own checking account, and being able to make better decisions about the people with whom he spends time.

Jenny's chin, emotionally bruised and pain-filled, is beginning to heal.

Now, after these past 17 years or so, Larry is beginning to respond with some care toward Jenny. **Could this be the birth of empathy with another person?** Larry has learned some cooking skills from his restaurant work, and one day he even made breakfast for Jenny. Recently he has begun talking with Jenny in a kinder and softer manner.

Perhaps, for the first time, Larry is beginning to "see" his parents. **More able to look beyond himself and his self-centered demands, he is beginning to notice the struggles of other people in his life**. Accordingly, there is more hope for a future in which Jenny and Larry can have a more positive, caring relationship. In such a moment of bonding, he would be able to see Jenny for who she really is.

He is not so filled with rage now, and it may be that Larry's negative representations of Jenny are subsiding. He is more able to see reality, the reality of his parents and the years of struggle that he and his parents had set in motion. For Jenny, she can now say that taking it on the chin, as adoptive mothers often do, was worth it!

A Counselor Perspective

Larry's anxiety has been a lifelong struggle for him and his parents. The causes of this generalized anxiety most likely may be genetic and biological as well as environmental in terms of relating to both his biological and adoptive families. The dynamics outlined in this chapter may only partially explain why Larry became so intensely upset with Jenny. Certainly, this deserves more understanding and attention in order to support adoptive mothers who are indeed taking it on the chin.

Further, in terms of treatment of Larry's anxiety, therapy with a well-informed counselor may bring to light some of the difficulties described in this chapter for more personal care and further resolution, primarily in the context of a relationship with his therapist. Ongoing review and evaluation by a psychiatrist with regard to accurate diagnosis and the possible effectiveness of newer medications is always wise.

Other treatments besides talk therapy or the use of medications may include the use of Neurofeedback. For some who have experienced trauma this is often effective in repairing brain function. EMDR (Eye Movement

Desensitization and Reprocessing), is another method of overcoming what may be deep-seated anxieties around early-life distress and trauma. These remain future possibilities for Larry to consider.

A Postscript to this Story About Absorbing the Anger of a Child

As one young parent stated to me, "You need to let your kids be mad at you."

Many parents today who are part of our millennial generation take a very cognitive approach to parenting. Simply put, **they seek to be consistently friendly and seek to persuade their children**, to convince them by a gentle argument that their behavior is somehow troublesome. It may be dangerous or hurtful to others; it may be self-centered and lacking in awareness of another's experience. But whatever, many parents approach their children with what they hope might be convincing arguments--employing a very cognitive method of change.

Usually the child is listening to the tone of the parent's voice more than the words and wondering how to get out of trouble or even out of the room. In some sense a relational misfiring is going on with such an approach. Parents usually fail at their attempt at persuasively arguing with a young child and the child, depending on age, may not comprehend or take in the values of behavior that these parents may seek to teach. Really, they pretty much miss each other, going right by the space of the other, like two trains on separate tracks zooming close by but never touching, and going in opposite directions.

Absorbing the anger of our children, letting them be mad at us, and listening carefully in order to understand a child's misbehavior is a tall order. For our purposes in this book, we are observing the ways in which very angry children face a very difficult challenge in adopting their parents. That kind of intimacy may be frightening to them, even sometimes terrifying. Accordingly, their angry misbehavior will serve the purpose of maintaining a safe distance from their adoptive parents.

More generally speaking, all of us who are parents will at some moment be called upon to take in--that is, absorb--a boatload of rage. We may need to learn how to do that, to hold our breath until the fiery confrontation subsides and stay alongside our children when they honestly want to hurt us, to bring injury to our hearts, and certainly to keep us at a distance.

But now, what about children who may be incredibly angry because they are carrying the wounds of starting life in families where first parents failed them? For whatever reason, they were taken away and put in a foster care home or perhaps, in other countries, they were placed in an orphanage where they learned to shut up on the outside and shut down on the inside in order to survive physically and emotionally and spiritually. These were their first lessons in living with adults who were sometimes dangerous, frightening, or absent, leaving them in dirty diapers, even for days.

And then by way of adoption, they come to join in on our family stories and slowly we began to take them in and begin to appreciate how difficult life has already been for them. Sadly, of course, we learn this not by words but by deeds, not by the words in a record of relinquishment or a report of adoption, but by dishes of spaghetti that are thrown at the kitchen wall, then broken on the floor; these are the hard lessons for adoptive parents to stomach.

Not reacting immediately with our own irritation but in the interest of both parent and child, instead, disciplining ourselves to act objectively, nearly without emotion, and to speak to the deeper issues at hand--this is incredibly difficult! (Remember the illustration of wearing the "white coat" of objectivity.) Consider, "Wow, you must be really angry right now. In a few minutes, would you please help me clean up the spaghetti on the wall?"

Practically speaking, the importance of this challenge of absorbing anger from children who are struggling to adopt their parents cannot be overstated. It may well be the most important skill for adoptive parents to master in order to form relationships that are as healthy as possible, that further the emotional growth of a hesitant adoptee, and that possibly brighten the future for the struggling, anxious adoptive family.

Let's weigh the considerable benefits of this parental approach, and then let's look at the downside of failing to absorb the anger of our children, a down side with painful, lifelong negatives. In what follows, I will present five good reasons to become "rage-absorbers" (maybe sometimes even "shock-absorbers"!) in relating to angry children. And in so doing, alongside of those positives, I will also consider the ensuing difficulties for adoptive parents if this skill is never learned.

First, let's return for a moment to that word picture where Larry was yelling right into the face of his mother, "I hate you! I hate you!" Jenny stood there and took it, without yelling back, without defending herself, and without scowling at him for the emotional hit she was taking on the chin.

At one time there would have been a tear in her eye that would betray her personal pain, but now, being worn and wiser, Jenny knew what to do: Nothing. No response. **She simply let Larry yell until the yelling slowly quieted down to silence, then to talking.**

Among the many reasons why this was a good interchange on her part, perhaps the most important, is that she let Larry speak and stay in his own out-of-control voice. As irrational and hurt and angry and wounded as he may have been, Jenny took it in. She may have needed a nap later in the day, but in this moment she took in, that is, absorbed the rage with which he hammered her. He later remembers that he really wanted to hit her but was able to hold back.

This then is the first good reason to absorb the anger: **Larry was permitted to stay inside his own voice, to speak his truth from inside his own skin and from the corners of his heart about his life experience as a young man who did not have the anchors that he needed to feel safe and secure about himself.** Of course it was her fault, of course it was his father's fault, of course it was the teacher's fault--we call this the projection of blame–because it was too much for him to carry blame about himself by himself.

Jenny's capacity to do nothing gave Larry the space that was needed for him to once again let her know that things were not well with him. It was a significant gift that she gave to her son that day.

Despite the many stolen sweatshirts in his closet, despite the chores undone, despite items stolen from his house by him or by his rascal friends, and despite the name-calling –"You bitch! You're not my mother!" – despite all these things, Jenny took the hits. She absorbed them as they slowly sank into the bottom corners of her heart.

She was wise enough to know that this was not about her; it was about somebody–maybe all the somebodies who have brought injury to Larry, birth parents for starters, Cindy for sure–but it really had little to do with the mother that Jenny really was, right then in the here and now of their relationship. So as much as it hurt, she learned once again how much pain there was in Larry's heart. In his own voice he spoke his truth, without interruption from a wise adoptive mother.

Now conversely, what might have happened if in a very usual, very understandable manner, Jenny had pushed back and disagreed and yelled at Larry and taken him on with her argument against his disruptive, angry behavior? Obviously at this time there was no respect at all for Jenny; she was simply the target for his rage. What if, steel against steel, they had battled things out to the point where Larry would probably have left, walked out of the house in a storm, and Jenny would have collapsed on the couch under a blanket in emotional exhaustion? What would we have then?

On Jenny's side she would have spoken her piece at the price of ongoing unmanaged conflict with her only son. She, who so much wanted to be a mother who was close to her child, she may have wept silently. But she would have lost ground in establishing anything that was warm and meaningful when there was little more ground to lose. Thus this may have been a despairing clash between them.

On Larry's side, he would once again become the orphan who thought that he had no parents, not really. Larry was good at reenacting becoming an orphan. This would be another occasion of failure for him, failure to be able to relate successfully to another person, and certainly failure to achieve what he really needed–the capacity to tolerate and then to enjoy the care of that other person.

Second, absorbing the anger of a troubled child will usually translate into less need to act out negative feelings. Simply put, when there is ongoing trouble in our own hearts we either talk it out or we act it out, or both. Sometimes, as with Larry, a child both talks it out and acts it out. Just as with any children, adoptees who struggle to adopt their parents may quite understandably hold back all kinds of emotional confusion and distress.

Maybe things are bad at some point, but they might have been worse if that little boy had never spoken his truth--the little boy living in a big boy body who seldom gave permission to other people to know what life was really like for him. Quite understandably, as hard as it may be to believe it, things could be worse when a troubled adoptee has no place to go and is unable to yell and scream and talk about the negative imprint that they live with when a mother by birth never becomes a mother by life.

Now, in the narrative of the first 18 years of Larry's life, he certainly did a good deal of what we call acting out by getting in trouble as much as he did. Not unlike many adoptees who struggle to adopt their parents, Larry had little guilt about taking money or taking those sweatshirts that somehow meant something puzzling to him. He acted out when he pushed so hard so often against Jenny.

And he acted out even more intensely when he packed himself in his car and simply left home. **Once more, he made himself an orphan**. Jenny and Thomas, to their credit, stayed with him in assisting his taking leave and assisting him along the way of his journey to another place. Quietly, Jenny fought all his efforts to re-create that word picture of the orphan on the street with no place to go and with no one in his life who cared about him.

Had Jenny and Thomas given in, given up, and washed their hands clean of managing Larry's angry outbursts, things may have been much worse for Larry; he may never know that. He may have been more destructive at home than he was, perhaps pitching a rock through the living room window. Or, a concern always to be feared, Larry may have attempted or died by suicide, taking his life from all of us as well as from himself. But the point here is that he did not do so. Things did not need to be worse because Jenny listened between the screams and gave Larry space to scream those screams, even when they were right into her face.

Third, Jenny's choice to absorb the anger of her son was another moment of potential bonding that may have facilitated a more trusting relationship. But this is not easy to see. By taking the hit on the chin, metaphorically, adoptive mother Jenny communicated to Larry that she could handle the depth of his rage. Also, he learned over and over that she would not relinquish him.

Larry may not even have known in a very conscious way how deep the well of troublesome anger may have been within himself. Nor may Jenny have been able to see how deeply distressed he really was. Nevertheless, what Larry learned again and again was that he had a mother who could handle his anger. She could do that. Further, Larry learned that she would be constant. He may have been testing Jenny to the brink to see if she would relinquish him. And he learned that, despite his fits of rage, she did not need to turn away from him--a profound lesson for him to learn.

And so, Larry learned that he could trust Jenny with the depth of his rage. And rage he did, on and on, especially in the middle years of high school, until he finally fell out and went his own way as the prodigal son,[17] driving away from home. Absorbing Larry's anger opened the door that gave him the opportunity to look away and even walk away, always knowing that mother Jenny would not abandon him no matter what he did.

So many times people told Thomas and Jenny that enough was enough and that they had already gone the

---

[17] See the parable, *The Prodigal Son,* found in Luke 15 in the New Testament Scriptures.

extra mile with Larry. It was time to cut him loose. Nevertheless, they persevered and stayed on the trail with their wayward son. There was just enough trust for them to do so.

Once again, let us suppose that Jenny got back in Larry's face and tore into him with an equal and opposite force. She would be protecting the tenderness of her own heart and would no longer put up with the emotional beating, the pummeling day after day that she experienced from Larry. Let us suppose that she refused to give him space to yell and scream and swear away at her.

So many things would have gone more wrong. Trust is critically important. To not trust another human being is to live in emotional isolation. Some call that the definition of hell. And never learning the capacity to trust means that such isolation becomes permanent. The road ahead is then set for significant disorders of the character for a young man or young woman.

One of the significant variables in personality that speak to the good quality of someone is the capacity for remorse, for feeling sorry for what they've done that hurts another. A little boy or girl only learns this lesson of the heart when he or she can imagine the pain that another child experiences as a result of his or her behavior. This creates the capacity for relating with care with other people, usually other children. But without trust something important never quite happens: relationships never get very far. Regret does not occur, despite someone's hurtful behavior. Usually, direct eye contact is minimal.

Some readers may recall the episode of "The Oprah Winfrey Show" when champion bicycle rider Lance Armstrong attempted to apologize for lying about the years of doping that contributed to the seven Tour de France victories of which he was stripped. Lance tried to express his regret, but he could not pull it off; he could not be sorry. And yes, there was a father missing in his life.

Regret is one emotion that none of us can fake, even if we try to look sorry in the courtroom. The judge knows. Sadness about bad behavior begins way back when trust makes room for bonding and attachment between a wounded child and adoptive parents.

Fourth, absorbing the anger of the wounded adoptee who is pushing hard to be troublesome indicates that being angry itself has a positive value. This may sound odd, and many people find this lesson difficult to learn. Anger itself is usually seen as a serious negative within a person, probably because anger is too often close to violence. That makes sense. However, unacknowledged anger may be the most dangerous.

Jenny was teaching Larry an important lesson when she was able to allow his anger within the boundaries against personal violence: "You may yell and you may scream, but if you hit me, I will call the police." She spoke these good words more than once to Larry as he navigated his way through his difficult early high school years.

Despite the bad press that anger usually has in any network of relationships, anger itself may be many good things. It is the experience, first of all, of self-esteem, namely that something really matters and "it really matters to me," and when I am angry, I know that I matter as well.

When anger rises up against all the-isms of bias, when anger rises up against the many plagues of Society that further injustice and poverty and disease and even death, **certainly anger itself is a positive value for persons and society and, especially, for wounded children struggling to grow up.**

Conversely, when an adoptive parent chooses to push against the angry outburst with a stronger defense or even condemn that child for getting angry, well, where will the anger go? How deeply will it be buried in the less than conscious spaces in a child's mind and heart? How explosive will that anger become days and months and even years from now? **Nothing goes nowhere**! With the judgment against anger itself, comes the judgment against the child itself: "The child is bad when the child is mad."

Now for those of us not so wounded in our development, stuffing our anger at children or at parents or at certain relatives may lead to distance and the distress of anxiety or depression or psychosomatic symptoms along with the development of a "false self" that protects us from being seen in a negative light. We may handle this experience in a variety of ways that seem more or less manageable in our day-to-day interactions with people.

But for the wounded child so much more is at stake. In Larry's case, for example, disallowing his experience of being angry would be dismissing probably half of who he really is. And he would then be left with few alternatives but to take his leave once again and stay away, because only then would he be safe from a further loss of self. Without acknowledging and respecting the aggression of the child, that little boy or girl may be left feeling lost and unable to find the nurture that leads to life.

To clarify terms here, **we think of rage as a visceral, very primitive gut reaction to a threat of some sort. It is an undisciplined physically experienced reaction. Anger might be thought of as more collected and more emotional in nature.** And aggression, which Larry often demonstrated, might be thought of as a more organized, more mature presentation of that anger. Even revenge has an organized quality to it. In both cases, aggression and revenge are forms of attachment, negative attachment, as they set the stage for engagement in one form or another with that present enemy, who is nevertheless an important person.

Fifth and finally is one more consideration that is vital to bonding and attachment, namely **the active engagement that happens when a parent joins the suffering of the child that has resulted in that anger. In one word, this is about the empathy of the parent.**

Here the dilemma is that we may not know the nature of that suffering at all, the early-on trauma that a child may have experienced. Sadly, sometimes we may never have such knowledge of that early painful narrative. Nor may the child be consciously aware of suffering too awful to know or too painful to remember.

Nevertheless, anger and its more organized counterpart, aggression, come from somewhere.

However these sit in the mind and heart of the child, when we as parents join in the suffering, wondering why the rage and what may be the deep wound underneath, we join with the child in teaching the skill of handling anger well, whatever the causes may be. Absorbing the anger of the child actually sets parents up to be partners in suffering with that child. As painful as this place may be, we then enter the world of child. That may be the best place to be seen, and, also, the best place to see.

Without the active engagement of adoptive parents who seek to find and discern the hearts of their children, little healthy emotional development can occur in their relationships. When an angry outburst separates, as it usually does, the child may win the moment using overpowering rage, but lose the war against isolation and the troubling inability to connect with parents and other human beings.

It is a significant challenge for adoptive parents to stay aware of the reality that their troublesome child is more than the one emotion of anger, prominent at the time. Yet many feelings coexist in our experience. Although they may not be seen in the moment, many other feelings and more organized emotions accompany the rage that sometimes bubbles over.

Without the active engagement of adoptive parents with these wounded children, usually their anger becomes more intense, a last-ditch effort to communicate their deep, abiding pain. Without an honest transaction with parents, the stage is then set for more trouble down the road of life. How sad that is.

So many times, adoptive mother Jenny took a hit on the chin as Larry struggled to put himself together to become a young man. Now these days things have quieted down. Less anger, more kindness, no more police calls–the drama of the last few years has significantly subsided. Larry is finding his own way with the support of his parents.

He has enjoyed a measure of self-respect, holding down a full-time job at the restaurant where he is making new friends that do not drag him down. Yes, they smoke marijuana together every now and then and yes, Larry certainly has a way to go to become the man he wants to be, with or without that high school diploma.

In the present day, that matters little to him. And it matters less to his parents, too, because **they "get" Larry.** They have been close enough to his personal suffering, sharing that suffering in the midst of the daily conflicts of the recent past. Today Larry is less the orphan who faces life alone, all by himself in the sea of other people.

Yes, adoptive mother Jenny has taken many hits on chin. Bravely, she took on the role of unconsciously reminding Larry, first of all, of his relinquishment when Cindy gave him up, as well as all of their own break in relationship when he was one. **These negative representations that date back to his preverbal life are incredibly difficult to rewrite.** But also, Jenny reminded Larry of frustrated teachers who sought to hold him accountable, of the female athletic director who had to expel him for stealing, and even of the policewoman who, on one occasion, spoke of the legal consequences that he might face.

But Larry may never go to jail because Jenny has helped him "break out" of the prison within himself that had trapped so much of his anger.

The bruises on Jenny's chin are starting to heal, finally!

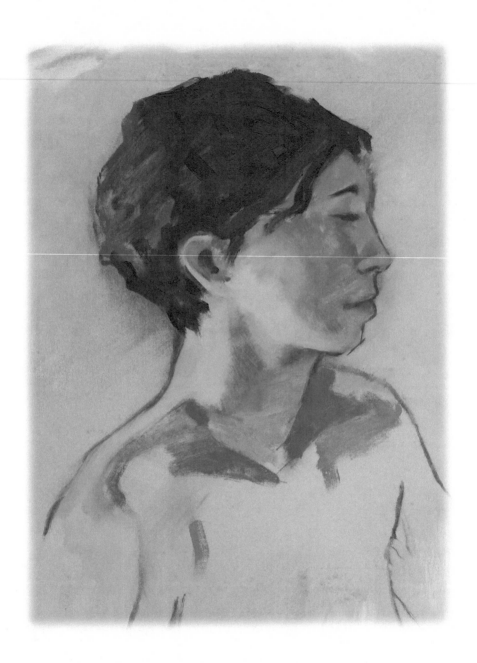

8

Yes, Adoptions Sometimes Fail

Tragically, some adoptions fail. The adoptive family never experiences sufficient connection with the adoptee, and the child is not able to join the family.

Many variables are at play in a failed adoption. But most likely, **the most important variable is the early-on experience of the child prior to the placement for adoption.** By this I mean the pre- and post-natal experiences that can range from strong bonding with reliable caregivers all the way to the tragedies of abuse and neglect. A child's trauma history may be so severe that it actually alters normal brain development, making it increasingly difficult for a child to bond to new caregivers.

Especially in domestic closed adoptions or international adoptions, the truth is **that a plan for adoption is a decision with significant risk, even when a child is placed with new parents at an early age**. That risk has to do with the capacity of the adoptee to form connections to adoptive family members and the capacity of the family members, especially parents, to understand the dilemmas of the adoptee and respond in a fitting manner. That relationship is where healing happens.

Few safeguards can be put in place. Adoptive parents may have very little idea about the nature of the child being adopted. The fate of their adoptive wishes is an unknown. Put differently, you simply never know whom you receive when you receive a child by adoption. Accordingly, sometimes this matching between parent and child becomes exceedingly difficult.

Sounds pretty negative, I know, but stories of failed adoptions are very negative. The purpose of this chapter is to offer to adoptive parents who face similar struggles with their adopted children a greater understanding of why plans for adoption may sometimes not succeed.

The relationship may be unworkable, stuck in ongoing conflict between new parent and new child, and secondarily between new siblings and new child. Here is one true story of one family's 14-month struggle to adopt a very frightened little girl whom we shall call Sheila. (Her first given Chinese name was "Chin.")

Alongside this narrative, as with one's given earlier, I will offer counselor-type reflections on it. And finally, I will review the various outcomes for the participants involved ten years after Sheila's second relinquishment and second adoption.

After nearly two years of home studies and negotiations and paying many dollars up front, Tina and John Wharton flew to China to receive this little girl. They were told she was only 14 months old, but in fact, she was certainly older. Although small, she had her two-year molars already, so was probably two years old or even older.

Flying with her back from China, Tina and John knew almost nothing about her early history and had no idea about what was coming. They were happy. But, looking into the eyes of this little adoptee, **they could see fear and confusion.**

There was never a smile on her face to accompany the joy that they were experiencing. But at the time they saw this fear and confusion to be temporary, believing that they could heal the broken heart of little Sheila. But they were wrong.

Now, ten years have passed since the day when Sheila was given to her next (third) parents. Yet the Whartons' guilt and hurt still lingers, even though they appear to be a relatively happy suburban family, living with the usual ups and downs of parenting and the usual stresses of making everything work for their three children by birth.

Adam is the oldest child. He was ten when Sheila was relinquished to her next set of parents. He remembers her as a family nuisance and was rather happy to see her go.

Daughter Bethany was eight when Sheila left. She was so hurt by the experience that still today, ten years later, she can barely talk about it.

And Ron, their youngest, was five years old when Sheila was handed away and gone from his life. His memory of it is somewhat vague but he does recall constant conflict with his new two-year-old sister who only really played with him to take away his toys. She played against him; whatever toy he had, she had to have two it. She would fight and fight until she possessed it.

Almost from the beginning of this attempt at adoption, Tina and John struggled to make sense of Sheila's behavior. In their minds she was completely obstinate and unwilling, not unable, to warm up to either of them as her parents. Tina began to worry when after several weeks of difficult behavior, it appeared that nothing was changing, that Sheila was no closer to them than on the day she joined their family. John similarly wondered why Tina would not warm up to such a good opportunity for warmth and care.

Both parents dealt with Sheila as best they thought they could, without results that they considered satisfying. Their hopefulness turned to considerable frustration as those weeks and months went by. They expected that Sheila would be a "normal kid," at least to some degree, and that the parenting they had done with their children by birth would meet with similar parenting success with her.

A Counselor Perspective

Tina and John appeared to be rather uninformed about the challenges that adoptive parents take on when they seek to adopt a child like Sheila. This little Chinese girl had spent approximately two years, the first and most important years of a child's development, in what was probably a back-country substandard orphanage after being abandoned by her parents by birth. The difficulties that little Sheila brought along with her to the Wharton home entirely surprised Tina and John.

Often adoptive parents themselves may glorify adoption and sometimes make light of concerns that social workers may present. Obviously and understandably, it is difficult to hear about the negatives in an adopted child's narrative. Nevertheless, without careful orientation and adequate post-adoption services, the Whartons were at a significant loss as to how to establish a working, positive relationship with Sheila.

Tina and John were taken aback by their own inability to "bring Sheila around," as John would say. They were told not to spank Sheila because of possible physical abuse that she may have experienced in the orphanage. Quickly, they turned to a behavioral method of rewards and consequences for her behavior. As John continued, "We tried everything. And timeouts were just a waste of time with Sheila." We might wonder how familiar Sheila was with being alone, given her orphanage story.

Also, we might note that a dynamic method of parenting, whereby the warmth of the relationship becomes the primary tool of change, appeared to be impossible. Similarly, with regard to a cognitive method, there was no ground to be gained by seeking to persuade Sheila to see things differently, in a more positive light.

The final straw in this tragic story was the day when Sheila bit Ron in the stomach and drew blood. "I had to pull her off like a dog, like it was a dog attack. Everyone was screaming, and I was screaming at Sheila, yelling, 'No, no, no, no biting!' And when I pulled her off, as Ron and I kept yelling at her, she just sat there looking at me and smiling. To me it meant that she had won," recalls Tina painfully.

That was the day when Mom and Dad made a painful decision that ended Sheila's time with this family. The adoption, the family's ongoing attempt to make a connection with Sheila, had failed. The day-to-day story of her living with the Whartons came to a very sad and guilt-ridden ending, accompanied with the shame that comes from being seen as failing parents. This, then, was the kind of goodbye that leaves a lump in your throat.

But why had John and Tina wanted to adopt in the first place? Things were going very well with them. They were happy with each other in a strong, committed marriage. They were enjoying watching their children grow up ever so quickly, pleased to watch them do the usual, the ordinary, and mostly the good. Certainly, they had all the normal family conflicts and questions about dealing with bad behavior and managing corresponding discipline that are all part of bringing children up. But overall it was "so far so good" in their home. Yet Tina wanted more.

Why? Well, she recalls, "It was my dad. He was three years old when his mother died and his father, my proud Mexican grandfather, took him and his brother to an orphanage but would never sign the papers to release them. So my father grew up in the orphanage until he was 18, because he was never really given up by my grandfather, legally anyway. My father remembers having very little food at different times, maybe just a piece of cornbread or maybe cornbread with syrup on it sometimes. He would tell us all the stories about Sister Veronica or Sister Mary. These were the nuns that became his mothers as he grew up in that orphanage.

278

"I always felt bad about what happened to him. And I knew that someday, if I were in a position to do so, I wanted to do something to get children out of that situation, maybe adopt, as I understood how hard it was for my dad. So we decided to try adoption. Now that it's over, like, ten years ago, I told John that when I get to heaven I am going to find God, and I am going to kick him in the shins. This side of heaven I will never know why God put us or Sheila through this. **I feel really guilty about what I put my family through in adopting Sheila. I can't let it go.**"

John added his comment about motivation: "At first I kind of just went along with it because it sounded like a good thing to do. I mean, our family was in a good place. Our kids were growing up well. Then at church, there was this push for adopting Chinese girls. There they were, running all over church, and they were so cute. It really looked like a good thing to do. So we did it."

At the time of Sheila's adoption, the Whartons knew almost nothing about her early history. They were given pictures of this little Chinese girl, including some of little Sheila, then still Chin, being held by several orphanage workers.

What they would learn about her history came later from Sheila's reaction to these photographs. Tina recalls, "By the way, these photos looked staged, as if a child in full winter dress was put in a crib to take the picture and then taken out. The crib looked like a backdrop of sorts. With regard to one photograph in which she is held by a rather young Chinese lady, Sheila would burst out saying, 'Dat my mama, dat my mama!' Most likely, this was the woman in the orphanage who cared for her. Most likely, little Sheila had been left on the roadside or at the door of someone's home because she was a girl." (Female babies are often abandoned in China.)

In the first days, it became very clear that with the exception of eight-year-old Bethany, Sheila would have nothing to do with adult women. Tina yearned to express maternal warmth, but she reports, "She did not want anything to do with me. She did not want me to touch her. She would push me away." Sheila was the orphaned child who was absolutely protesting the much needed warmth and affection of another.

But with Bethany it was different. Bethan, with her very dark hair, looked like that orphanage worker identified by Sheila as her "mama." Quickly she turned to Bethany to be that mother. This was a heartbreaking experience for Tina and a life-changing,

overwhelming experience for Bethany--really too much responsibility for an eight-year-old girl.

"Sheila loved men," said Tina. She had no problem relating superficially to men with what we call indiscriminate friendliness. This is the behavior of a rather disconnected child which is an adaptive attempt to seek out attention and care. It involves being very friendly with anyone, indiscriminately, friend or stranger, in such a way that the person is pleased with her smile and rewards her in some way, if she is truly successful. Without concern at all for her own safety, she would approach men with her cute, endearing smile.

She was fine with John, her newly adoptive father, but in a somewhat indiscriminate way. Her method of relating to John, according to him, was usually a subtle or not so subtle attempt to get her way. This adoptive father felt like he meant little to her except to manipulate him to get whatever she wanted at the time. This was a significant disappointment for John.

A Counselor Perspective

At this point it is important to notice how far away all might be from the real Sheila who has been so carefully protected by Sheila. John reports his undoubtedly negative experience of Sheila towards the close of their 14-month ordeal. As I listen to John's report, I am then twice removed from the reality of who Sheila is: a frightened and confused and angry little girl.

At this point it becomes critical to remember that in the time that Sheila lived with the Whartons, first and second and third accounts of the kind of person Sheila was failed to appreciate and understand the real Sheila so carefully hidden. As Sheila is described in this narrative, it is important to wonder what these experiences were like for her.

A problem with food became immediately evident. Sheila would carefully guard her bowl of Cheerios. She would yell and scream if anyone got near it. At every meal, breakfast, lunch, and dinner, she would ask for "more, more, more!" Sometimes she would eat so much that she would purge that meal, vomiting as she ate far beyond a satisfied stomach. **Tina and John empathically interpreted this as a sign of the early deprivation that Sheila must have experienced.**

As she grew older in her 14-month stay with this family, she would hoard her food, keeping a supply of some sort in her room. She seemed to have no trust that food would be there the next day. This reality certainly indicated significant trouble in the first years of her life before she traveled across the Pacific Ocean with two strangers who wanted to be her parents.

It was almost impossible for the Whartons to go to a restaurant. Sheila would look around the restaurant, watching the people who were eating food, while she waited, with none. Tina would reassure her that the food was coming, but Sheila could not believe it. Her head would become hot, not just warm but hot, so hot that she would break into a sweat.

Her hair would become wet and matted down; she would be beside herself with anxiety about her perception that she would not get food in the restaurant. There seemed to be no way to console this little girl, this orphaned girl who struggled to trust the words of her parents.

A Counselor Perspective

Sheila's behavior deserves careful consideration. Despite her being fed every day, the capacity to believe differently about not having food was a real challenge for Sheila. She was stuck in a world without trust, a world of near starvation where she had no internal assurance that there would be bread for tomorrow. She seemed to be inconvincible, unable to internalize her new reality.

Here again we have a window into her past experience, prior to age two. Being fed, our most basic human need, seemed to have never been a certainty for Sheila in those first months in the Chinese orphanage, if indeed, that is where she really was in the first weeks and months of her life. We can only infer what it may have been like for Sheila at that time.

We also should take note of the truly empathic moments when Tina and John and their children tried to imagine what life was like for Sheila at that Chinese orphanage. Their attempts at imagining the early days and years of her life put them in a place where they sought to understand why Sheila might behave the way she does, rather than, un-empathically, stand more at a distance and judge her behavior harshly and label her negatively as well.

Judgment of Tina and John as parents or of Sheila as a struggling child would merely serve to label them in an unfortunate manner and stop our wondering more about both parents and child. In my experience, when we finally truly understand, judgment goes away.

Once at a Bible study, Tina recalls, Sheila was playing on the floor with some toys. She reports, "I wanted to keep her close to me. I did not want her to be with other people because I was working on her bonding to me and not to everybody else, which she would do in a superficial fashion."

At some point in that hour, Sheila took a napkin off the table and approached a man sitting nearby. She then knelt down as a near two-year-old might do and began to wipe his shoes.

She knew about people who shine shoes. Perhaps she was a prop for such work whereby someone would take her from the orphanage and allow her to sit nearby to draw sympathy and customers to the shoe-shining operation. Certainly, this would be a guess; however, her behavior was clear. Somehow, in some way, she had observed the skill of shoe shining in her very early days. This would speak in some way to the mystery of what happened in the first two years of her life.

John reports, in a disappointed voice, that when Sheila got out of control there was no way to hold her down and help her collect herself: "Although she was only 25, maybe 30 pounds," he recalls, "she was incredibly strong. She was so strong that as little as she was, it was always a battle to somehow restrain her until she calmed down. Then usually, exhausted, she would crash and fall asleep."

It is important to wonder what this experience was like for Sheila, on her side of the relationship. **It quickly became apparent that Sheila seemed to be driven by her basic need for survival.** For her so much was at risk that she behaved in a way that somehow made sense to her, but not to the Whartons (or third hand to me as the listener to this report). Except for her connection to Bethany, for reasons we can only surmise, she needed to keep her family members at a distance.

As John and Tina experienced it, Sheila became a tornado that spun through their home, wreaking relational havoc in her path wherever she went. Understandably, they worried.

Adam thought of her as a chronic nuisance. Ron was usually fighting to keep his toys--any of his things--and saw Sheila as a would-be threat, a thief whenever she had the opportunity. He reports, "I was relieved when she left our home. At first, I tried, but it didn't matter. Towards the end I realized that it didn't work [to try to be friendly]. Maybe I was a little sad, but mostly relieved because she was an annoyance for everyone."

John recalls, "It was so much work, never like bringing up a kid normally. It was never natural parenting."

Seeking to understand Sheila's behavior in relation to him, John wondered what it was like for her to be in that orphanage. "I'll bet she would stand up in her crib, if she had one, scream and scream and scream until someone noticed. That's the way it was for her. And probably, food was a big deal there because there was never enough. I can see that in order to survive she had to be this way. We kept hoping that we could have a breakthrough of some sort--that she could change. But I guess she just couldn't."

As you can see, John's comment here starts out empathically, but ends with sorrow that in relationship to him, nothing changed.

A Counselor Perspective

In a personal narrative such as this, we must take care to reflect upon the different levels of observation going on. Tina and John, as well as their children, were reporting to me what their experiences of Sheila were in those 14 months she stayed with them.

The real Sheila lies hidden beneath their words. This real person, even at age two, may have been carefully protecting her truth, her real story, from observation. Writing this book, I am two steps away from the real Sheila and, as a reader, you are three steps away from her reality.

Put differently, we must take care to pay attention to the series of lenses through which we see Sheila and wonder about the eye of the beholder. As each relation has two sides, wisely, we must listen to and wonder about both sides of this story as best we can.

Hopefully, then we can understand more clearly the nature of each person's relationship with Sheila. We can make inferences from a review of Sheila's behavior, especially with food, but we must remember that an inference is not the real truth about Sheila's many possible motivations for her behavior.

For Bethany it was very different. Sheila allowed only Bethany to give her a bath. She formed a connection to Bethany, her new roommate, throughout this 14-month experience, allowing only her to be that orphanage helper who tended daily to her basic needs, like the one in that photograph whom Bethany resembled.

According to Ron, "First it was nice to see that Sheila was being cared for, but then later, it was like Bethany was taking Sheila over the rest of the family."

When Tina and John were asked whether Bethany had gotten over this experience of 10 years ago, both quickly answered,

No, she has not. She is the only one that still has a picture of Sheila hanging on the wall in her room. She still has a little stuffed baby rabbit named "Bunny" in her room. And she used to say, "I wiped my tears with Bunny's ears and that was why Bunny's ears were so dirty." But now she will not talk about it, not in front of us. She doesn't want us to know how she feels."

It is certainly clear that these parents realized rather quickly that Sheila was a different little girl with significant problems and that they needed outside resources. "We had three different counselors who tried to help us with this," remembers Tina, "but none of them were able to help us and they pretty much said so."

"One of our friends told us that we should go to the hospital and get a good assessment of Sheila," Tina continued. "So I took her there and spent two hours with a therapist there who was going to assess her attachment issues. And so she gave Sheila two toys and asked her to give me one of them. So politely, with a smile on her face, Sheila came over to me and handed me one of the toys with that smile. Then she was given some food and was asked to share the food with me. And again, Sheila came to me and handed me some of the food. The therapist was then quick to conclude that this little girl had no significant attachment issues. She should be fine. But she had no idea what immediately followed.

"Out in the parking lot when I opened the door to put Sheila in her car seat, she kicked me in the shins. Ouch, it hurt! (Tina's report of this incident perceives Sheila in a certain way that comes along with such physical injury. **Sadly, the real Sheila remains unknown.** She had been obedient in the therapist's office because of her need to control her environment, ensuring her survival.)

"And I knew right away that the hospital people would be of no help. And then we called you (in reference to me, your author). I remember us talking to you and explaining what the year had been like and what we were dealing with as a family, and how Sheila was really breaking us apart, and in that conversation, we talked

287

about the possibility of letting her go, and anyway, that led to the end of this after 14 months."

John went on further to talk about his sense of guilt and disappointment: "I would get so angry with her, so angry. She was so disruptive, and she could be so mean. We just couldn't believe it. Sometimes, I would play with the kids and hold them up by their feet and let them giggle. And I tried to do that with her. And at times she would let me, but usually she would fight every attempt I might make to play with her. It's hard to admit this, but it's true: sometimes Sheila would really get to me."

And then Tina chimed in: "I remember there were times when I wished that I could find a box big enough, and I would put her in the box and seal it and send her back all the way to China. That is how she made me feel."

Both Tina and John also rehearsed their fears about Sheila's possible future with them. "What's going to happen when this girl is 16? John wondered.

And then Tina remembered, "She was very, very angry, very angry, angry to be here."

"People judged us" John recalls. "We were thinking about relinquishing her, and people would ask us, 'How can you do that?' They saw her in a different way. In a different setting, she was as sweet as could be, and she would sit in their lap and smile and giggle and be a little angel as far as they were concerned. (Again, what we call indiscriminate friendliness.) They didn't know what it was like at home. They didn't know what kind of a violent little girl she really was. She could put on quite a show and fool everybody. But then we would come home, and she would just terrorize the house."

John concluded, "We could never get her to be just a normal kid. You know, love and affection and calmness, just being part of the family. We could never get her there."

A Counselor Perspective

Let me say again: Clearly at this point, as well as in what follows, we can see that the descriptions presented by Tina and John as well as by their children are their individual experiences of living with and dealing with Sheila. And it certainly looks like Sheila is the problem, Sheila is the instigator, Sheila is the unmanageable child, plain and simple. We can understand why such accusations took hold. We might even have an affinity to similar judgments.

*However, **it may be more fruitful to paint Sheila in less negative colors**. It may also be more fruitful not to ascribe parental failure to Tina and John, as they ascribed to themselves with the load of guilt and shame. We might more usefully understand the problem at a deeper level.*

Paying close attention, without judgment, to the critically limited relation between these family members and Sheila may help us see more clearly why this complex of relationships could not succeed. In so doing, blame follows in neither direction. Neither Tina and John nor Sheila would then be given negative labels to live with for years.

Tina further recalls: It got to the point where I was so frustrated and sad, I'm embarrassed to say, that I would look at the clock and it would be noontime. And I would say, 'Well, it's five o'clock somewhere else in the world,' and so then I would pour myself a drink. We knew other parents who were adopting and they were having troubles, too, with their daughter, but they got through it. Anyway, we would talk often, and I remember calling [that mother] and saying, 'How is she doing?' And she would say, 'Well, I just sat down to have a drink.' And I would say, 'Well, I just did too.' And it would be 2:00 in the afternoon."

John continued, "Sometimes, I would play with the kids and hold them up by their feet and let them giggle. And I tried to do that with her. And at times she would let me, but usually she would fight every attempt I might make to play with her. Sometimes Sheila would really get to me."

And then Tina chimed in, "I remember there were times when I wished that I could find a box big enough, and I would put her in the box and seal it and send her back all the way to China. That is how she made me feel."

"Well, after that visit to that lady, we hoped that would make things better. But, it didn't. Even the day that Sheila was handed over to us in China, she was not happy, she was yelling and she was screaming and she hated what we were doing. We hoped that that would change, but really, it never did."

A Counselor Perspective

Although the Whartons found no explanation for Sheila's behavior, a deeper look at the trouble in relating to each other may have been helpful. A skilled family

290

*therapist, specializing in these difficult adoptive dynamics, might have been beneficial much earlier in this story. And later, **such a resource might have helped even to explain from a relational perspective the nature of the mismatch here, thereby avoiding the need to blame Sheila or themselves**. Within the framework of these specific existing relationships, there could be no peace. As they were constructed, these were the connections most deserving of our attention for learning and for changing.*

This was their journey. From hopefulness about creating change in a loving family they moved to disappointment and confusion and frustration as they failed to help Sheila manage herself, then to anger and embarrassment, and then, finally to utter despair and sadness and fear as they realized that they could not find a method to help them relate to this little girl. Doing so appeared to be impossible within the setting of their family, the family that she was, in their words, destroying.

On several occasions Tina and John had reported these difficulties to the original caseworker. Once again, she was little help. However, the day did come when she called and reported to Tina and John that there was a couple who might be willing to take on the challenge of parenting Sheila. In this family, the Rogers family, there was one 16-year-old daughter, but no younger children who might engage Sheila in a competitive, adversarial manner.

And then she was gone. It just did not seem to matter to Sheila that we had given 14 months of our lives in an attempt to love her: we did not matter either," John lamented with sadness in his voice. These were his last words on it, a painful ending to a tragic story.

Lingering Collateral Guilt and Sorrow-- Ten Years Later

Although my intent with this extended interview was to gather information about this example of a failed adoption, as it turned out there was therapeutic benefit for the Whartons simply from their talking about Sheila.

One method of keeping something unreal is to choose to not talk about it. And keeping silence about the story of Sheila was now their method of coping. How tragic.

The everyday problem of dealing with Sheila certainly ended with her walk in the park with her next parents. The traumatizing effect that Sheila had on the Whartons was finally contained and the everyday disturbance that she had created was finally over. So, the immediate anxiety that each family member carried was put to rest.

But the Wharton family was forever changed in some painful ways, wounds that they had pushed away until this interview opened the opportunity for further conversation and the beginning of resolving some the difficult emotions that surrounded these troublesome memories. **A series of conversations now offered the possibility to think more carefully and nonjudgmentally about the nature of this tragic mismatch.**

The new normal was to be forever different. It was a significant relief from anxiety for everyone, everyone except for Bethany and perhaps for Sheila. One by one the ongoing experiences of each family member came into view.

We learned from Tina that to this day she lives with both guilt and shame about their decision to relinquish Sheila as well as ongoing sadness about the necessity of doing so. To some degree, she blames herself for the family's inability to stay with the challenge of helping Sheila with all her struggles with relationships. In terms of shame, she feels diminished by the embarrassment that is the public part of such a story.

Tina remembers that for Sheila, anger was nearly always there, and impulse control was seldom there. All too quickly Sheila became the most powerful person in the system of the family. And, unfortunately, as Tina recalls this, Sheila "needed to push all of us away." Sheila's way of keeping everyone at a distance was to continuously create conflict with one family member or another, except with Bethany.

We can infer that Sheila needed this protective shield at that time. This kept her vigilant and quick to externalize blame as she continued to create a troublesome atmosphere. Tina saw all this unfolding. As chronic frustration moved toward despair, Tina felt a great deal of sadness and personal disappointment in herself.

Remember, her lifelong dream was to "rescue" a child from the difficulties of orphanage life. Her fantasy was that of warming up to that child in such a way that both could enjoy and benefit from that place in her neck where the bonding from the child and the attachment from the parent takes place. That fantasy of attaching to

293

an orphaned child remains a fantasy to this day. Even now, Tina is not far from tears about the lingering lament in her heart.

The Wharton family was not able to survive the destructive impulses that Sheila regularly displayed in their daily family life. At times they could not absorb Sheila's anger without the wish for retaliation that usually comes in such moments. Sometimes parenting is precisely that–absorbing the anger of our children, as difficult as that may be. **To do so, to maintain neutrality in the midst of such destructive behavior is a tall order for any of us as parents**.

John is now able to speak openly about this major disruption in their family life. He is a decision-maker who had seen this profoundly difficult decision coming toward his family for quite some time. He certainly tried to remain positive about the possibility of a shift in Sheila's attitude toward them and resulting behavioral changes that he hoped and prayed might come about. But as her would-be father, John was not allowed to find a way to her heart.

He became especially aware of the way he was losing connection with the other members of his family as the weeks and months wore on. Adam and Ron were slipping away, and slipping away from each other, keeping distance in their rooms, creating very private lives away from the tension in the family room. And, for John, understandably, this was intolerable.

According to Tina and John both, their oldest son Adam "carries depression. He has for a long time. And we do not know how much of this is related to our experience with Sheila, but we wonder if it has something to do with it. Adam kind of hid in his room and really never came out. So, he has been depressed for a long time. And we are not sure why."

Now a college student, Adam had this to say: "At first I was really excited about it. I thought it was great that we would have someone from China join our family. But even the first night, Sheila was throwing fits and not happy at all. Really, she was screaming all the time. My parents took her to several therapists, and even once to a priest to get help for Sheila, but nothing worked. I don't remember too much about it, but I do remember being relieved when Sheila left, but also sad that it could not work. I tried and I tried to care; she was screaming all the time. So, then I stayed away. Really, I gave up because there was nothing else I could do."

Adam was about 11 years old when Sheila walked out the front door for the last time. Looking back, Adam recognized his family's willingness to reach all the way to China to care for this frightened and confused and abandoned little girl as a real blessing to her. Now he sees that his family was a "stepping stone" in Sheila's life so that she could be better cared for here in the United States, even if it was not to be by his own family. This is a good way to bring some closure to this wounded family.

Adam was asked how his experience with Sheila as his younger sister for those 14 months might have affected his growing up. His response was immediate:

"Well, in my life I have always been kind of timid. You might say that I am a shy person. And I remember when I needed to stay in my room to get away from all the hassle with Sheila. And so now maybe I am a little more timid because of it (the family struggle with Sheila). I'm not sure, but maybe that is one way that it has affected me. Sometimes I am more fearful of people. Sheila was afraid of people, too."

Although somewhat detached, Adam was able to express his identification with Sheila, seeming to understand how hard it was for her to be with people. In part this may be his own ability to see himself in her as a person who struggles socially. At any rate, Adam's memories of life with his then new little sister seem to include a measure of tenderness.

Certainly, there was relief when she left, but Adam remembers something deeper as well. "There was something about the pain of separation that I saw in Sheila, and that memory has stayed with me." Although Sheila saw her brothers as potential threats who might take her food and diminish her life, part of the tragedy of this failed adoption is that she could never see the brotherly love that both Adam and Ron might have offered her.

Ron was the brother who was always doing battle with Sheila until the day she bit him and ended her time with his family. It was not only the battle for his toys; it was also the battle for the love and attention from his parents that a five-year-old would want and need in order to grow up well. Now, ten years later, Ron still remembers the relief that he felt when she left permanently. He said that relief was the only word that really fit then.

However, now at age 15, he can see things differently. He can now recognize how frightened Sheila was back then. He sees what a five-year-old could not see, namely that Sheila was out of control because of the suffering that we wonder about, that we try to imagine. Now an older Ron has the ability to be much more sensitive to his childhood foe.

Bethany's story differs qualitatively from that of all the other family members. For Bethany, what happened ten years ago is just as if it were yesterday. Tina states, "Even today, Bethany does not want to talk about it in front of us. She still has a picture of Sheila hanging on the wall in her room." Tina and John both are well aware that Bethany has not gotten over the relinquishment of Sheila. They know that to this day, the day of this writing, Bethany still carries Sheila in her heart.

Here are Bethany's own words, an extensive soliloquy about the experience:

"When Sheila joined our family, I was very excited. I always wanted a sister, so I was so happy that that was going to happen. The first few months were very exciting for me. I was excited to wake up every day and see if she was awake. We shared a room, and I would say good morning and help her get dressed.

"I remember she cried a lot. Actually, screaming is probably more appropriate. We had this little playpen for her that I remember she would just scream if she was in there, but when she was out she was okay.

"She was very protective of her food. She would scream and cry whenever anyone came near it or took it away. My mom explained to me that this was because she probably didn't have enough food in the orphanage. I

297

felt so sad about that. So, I would give her some of my food.

"In the middle months, I remember she was very mean to everyone but me. She did not like my brothers at all, she would like, fight them, get them in trouble, etc. I was very sad that she did that because she was so sweet to me. She was always very mean to my parents, and I remember how hard it was; They were wondering what they could do to make it better. I did not understand that because she loved me, and we got along very well.

"Towards the end, I could sense that there was something wrong. My parents whispered a lot and would not tell us what was going on. When they told us they were looking for another family for Sheila, I did not know what to say. I kind of knew something like that was going to happen. She made life very difficult for the rest of the family.

"This is something I remember very clearly, possibly the most vivid memory I have of her. I remember being very calm when they told me. That night, I went into Sheila's crib with her after my parents were asleep and just started crying. Sheila looked at me and almost it looked like she was about to cry, too. She held my hand at one moment and asked, 'Sissy, what's wrong?' And I said, 'It's okay. I'm just tired. I love you.' And she said, 'I love you too.' We both fell asleep shortly after that, and I got up early and went back to my own bed.

"The day she left is also something I remember clearly. Her new parents came to the door. I think I remember her new mom crying when she saw Sheila. Then my memory goes forward to when I saw her get in the car with them with all her things. I remember she was wearing this little blue dress with the Disney Princess Ariel on it. It was mine, one of my favorites when I was little. I stood there as I watched them drive away, and I could not stop crying. My dad had to carry me inside because I was so upset.

"Sheila's presence in my family as a whole was pretty negative. She hated my brothers and my parents. She was nicer to my mom than she was to my dad. They fought more than I have ever seen in those few months. I remember that we all had the attitude of 'Oh, it's just the first few months that are hard; it will get better.' I just remember when the whole family was together, everything was very tense.

"For my mom, I think she was as happy as I was at the beginning, but then was very sad because Sheila lashed out a lot and my mom didn't understand what she was doing wrong. My dad was very sad because she did not like him at all. I think he expected to have another sweet little girl like I was to him and getting the complete opposite from Sheila broke his heart.

"This whole situation affected me greatly, and I don't think I've realized that until recently. When it first happened, **I just remember being very sad that I didn't get the sister I wanted. My family was so relieved, but I was heartbroken**.

"I loved her so much. I think there was a part of me that blocks the memories of being so sad. I tried to remember it was a good thing, which it was of course but I just block the feelings of being so devastated. It is a very hard thing for me to talk about now. When I do talk about it, I realize how much it really did affect me because I can't keep myself from crying.

"My mom contacted Sheila's mother, who said that Sheila asks about us. She said Sheila wants to talk to me and know our family a little bit again. When she told me that, I could not stop crying on the phone. They were happy tears, because I would love nothing more than to be a part of her life, but also just tears because I felt like I was reliving the heartbreak I went through the day she left our family."

It was on a November Monday that I recorded Bethany's soliloquy. Two weeks later, just as I was writing, for the first time in ten years she and Sheila met each other on the local college campus where Bethany studies. Tina was well aware of Bethany's wish to see Sheila once again. In a phone conversation with Mrs. Rogers, Tina learned that recently, on several occasions, Sheila had asked if she could see the Whartons once again. Well, the photos that were sent show wonderful smiles as these two embrace each other in a way that looks deeply happy and satisfying, sisters still.

This meeting, as we discussed it, was not about some kind of closure for Bethany to the difficulties of ten years ago. A much better metaphor might be that Bethany and Sheila, as "long lost cousins" of a sort, enjoyed a deeply moving reunion. Their future as such will hopefully include ongoing conversation and time together for an ice cream cone.

Both of them are happier and emotionally more complete today than either was just before their first embrace on that college campus. Already, each speaks of how rewarding it would be for both families to meet each other once again in such different circumstances and to celebrate the young lady that Sheila is becoming at age 13. Her load of emotional freight, the baggage that she carries today, is certainly a bit lighter. Accordingly, her smile now runs deeper. And today Bethany's heart may be more at peace.

A Counselor Perspective

First, the dilemma with labels, specifically with diagnostic categories, is this: Attributions to a person, child or adult, come along with a list of prescribed behaviors that are interpreted in such a way that the prognosis for recovery may be quite mixed. Put differently, a given diagnosis may misunderstand someone like Sheila and suggest a challenge nearly impossible to overcome.

It would've been relatively easy to label Sheila as an example of that frightening term, reactive attachment disorder (RAD). And along with that would come a very guarded, even pessimistic prognosis about change, about any possible interpersonal success in the future. Her parents would be told that it would be nearly impossible for her to change much, just as the three therapists that they consulted had reported to Tina and John. The tragedy here, among others, would be that Sheila would never be deeply understood.

Certainly, Sheila may have lifelong challenges because of the lingering effects of her history of traumatic experiences on her brain development. Nevertheless, the attachment that she allowed from Bethany contradicts an inability to bond to another human being. But this may have been puzzling and overlooked, with unfortunate results.

Labeling Sheila, seeing her exclusively as the problem with a certain diagnosis, leaves no room for a careful examination of other participants in relation to her. Doing so fails to see the way in which the problem to be addressed is in the relationships themselves.

Possibly a more troubling problem with labeling in this way is that such diagnostic attributions locate the problem to be addressed within the person, suggesting that no matter where such a child might be, the problems connected to this diagnosis would once again occur. In Sheila's case, a given diagnosis would have been misleading.

This method of single person labeling also contributes on the other side of the relationship, labeling parents or caregivers as failures in their attempt to help a child, precisely the judgment that fell upon Tina and John. They judged themselves, and folks in the neighborhood stepped right up to judge them as well. What a tragedy, so unfortunate, and so unnecessary.

*Second, **it is obvious, now ten years later, that Sheila could never have gotten beyond the psychological defenses that protected her need for survival while she lived within the Wharton family**. Most likely there was too much orphanage-like competition in the family with two brothers and the sister she befriended. She needed to be the center of attention, and she needed Bethany to provide daily affirmation.*

Ultimately, we can only guess what the reasons might truly be. Perhaps she believed that she needed to fight for

302

her daily bread, though that was obviously not true. There was always plenty of bread for the day. But with daily competition, as she experienced it, there was no room for the slow-moving development of trust with her parents and her brothers.

Only Bethany was exempt from this rule of life for Sheila. And her capacity to bond to Bethany does, of course, speak against a harsh and negative diagnosis. Unfortunately, with the Whartons, Sheila may have felt trapped in circumstances that she could not manage successfully. If this were true, it would certainly speak against a harsh diagnostic label. Better that we think that this was no one's fault. Better that we think that blame might lie in the mismatch within the relationships themselves.

Unfortunately, with the Whartons, these relationships were set up not to work. **Responsibility for this tragic mismatch may lie at the feet of those who arranged this adoption.** To offer no significant post-adoption services to them seems unthinkable, given the struggles that adoptees from nations such as China often face.

Today Sheila is an honor student in the eighth grade. She is also a very good athlete. She is in cheerleading competitions beyond the walls of her own school. Pretty cool. But understandably, she continues to struggle with relationships and certainly still has work to do to give her current friendships more depth and make them more successful. Pretty understandable, given the hard start that she had in the first two years her life. In summary, she is in the process of becoming a delightful young lady.

The most important variable that may account for the shift in Sheila's ability to quell her anger is that of moving to a family where she is functionally an only child. A much better match. She has an older sister who is 13 years her senior, old enough not be a competitive threat. Still she did push this older sister away, especially at the beginning of her experience of being parented by Mr. and Mrs. Rogers, her third such experience of being parented.

In her new family, Sheila was able to get beyond her competitive need to control every aspect of her environment where she would try to control others to get what she wanted. She no longer needed to fight for that position. She had it. Her lack of trust and her lack of impulse control began to slowly subside day after day in her new family environment. No other children were around to take her food. No other children were around with whom to fight over toys. As the queen of the hill, she did not need to fight or be fought. She could declare herself the well- fed winner!

Third, we can now imagine the Wharton's relief from guilt, to a very good degree, for the decision they had made to relinquish Sheila to her next parents. Her positive turn in trust and in behavior stands to confirm that they made the correct call on Sheila's behalf as well as their own.

Of course, this was not their first concern at the time of the relinquishment; they made their choice, first, in order to protect their family from the explosive breakdown that it was experiencing. Sheila was so powerful as to harm their family as family. Nevertheless, their choice brought the significant collateral blessing that Sheila would be placed in a family environment more fittingly matched to her specific needs.

In this new network of relationships, she could move beyond her defenses to accept the care of a new mother and a new father, and, more recently, the affection of an older sister. This was primarily good for everybody involved, except for Bethany who carried her sorrow for the ten years following, until yesterday when, once again, she could embrace Sheila and restore daily life to their friendship.

Fourth, let's look at the efficacy of different methods of parenting in this story. It is useful to notice that when the Whartons observed that "nothing works with her," they were alluding to the reality that no effort of theirs brought Sheila to a place where she could receive affection from them as parents.

Again, as with Humpty Dumpty, "All the king's horses and all the king's men could not put Sheila together again." They were seeking an emotional connection with Sheila, but we might surmise that it was far too frightening for her to engage. For her to open her heart to them in those early months of her life would have been far too overwhelming; she would literally be fearing the loss of her bread.

Sometimes, especially for abused and neglected children, some things are just too painful to know in a conscious way. We can only wonder how much this was true for Sheila in those 14 months of her early life. No matter how much Tina or John, or her brothers, Adam and Ron, did their best to love Sheila into an emotional connection, at that time in her life, given the family dynamics that she faced, she just could not go there. They could not love her into loving them back, much less behaving in a less destructive manner. Love by itself could not get the job done within the Wharton family setting.

Furthermore, when it comes to persuading, at that time trying to help Sheila cognitively think differently about her behavior was pretty much a dream at best. We may recall that moment in the restaurant where her parents were trying to convince her that her food would come, that the waitress would soon appear with the meal that had been ordered. Sheila could not change her belief that the food might never come and that she was therefore quite right in her panic about being fed. No convincing. No possible change of mind.

Sheila was living her life on full alert, vigilantly scanning the environment around her. In her life thus far, she had been unable to establish what we call object constancy, a developmental accomplishment whereby a child can believe that the people in her life today will be the people in her life tomorrow, especially when they are out of sight. With such a frightened adoptee in their family, the Whartons were at a complete loss about how they might help Sheila believe that her life experience could be different.

When the realization is clear that an emotional attachment is not available at the time nor will any attempt at a "friendly argument" effect change, the only parenting method left may be a behavioral influence regiment–a method of rewarding the good and extinguishing the bad. Usually when adoptive parents default toward rewards as their primary method of parenting, they get somewhere.

Consequences are necessary, but they seldom change behavior. But with Sheila it was not to be so. She would scream her way out of the punishments for her bad behavior. Consequences had very little effect on Sheila. Try as they might, the Whartons once again met with failure.

Sheila's fear may have been so great and her defenses so strong that little could be done to influence her to become part of this family in a way that would work or begin to help her to believe differently about her circumstances or accept the authority of her parents. Both Sheila and her adoptive family were trapped, and neither could find a way to break the deadlock that they experienced.

Only Bethany was left with an attachment to Sheila sufficient for Sheila to feel safe. With Bethany she could lower those defenses and begin to speak some of her truth, if even in an awkward, guarded way. She could cry with Bethany.

Fifth, and unexplored, is the question of whether some medication, even at such an early age, might have been helpful. Few parents are willing to go the path of medication in the early months and years of an adoption, a resistance that is quite understandable. Further, the fear that the medications may somehow have a negative effect in the future would be an understandable further roadblock to a consultation with a child psychiatrist. Nevertheless, psychiatric evaluation is always useful.

Him (A psychiatrist is a physician who can prescribe medications for certain kinds of behavioral change depending on the working diagnosis that he or she starts with. A family physician is seldom trained in the careful delivery of medications that might be useful for a child like Sheila. A psychologist is a clinical professional who is trained in testing and psychological assessment as well as skills in counseling.)

Some parents have found therapeutic benefit from the use of medications that manage a child's anxiety so that the child has more capacity to deal with his or her own struggles, for example, with impulse control. Further comments about medications are beyond the scope of this book. As a trained therapist, I can really speak no further.

Also, the effect of trauma on the development of a child's brain needs thoughtful consideration. To whatever degree a history of traumatic experiences derails normal brain development, a child may face significant limitations in forming relationships. To some degree the brain may remain pliable and capable of repair, but **the hardwired effects of such trauma may be very difficult to overcome**. In some instances, neurofeedback has proven useful in such repair. All of this needs to be mentioned as part of the mix in struggles like Sheila's. Fully appreciating and understanding this concern extends beyond the reach of this book.

Final Reflections

As tragic as it may be to relinquish such a child from a family like the Whartons, at times such a choice is the correct decision. The network of relationships within the Wharton family was being strained to the point where family members became distant from each other. And quite correctly, Tina and John needed to remove Sheila in order to reestablish their vital connections to their original children, including Bethany who continued to be so loyal to Sheila.

When your children escape to their private rooms, when your family room is empty of family in order to avoid conflict with someone like Sheila, then the time has come for the failure of the adoptive match to be named and recognized and sadly accepted. Wise adoptive parents will recognize the limits of their own ability to create change in the life of a troubled child. As with Sheila in the Wharton situation, sometimes it is not possible to succeed.

In a mostly unspoken way and despite how we might think about adoption as forever love or a permanent home or eternally yours, the truth is that initially all adoptions are on probation. It certainly makes sense that adoption case workers would not say much about this reality, but the conditional nature of adoptions is nevertheless true.

Adoptive parents do have an option to relinquish that parents by birth do not have. This is not to say that such a comment ought to be made at the beginning of any adoption, as if to say "Well, if it does not work out..." Of course, the expectation is permanency in placement. But as this case study has shown, there are times when the complex network of relationships, in which individual needs of different family members are so unique, may preclude a successful adoption.

Once again, it is important to emphasize that the relationships themselves need further review in order to understand the tragic failure to create a satisfying adoptive relationship. Understandably, we can never know for certain who a person is; we can only approximate and infer from certain behaviors who that real young person might possibly be. To blame or label a child as simply disordered, as accurate as a diagnosis may sometimes be, or to blame adoptive parents as failures in their ability to parent--neither is helpful.

Aside from being accurate or inaccurate, they set the stage for very single-focused observations of the persons who participate in adoptive relationships. And most critically, careful observation of the fit, the match or mismatch between the relational participants is overlooked. The real problem lies as much within the relating as inside the individuals involved.

Empathy towards all family members involved is the single most useful response that can be made in circumstances like those that the Whartons faced. John and Tina Wharton were unprepared for what they were about to face as they received Sheila into their home. Naming that lack of preparation on behalf of the Chinese adoption agency involved might be the first place to look for trouble ahead.

Nor were their children in any useful way prepared for the arrival of not a simply cute little sister but rather a sister who was unable to connect with them.

And of course, Bethany was an exception for Sheila, which should alert us to the possibilities of what Sheila might be able to achieve in a different family, a different match that the Rogers family had to offer.

Being empathic with the Whartons means wondering what it was like for them as parents to be so puzzled as to how to assist Sheila in the midst of her great distress. Tina was the most motivated of the Wharton family members to adopt a child from China. Initially, she had the greatest emotional investment in helping this little girl join their family.

When it became evident that all was not well with this relationship with Sheila, Tina experienced the disappointment, anger, and great frustration around guessing as to how she could help Sheila open her heart. Soon she began sensing her own personal guilt and sense of failure as the family relationship with Sheila became more negative and more intense. Her tears are still there, under the surface, ready to be cried.

For John, the surprise at the relational difficulties he faced with Sheila was greatly unsettling. He had never anticipated such an experience with a child. He believed it to be his own responsibility to do what he could to somehow make things better.

However, his expectation and his wish that Sheila would become a "normal kid" was pretty much dashed to the ground because Sheila was anything but. John watched as his wife settled into sadness about the difficulties of a relationship with Sheila for both herself and for her family.

John also watched with sadness as his two boys hunkered down in their rooms to stay away from the tension that Sheila created in the family room. And he saw how Bethany was caught, struggling with her competing loyalties to her family and to Sheila.

Bethany did appear to have momentary connections to the real Sheila. Remember those words "I love you too," spoken by Sheila to Bethany the night before her second relinquishment? Those words seemed to be coming from the heart of this little girl.

Bethany's struggle, sometimes defending Sheila at the price of pushing her own brothers away, made for a dilemma impossible to solve. As John saw this, his sadness and anger turned to discouragement with anticipation that one day sooner or later, this turmoil in relation to Sheila would have to end. And sadly, it did.

Sometimes adoption matches do end in failure. Sometimes they must.

314

9

God on the Block

God is on the block for many adoptees. By this I mean that the reality of God as a benevolent deity may be difficult for adoptees to accept and believe.

When, at the beginning of life itself or after months or even years of foster care, there is an exchange of caregivers, something quite spiritual is at stake. Certain spiritual questions may naturally come to adoptees' minds when they become consciously aware of their circumstances and learn (hopefully at a young age) that they are part of an adoptive family.

Up until this chapter, we have taken seriously the plight of the adoptees who are resisting the love of their parents. We have taken seriously the struggle of the adoptive parents to appreciate and understand why it may be so difficult to connect to their children. Underlying both are spiritual concerns that we now take just as seriously.

These are the questions that are usually asked over and over again. "Why was I relinquished or taken away or given away when I was a baby?" This is an inquiry of ultimate concern. "Did I not matter enough to my parents, my birth parents? Did I not matter enough for them to fight harder for me, to keep me, and to love me as other parents do?" For the adoptee, this Why? question may include a spiritual inquiry that relates directly to his or her value as a person to God, if God is there.

Adoptees may be told that they were "chosen," but they know quite well that, prior to being chosen, they were surrendered and taken or given away. (Today it's not even necessarily true, since few adoptees are actually chosen by adoptive parents. They can say "yes" or "no" to a child, but this is only choosing to a limited degree. Birth mothers usually do the choosing, deciding from several portfolios who the adoptive parents will be.)

Adoptees may be told that they are now "special," but on the face of things they would certainly rather be simply "normal", normal children in a normal biological family.

So, adoptees are persons who have sustained an emotional injury which is, at the same time, a spiritual injury, sometimes immediately, perhaps even on the day they were born.

The next question naturally comes: "What's this with God that God would allow such a difficult beginning for me, just a child?" "Maybe God is not even there; or maybe I'm just not very important. Maybe I do not even matter to God." These are very painful thoughts, seldom spoken out loud. But they are there for the taking, reflections that arise from the silence of wondering.

Now certainly, all of us at one time or another wonder about our sufferings, the hurts of living, especially when evils like cancer come our way. It's common to the human experience to question God and God's plan because certainly life is unfair and sometimes even miserable.

But what may be unique to the suffering of the adoptee is that from the beginning, sometimes from the moment of birth, the adoptee is set aside for one reason or another and offered to other parents. From the beginning, the adoptee is a secondhand person, so to speak.

Attributing to God a plan for the relinquishment–Ouch!–and the adoption–Yikes!–of a child puts belief in a loving god in a rather precarious position with the child. The practice itself of arranging relinquishment and adoption sets up a unique separation between child and first parents that is so contrary to the notion of God as love.

All people likely voice concerns about God and God's love or presence, and in some ways we all experience some measure of suffering, inquiry, rejection, harm. At the same time, even if we experience our birth parents as less loving or more harmful than they ought to be, the *structure itself* of relinquishment and adoption precipitates a particular kind of encounter that those who are not adopted do not face.

The adoptee's interpretation of reality might be that God is neither kind nor loving, but instead, if

relinquishment is in God's plan, watch out for God because God may wound you again. Understandably, this painful reflection puts the adoptee at spiritual risk in terms of seeing God in a positive manner.

From this perspective, a child's personal understanding of God, as it may develop over the years, may not provide a resource for comfort and for guidance. As the adoptee becomes more aware of the reality of his changed split-life experience, negative and painful perceptions of God may challenge a belief in cosmic benevolence or divine concern.

Or, it may be that the adoptee takes the position that, although the failures of earthly parents are clearly seen, God is seen to compensate for these difficulties. Unrealistic, even magical ideas about God may serve the purpose of balancing the daily difficulties of being relinquished and adopted. In this case the adoptee's idea of God may be that God compensates in some way for the struggles of living. God is then unlike anything or anybody on Earth.

This is doing theology from orphan perspectives. Empathically, the task here may be to appreciate how understandings of God will vary in terms of how gracious God might be and how difficult God might be for the adoptee. Obviously, children who begin life without parents will certainly live with ambivalence about trusting God as God is presented to them.

For adoptive parents who take an interest in such things, this is a challenge for conversation that is difficult and yet quite important in the spiritual life of a child, a relinquished child. Bear in mind that, better than most, children such as this one would understand the words of Jesus on the Cross when he uttered, "My God, my God, why have you forsaken me?" They know forsaken.

In this chapter, we will review some of the spiritual challenges that come alongside being relinquished and adopted as well as several that come alongside being adoptive parents. But first we consider two working definitions.

About the term, *spiritual:* Every now and then, in conversation with adoptees and birth parents both, the word spiritual enters as the adjective that best describes the ongoing connection between first parents and relinquished, sometimes called lost children. "Something is there that is also missing," they say. As I listen, I hear these members of the adoption triad trying to describe something for which they struggle to find adequate words.

Spiritual, as used in this conversation, refers to experiences that are both deep within as well as "out there" – a reference even to space and time in the Universe itself. The part within may have to do with one's foundational identity. It relates to being brought into the world, for adoptees, by lost people with whom their lives began. "Who am I? And who am I as an adoptee?"

And the part "out there" may have to do with their place in the Universe. "What place do I have in this world in which I live?" "Do I even have a place here in this universe?" "Where is home?" Or, "I feel lost, like there is no place for me." "Where do I really belong?"

Or, in between the inside and the outside of spiritual life as described above, **the term spiritual may reference the sense of presence unlike anything else.** This would have to do with a certain awareness of not being alone, of being with another, a power, a force, or more personally a mirroring of ourselves that is indescribable. It is a sense that we are not alone when we are alone. We are in "the presence of another." By this way of thinking about or sensing God's presence, the adoptee would find solace, the shalom, the peace for which we might all be searching.

For birth parents within the older closed adoption system, their use of the term spiritual sometimes sounds like a reference to the way in which they continue to stay connected to their relinquished children, despite the reality that they are no longer attached to them in this world. "It's a spiritual connection that I still have with the son that I relinquished 30 years ago. We are still connected somehow in this universe."

Especially with yesterday's method of adoption placement, when it appears that nothing is left of the relationship, **birth parents sometimes say that it is only the "spiritual connection" that remains in place**. And, when reunion does finally occur, as it does for some adoptees and birth parents, the flood of emotion so often witnessed is, in part, the resolution of their spiritual distress. They are seeing God as one who finally answers prayers for reunion.

Let's consider, too, adoptive parents. I sometimes hear about the "spiritual" underpinnings of their decision to receive an orphaned child into their family. It sometimes sounds like this: "We just knew that God wanted us to do this, to adopt a child as we formed our family. It was God's plan for us." Certainly, it is then believed that following God's will would bring blessings to the adoptive family.

By the term *ultimate concern*[18] I mean attending to those deeply existential matters of living and dying importance. These are those ultimate wonderings that we sometimes ask about our experience of living between our births and our deaths, and about our places in the Universe, about what ultimately matters, especially including ourselves.

In this chapter, we consider some of the ultimate spiritual concerns that relate directly to the struggles that children sometimes have adopting their new parents. The term also relates to the struggles that parents sometimes have finding a way to successfully adopt their children.

Seven Spiritual Questions that Circle Around Adoption

Each of these questions comes from a place of personal suffering where God may be on the block of our negative judgments. Some people, in the midst of their personal suffering, may sense a need for God and for experiencing moments of divine care. For others, questions about God may never be asked.

---

[18] These words are, in the scholarly literature, actually "technical" words coined by the Protestant theologian Paul Tillich to refer to what is a matter of life and death, or as he put it again technically, our "being and non-being." Those things that are ultimate are things related to our being and non-being.

But for many, especially adoptees in the midst of their very human struggles, they may think of God as an uncaring birth parent who turned His back upon them in the early days of their lives, ripping them away from their first parents.

Many people ask one or more of the questions that follow because they are human questions that may challenge any of us at some point in our lives. However, the particular issues and life experiences around relinquishment and adoption, for everyone in the circle of adoption, make these questions more likely, more prominent, and often more painful. They are not academic.

First, from pre-adoptive parents: "Why are we an infertile couple?"

There they sat, one couple among a dozen or so other couples in the sanctuary basement. This group was intended for friendship and mutual support for so-called young couples who gathered once a month. They sat quietly because the other couples were quite busy describing their children, including babies who radically changed the focus of their lives.

Several new births were celebrated with a basket of congratulations cards and some baby gifts. As the evening unfolded, the couple felt themselves withdrawing, emotionally backing up to the wall behind them, because for the last two years all efforts at becoming pregnant had failed. Infertility was now their personal agony.

They had tried in-vitro fertilization (IVF) at a cost of about $18,000. Harvesting ten eggs produced only one that was viable. And that one viable egg failed to become a pregnancy. So now each day they carried this sense of deep discouragement. The challenge of grieving the loss of that never-born child who would look so much like them, who would keep the family genetic line going forward, who would naturally be and act as one of the family – that grieving was still before them.

It is quite understandable that they would bring their lament to God, questioning God very directly and wondering aloud to each other: What is up with God who is supposed to be so loving and caring for us? It looks like it will take a miracle for us to become pregnant. We are not ready to think about adoption. Will more prayer somehow turn things around? Or, are we really in for it, never having a child 'of our own' as awful as it is to say that?

This couple was challenging God, putting the Almighty on the seat of judgment, the block of harsh confrontation about how God had let them down. They were being denied the child that they had dreamed of for the first few years of their marriage. And now, instead, they were dealing with the injury, the insult, the embarrassment of infertility.

Their marriage suffered as intimacy, closeness to each other, also brought them close to their personal pain and discouragement. Sex became mechanical. He was angry. She was sad. They were in different spaces and distant from each other. It hurt so much. And, understandably, God was under judgment.

Second, from the adoptee: "Why was I even born?"

The Hebrew Scriptures contain the saga of Job. In it we learn the story of a man sitting in sackcloth and ashes who has lost nearly everything–his great herds of cattle, all his children, and even now his own health. Job had "painful sores from the soles of his feet to the top of his head" (2:7). He scraped them with broken shards of pottery. In his suffering he states graphically that he wishes that he had never been born: "Why did I not perish at birth, and die as I came from the womb?" (3:11).

His life had been drained of all that was meaningful to him and he wished that he were dead. Like some adoptees, he may have felt suicidal, as he saw no reason to continue to live his life. This was a powerful and negative place from which to review his life and wonder about God's involvement.

God had given much to Job, his life had been full with wealth and with family and with all the pleasures of Creation. And then, it was all taken away and **Job was left orphaned by God.**

Some adoptees can relate to Job's question and judge the day that they were born. For most adoptees, their birthdays, for example, are a very mixed experience as they may commemorate their loss as much as they celebrate their life. Job's experience was the opposite of a birthday party, wishing that the day of his birth had never happened. Job's lament in the Scriptures is his cry of despair, of too much suffering for one person to bear. He comes to that place where he asks, "Why should I live?"

There are times when this is the question of the adoptee as well. **How does one go forward when it appears that there is no place in the universe where he or she is really "at home"?** What happens when adoption is truly adoption for parents but, for adoptees, adoption is experienced as a program of foster care at best? These are questions driven by personal pain and serious doubt about God as a loving God.

The adoptee is challenged at the core of his or her being to discern an answer to that question, "Why was I born?" It is hardly an academic question. There are times when teenage adoptees cannot see the horizon beyond their immediate hurts and painful disappointments. These are the occasions when they are most at risk of thinking about suicide because their lives feel empty and devoid of meaning.

Unless they believe that they matter to someone, that they have value in the life of an adult, at least one adult, whoever that caretaker might be, their most honest answer to this question might be, "I don't know why I was born, and I don't see a good reason for me to keep living."

This sounds very much like the lament of Job. And, from a spiritual perspective, if the beliefs of adoptees do include a belief in the existence of God, they may see God in a rather negative light as they wonder whether, in the face of their own suffering, they matter to God. Accordingly, the word spiritual and the word painful may be closely aligned for some adoptees.

Of course frustration and sadness, anger and hurt, are prominent in this Job-like inquiry, asking God this tough question. But we need to also notice that embedded in these questions, as asked by the adoptee, is the sense of longing, the longing to be connected, to be connected to someone who loves and cares, and to someone who can offer an explanation. The longings that drive these spiritual struggles are the songs of the orphaned heart.

Third, from the adoptee: "Why was I relinquished and why was I adopted?"

Adoptees ask these pressing questions as they consider what has happened to them in their lives thus far. As God or Destiny would have it, they have suffered an injury right away, early in life. Here we use the term destiny to refer to a reality beyond words that may pull us forward into living life with a known future, even if not known to us.

And as an adoptee would usually see it, his or her ordinary pathway for life has been disrupted, derailed so that his or her first parents are gone, at least to a great degree, even in an open adoption. They may be dead, they may be unknown, or, especially in international adoptions, they may be unavailable. Or, simply, these first parents may be unable to parent for a variety of reasons. But still, "Why"?

Whatever the reason, the result is still that the usual bonding and attachment, prenatally and postnatally, with parents by birth is lost, early in the child's life. In the plan set forth by God--or Destiny or Higher Powers in the Universe, however the divine is thought to be--the adoptee is challenged to slowly face and accept the reality of living a different life in a different family, separated from his or her original parents, and to adopt new and different people as a second mother and father.

It is not uncommon for many children, adopted or not, to have fantasies of being rescued from their current family circumstances and brought to a place where, as kings and queens, they live wonderfully happy, fanciful lives. But for adoptees, it goes deeper. Fantasies of being rescued and restored to their parents or families of origin may be a significant part of their early life experience.

"Do I matter enough to my first parents that they might ever come back and find me?" Usually, in the course of adoptive development, adoptees report such rescue fantasies. Then once again, the adoptee faces the painful reality that there will be no rescue. They are where they are in their adoptive families. Nevertheless, these fantasies often stay alive for years. Wishes die hard.

Fourth, from the adoptee: "Where is home?"

As an ultimate spiritual concern, many adoptees are challenged to wonder about their place in the Universe itself. Being adopted raises the all-important question: "Where do I belong?" "Where is there a place for me where I really fit and where my roots can go down deep and help me become a grown-up?"

Home is certainly a place, a physical space, but it is that place because of the people there–the network of family relations where we belong to the people there. In this sense the people make the place a home.

Consider the behavior of many adoptees around the holidays. These are times of family togetherness, of celebration of belonging to each other, of gifts that are given in the context of familial closeness, of being home together. Lots of times, adoptees find themselves withdrawing, pulling away from the festivities, as if to say, if only to themselves, **"I don't quite belong here like everybody else does. I just feel weird in the Christmas family picture."**

These are often comments never spoken and, unless adoptive parents take the initiative to begin a conversation about these home-making concerns, the adoptee may experience little understanding, guidance, or encouragement.

Or, consider the difficulty some adoptees have describing the occasional family reunion, especially if they are in their teens and 20's. One such adoptee, Alayna, remembers being 12 years old and going to a reunion that included nearly 75 people. Generations of people laughing and participating in playful conversation, remembering parents and grandparents and hearing the stories of life long ago. Hamburgers and corn on the cob, covered picnic tables, and all the rest, the homemade salads, red Jell-O, and desserts that were family recipes.

Alayna recalls stepping away from it all for a few moments, standing under a tree by herself, and becoming aware that in some way, as loved as she might be by these people, she did not quite fit. She looked different. She was different. She swallowed hard as she returned to play with her cousins in an open field.

Where did she belong and to whom did she belong? Only in her fantasies could Alayna see herself with other people, with her birth parents and their families. She wondered what a birth family reunion would look like. She was part of two families and she knew, then at age 12, that she was living with both reality and fantasy, and that she did not fully belong to either one. She was alone; part of her was still an orphan.

A house becomes a home by degrees, as on a continuum. It is home when it is the place where there is safety, the chief security of knowing that you have a place there, not simply a room but a presence. In a home, a child is known deeply, valued greatly, and comes to believe that he or she belongs there. That child learns by everyday experience that he or she also belongs to the people there; they belong to each other. The warmth and security and the care of home are vital, both to children growing up and to adults whose lives continue to evolve.

And home is the place as well that fosters spiritual life. When a child experiences home in this rich fashion, that child naturally internalizes the spiritual beliefs and personal values that guide family life. The strong relationships between parents and children become the vehicle by which these beliefs and values are transferred.

And when children adopt their parents with strength, this process of internalizing their beliefs and values usually goes well. Of course, many variables contribute to developing spiritual life. But for our purposes, we take notice of the importance of home in an adoptee's spiritual development as the place where much of this takes place.

Fifth, from adoptive parents: "Why is there so much suffering in our adoption?"

As adoptive parents who are struggling with their children look around, they usually see many adoptions that appear to be "working," where parents and child are connecting well and where these adoptees seem to be growing up more successfully. And then, they might also assume that in non-adoptive families things go even more smoothly, leaving them feeling hopeless.

In these troublesome comparisons, nagging doubts come to mind and heart. "What's wrong with us as adoptive parents that our son is acting out so much and unwilling to really let us in to really love him?" To them, adoption looks to be a considerable gamble, and in their own experience they have lost the bet and are now parents to an unwilling adoptee.

Blame needs to go somewhere, and so at times adoptive parents blame each other for this perceived failure. Moms blame dads and dads blamed moms for the adoptee's obstructive behavior. And their marriage suffers. Or, blame simply stays with the child who becomes the target for the anger the parents experience.

Or for our purposes, God may get the blame. God is on the block of our judgment for this family suffering. And blaming God may serve the purpose of protecting everyone else from the anger and the discouragement that adoptive parents feel.

At other times, agencies of adoption become the target for judgment. "We were never prepared to deal with a child like this! No one ever told us that it could be this difficult. No one ever warned us of these struggles–that our child might not adopt us."

At this point the resource of post-adoption services comes to mind. Usually this assistance, although helpful, is so much less than is needed to train adoptive parents to manage their limited attachment to their children. Helping these adoptive parents facilitate a different kind of relationship with their adoptees is a considerable challenge (and the goal of this book).

Sixth, from adoptive parents: "God, was this not Your plan?"

"We thought that this was your plan for our family. We believed that we were following your leading, Lord! Well, did we get it wrong? Is this what your plan is for us? It is much more punishment than a blessing right now." By attributing the decision to a divine plan, parents reassure themselves that, first, a plan to adopt was God's idea; second, this plan has God's blessing, God's seal of approval: and third, it has the promise of God's blessing and direction.

By this way of believing, God is very involved and very responsible. Sometimes when asked to explain this comment further, adoptive parents will respond, "We just knew that this was the right thing for us to do. This was God's leading in our lives." Not only did God get things started, but God evidently committed to give the wisdom and strength needed to assist adoptive parents in the daily practice of doing adoption itself, or so they thought and believed. Yet now they feel like they have been led to the end of a box canyon.

It is useful to notice that such a comment, "This was God's plan," is how the adoptive parents interpret things. Certainly, they sensed something and named that experience as God's leading for them. And along with that belief would come the expectation that "it would not be really, really hard," as God was putting things together for them. But now, their present reality of a difficult adoption puts God in a different light and does not notice that this was their plan as well.

To learn that divine support would be so much less than was needed in a given adoptive family is a considerable blow to adoptive parents, a spiritual wound that they may carry all along in the parenting of an adoptee. It would appear that God has not come through with what adoptive parents needed in order to successfully develop a relationship with their children that would be more redemptive than it appeared to be.

Notions of the imminence, the closeness of God, were seldom experienced. And notions of the transcendence, the great distance between humanity and God, may have been experienced as the abandonment of God. The silence of God then becomes a spiritual hardship to bear. Here the experience of divine betrayal parallels the experience of their child. Adoptive parents are given the opportunity to understand the pain of their children at a deeper level.

Seventh, from the adoptee: "What, then, is the purpose of my life?"

This is the question of most all young people who struggle to make sense of things. She knows that she does not know what her future holds but, nevertheless, she wonders about the purpose of her life. What is her life for?

Many children review that possibility of being like or not like their parents. Some say yes and some say no to the option of picking up the life purposes of their parents.

But for adoptees, which parents? Some adoptees, especially when they wonder in fantasy about their unknown and unrecognized first parents, may have a significant impulse to be as those first parents have been, if even in fantasy.

For example, **many teenage female adoptees are pleased when they become pregnant**: "I was happy when I found out I was going to have a baby." This may sound surprising as it is so opposite of the fears and anxieties of most teenagers about pregnancy. But further reflection as well as the direct report of pregnant adoptees helps us understand that in such a narrative the adoptee has become her mother or at least the fantasy of her first mother.

This pregnant teenage adoptee also has a direct connection now with someone who looks as she looks, who has the same blue eyes that she has, or the same hair color or silly smile that she sees every day in the mirror. In these ways pregnancy may be a solution of sorts to the deepest spiritual longings of a teenage adoptee.

When the relinquished and adopted child grows up well bonded to his or her adoptive parents, when life in the adoptive home is relatively good and satisfying, when the relationships that develop within the network of the family are enriching and supportive, an adoptee might well carry forward the purpose-giving attributes, positive attitudes, and spiritual rituals of their second parents.

These adoptees have internalized these descriptors of their adoptive parents and are able to test out their own passions as well as their own skills as they move toward becoming productive adults finding purpose in their lives. They are noticing those meaning-giving attributes of their parents and, shall we say, adopting them.

However, when adoptees struggle to adopt their parents as the resources, both emotional and spiritual, for their own development, **they may also struggle with finding purpose in their own lives**. Meaning-giving activities may be in short supply when no parents are taken in deeply and then as living as a spiritual orphan continues.

Certainly, signs of trouble in the adoptive relationship include little sign of a conscience and very limited eye contact on the part of the adoptee. In the case of conscience, the personal values of adoptive parents may hardly be taken in by adoptees in such a way that they adopt them as their own. These adoptees may struggle a great deal to adopt any values that are beyond the value of their own survival. Without such core values, finding meaning-giving experiences in life may be more difficult.

And, as well, very limited eye contact may be the red flag for a very limited connection where fear remains the primary concern of the adoptee. If that is the case, without the strength of person that relationships provide, as adoptees feel lost in their lives, their conclusion may be that nothing matters and that neither do they. We are then back to the despair of Job, their lament of being alive.

In the first six months of his life, Johan was placed in a foster home with elderly parents who kept him fed and clothed and warm in bed, but seldom touched him at all. His bottle was propped up on a diaper as he lay on his back staring at the mobile floating above him. His diapers were regularly changed, but beyond that these older folks gave him almost no attention, certainly very little skin-to-skin contact.

Johan was not unlike many of the seriously underweight and under-touched adoptees from Romania of the early 1990's after Nicolae Ceausescu was executed and the orphanages in that country were opened for the adoption of previously unwanted children.

It was immediately obvious to Johan's adoptive parents that he could barely lift his head and the hair on both sides of his head was simply rubbed off. The bonding behaviors of finding comfort in his mother's neck, cuddling, and finding warmth and rest on his father's bare chest were noticeably absent.

Johan's adoptive parents sensed that being his parents was going to be a significant challenge. And certainly, that became the case. There was very minimal eye contact from Johan. He seemed to be a little boy very much unto himself. As the challenges of school came before him, although he tested at mid-level intelligence, he had little motivation to do much of anything at all, much less his homework. Johan felt little purpose in his life. **At one point as a teenager, he informed his parents that he did not believe in God.**

Well, that makes sense. Not only was there a significant distance between Johan and people in his life, but there was also a significant distance between Johan and any inward sense of a caring, loving God. He could not report any experience that he would consider spiritually positive, given the way that people around him use that term.

Spiritually speaking, Johan was still very much an orphan. His first experience of life without touch in foster care was, among many things, a profound spiritual tragedy.

Hell itself is sometimes described as ultimate abandonment-- being ultimately separated from everyone else as well as from God. In this sense, sometimes life for the adoptee is a living hell.

Johan had good reasons not to believe in God.

For him, it was "enough of Sabbath worship." In the sanctuary he was told of divine care and personal guidance for living one's life, of the richness of religious tradition and the importance of ethical values. In services of worship, Johan learned about how his adoptive parents saw things. But for him, their spiritual beliefs, their religious practices, and their altruistic values–these made little sense to him because they did not fit his life experience.

Johan knew something of abandonment, of God turning God's face away from him, of parents who did not "get him," as well as of ethical values that seem so hard to follow. At some level Johan knew that accepting these spiritual perspectives and religious traditions would feel dishonest. It would be an act of joining his family at a deeper spiritual level and so, of course, he struggled to do so. But what fit for them did not fit for him.

At one point in his junior year of high school, Johan flatly refused to attend Sabbath worship. In one sense we might think of this as declaring his own independence, as stepping away from his family to become his own person, his own adult, shall we say. And it may look that way.

But for the adoptee, separating, leaving home is different. For Johan it was an important moment when he brought his truth, his very different truth, to the family table. So far from maturing and leaving as his own continuing development, this was an expression of his own spiritual suffering.

Johan was wanting to find more solid earth on which to stand, more clarity about his own spiritual identity in relation not only to his adoptive parents but, in his case, to his parents by birth, unknown to him. They may have had very different ways to see one's place in the Universe. Johan put his foot down to stop what felt to him like a charade, a religious façade that did not fit the person he saw himself to be.

As is usual in adolescence, the importance of his own self-definition was coming to the front burner of his awareness. As loving as his adoptive family had been, Johan was challenged to sort out and declare his own truth about God as he understood how God might be.

From Johan's own perspective, God was not simply kind and benevolent and always caring. For him, God at best was a tough parent, sometimes neglectful, and even abusive. Of course, this did not square at all with what he was taught at home or in worship.

He had developed the courage to begin to speak his own spiritual truth about his experience of living in a world of complexities where very little was as simple as people pretended to make it. His was a personal struggle, an ambivalence of trying to love his adoptive parents on one hand and trying to stay away from them on the other. His spiritual life did not match their spiritual life very much at all. Johan was growing up, but he was growing up differently than how he would have, had his relinquishment never occurred.

There are no simple answers to these inquiries about the nature and being of God in the life experience of the adoptive family. Nevertheless, these are the questions that are asked, especially by adoptees and adoptive parents. They must be asked. They are asked because they address the ultimate spiritual concerns of living within that family.

And, as we can see, they are primarily existential in that they have to do with the here and now lived experience as adoptee and as adoptive parent. (For our purposes in this book, we leave the spiritual concerns of birth parents in the background. They are people who usually attend to the loss that they have experienced as surrendering parents.)

Questions without final answers--Sometimes they haunt us and refuse to go away. They recycle in our consciousness and we struggle without understanding--that's the human condition. We come up with possibilities that may work even for a while and then, as life continues, those solutions are no longer viable. So we ask again.

We all need a reason to get up in the morning and it may be that for the adoptee this is especially true because the split-life relinquished and adopted experience is always at risk of removing purpose in living and value as a person. These are such important factors in living and loving life that such questions don't go away, even without final answers.

Spiritual Recommendations for Adoptive Parents

Attentive adoptive parents do well, first of all, to remind themselves that young children quite naturally take in **the religious rituals of family life.** These can be defined in different ways.

For Christian families, the usual activities of devotional time, family prayer, and the reading of the Judeo-Christian Scriptures may be a daily practice. Weekly they assemble themselves together with like-minded others for worship. Anticipation is shared around the Advent wreath. Children take notice and become curious about the meaning of such activity.

Within the Jewish community, the calendar of spiritual celebrations, Yom Kippur and Rosh Hashanah, for example, guides family life, and children take notice. The family gathers around the table for the Passover Seder. The children ask why that night is not like others, and parents rehearse the story of their heritage. The candlelight of the Menorah is rich, aflame with meaning.

In the Muslim community, the daily ritual of call to prayer by kneeling in respect to Allah, the God of the Old Testament Scriptures, marks persons and families with a clear religious identity. Children become aware of the fasts and reflection of Ramadan and, as in other religious traditions, participate in distinct ceremonies surrounding life events

In all these instances, engaging the power of such religious rituals forms and strengthens a child's personal spiritual identity, both as a young person and as a member of the larger faith community. **The practice of such daily, weekly, and yearly habits and celebrations would certainly strengthen the adoptee's spiritual awareness and developing identity.**

And, what about spiritual conversation? Though many in North America live in an increasingly secular post-religious world, these spiritual questions don't go away. Children still bring their wonderings to the table. They will quickly learn whether are not these questions are welcomed.

"Daddy, where did the world come from?" "Mommy, why do we go to synagogue?" "How far away can a rocket go in Space if it keeps on going and going?" "Will the sun always keep shining?" Or, "Who made the moon and the stars?" Or, on the Christian celebration of Easter, "How could Jesus rise from the dead?"

Out of the mouths of curious children come these inquiries about the nature of reality and the things that people believe. These delightful invitations to big questions can open the door to greater conversation with children about God, however one thinks about God. But if these questions make parents anxious and are met with a frown and hesitation, the conversation goes nowhere. It disappears.

All too often children quickly learn that neither religion nor politics can be discussed in a thoughtful objective manner. Sadly, it doesn't take long until talk about the spiritual is trained out of life at the kitchen table. The discussion of beliefs and the values of living that come from them--the Ten Commandments, for example--is important in the formation of a child's spiritual identity. Having conversation, **spiritual conversation,** is a wise thing to encourage in family life.

And then, there is **the value of testimony**. As parents, it is a good idea to challenge ourselves to speak to our children about our own spiritual perspectives and experiences, both past and present. Whether it be the presence or absence of God in our personal life stories, it is good for our children to hear us speak of these things.

I often reflect on how war veterans so often are only able at the end of their lives to speak of the trauma they've experienced. It is quite reasonable to not bring up the horrors of war, to wish them away, to forget them. And yet they are remembered in a person's life, these moments of spiritual struggle and trauma and survival. Even years later, stories of the past may bring tears to the eyes of our elders.

These testimonies are rich with meaning and speak with great depth to the heart of the human struggle. To whatever degree we are able to tell our stories, we then can create opportunities for faith to move from one generation to the next. In some ways our silence about such things is understandable, but unfortunate, because hearing these stories would have great value to family members, especially children, and especially relinquished and adopted children.

And then, **there is the challenge of challenging.** By this I mean that all of us who parent children are teachers as well. Attending to the spiritual life of the child might certainly include challenging boys and girls to wonder, to be curious, to struggle with the reality of not knowing.

Taking the lead in a child's spiritual life may take the form of questions like "Samuel, what do you think about people who take Christmas packages off the front steps of people's homes?" And then, a bit later, "Sam, why do you think they do that?" Such a little inquiry about something they see on the news at Christmas time would certainly open discussion in which parents would learn more about their children rather quickly. And further, they would facilitate a discussion about values by which people live. It would be so interesting.

But above all else, **there is love, the parental affection that seeks the heart of a child.** The most significant frustration for some adoptive parents is that of getting through to their children that they truly love them, that they are attached. Sometimes these children cannot believe or trust that it is true. And sometimes it seems to be impossible to get through the wall of defenses that disallows a child from adopting his mother or father with any strength. In this spiritual dilemma, the bonding and attachment of the child to her parents is minimal, just as with Sally Anne in the opening pages of this book.

"I know I shouldn't, but I just want to yell, to scream, to somehow get through to her how much she means to me, that I love her deeply. But she doesn't seem to get it." This is the lament of Sally Anne's mother who is so invested in making that vital connection between her mother- heart and the heart of her child.

Nevertheless, acts of love need to continue day after day, nourishing the ongoing relationship, because it is the relationship that brings life. It is the relationship that offers warmth. It is the relationship that offers security. It is the relationship that offers daily care.

The warmth of a hug or a soft word spoken kindly or a reward for good behavior, or even a gentle consequence for bad behavior, all of these must be seen as attempts to build the relationship that heals and restores and offers the adoptee the experience of being loved.

There is no substitute! In that child's spiritual life, the cognitive notion of a loving presence then becomes experienced in such a way that a child may begin to "get it" that there may be a God who loves the same way.

So we come full circle, remembering that for many adoptees God is on the block in ways that are confounding and difficult, even impossible to resolve. The idea of a god who is kind and loving flies in the face of the experience of relinquishment, of what adoptees might think of as a decision, a divine plan for abandonment.

All that stands in the way of this conclusion are the arms of adoptive parents who reach out, sometimes hoping against all odds that their offer of healing closeness will be taken.

In the divine plan for adoption lies the possibility of a more benevolent view of God. By this way of seeing things, of making sense of things, there may be room for spiritual experiences that are the opposite of being abandoned. The adoptee may find a way to the spiritual act of courage that is needed to allow love, to allow the love of adoptive parents, to allow the love of God.

10

How Wise Adoptive Parenting Looks

So, what are some good things to recommend to adoptive parents who are struggling with difficult adoptive relationships?

Clearly, so much usually happens before adoption in one way or another. We've seen that to whatever degree this is the case, an empathic appreciation of adoptees' experiences as they face challenges is critical for change. And further, the nature of a relationship adoptive parents construct with these children sets the stage for possible healing and forms the context for good parenting choices.

Parental actions and responses will then flow less from guessing about what to do and more confidently from knowing what to do. Realistically, we are always guessing to some degree, but, ideally, we can gain more confidence in those guesses.

In this chapter, attributes of wise adoptive parenting will be presented with a positive twist while we acknowledge that it is not easy for parents to face the challenges of changing as both persons and parents in order to care for and respond, more effectively, to their children, wounded adoptees.

What does wise adoptive parenting look like in the face of the usual complicated struggles with closeness, battles for power between parent and child, as well as other aspects of successful adoptive parenting?

Ten Attributes of Wise Adoptive Parenting

Attribute #1- Wise adoptive parenting requires the ongoing effort to continue to understand, more and more fully over time, the many personal motivations for choosing to adopt a child.

At times, adoptive parents may resist examining their own motivations for the choice of adoption. Intentions may be both conscious and unconscious at different times.

Often, a husband and a wife may have quite different motivations for this decision to bring a child into their lives. But when adoptive parents cannot begin to wonder what motivates their desire to adopt a child, they may stumble along and sometimes trip over roots that go deep into the ground of their own being as persons.

Sandra was one such adoptive mother who took it on the chin when her relinquished and adopted son yelled, "You are not my real mother!" in the middle of a fight over helping with dinner dishes. Time and time again, Sandra had heard that this was an often-used adoptee response, one of the many weapons in the arsenal of defending against the fear of closeness between mother and child. Her son was also naming his truth that real mother had different meanings to him.

There was something about being a real mother that touched Sandra to her very core. She had more grieving to do around the insult of infertility, her own inability to become a mother by birth. Now, sadness and anger had become her present-day diet of distasteful emotions. Her son had hooked the source of some of her own suffering.

As she began to ponder these moments, she was able to notice that part of her deepest motivation for adopting was that of fixing her broken reproductive self. However, adoption is never a cure for infertility. Mourning the child by birth, never to be born, was still before her. And, unless she resolved some of this necessary grieving–**the word means "letting go"**–she would not know her own sadness, and she would not know of her need and expectation that her relinquished and adopted son would become a substitute who would fix what felt so wrong.

Taka has a different story. For in his Taiwanese culture, having a son was a most important part of becoming a successful man. After the birth of two daughters, he decided to request of his wife that they adopt a Taiwanese boy to complete their family. Further, it was important to him that the adoption be secretive. So much so that his wife feigned a pregnancy, little pillows under her dress and all, so that their parents would not reject the child as "not of our blood." This was quite an endeavor, yet they were successful in this secretive project of adoption.

349

Little boys are difficult to come by in the Taiwanese male-dominated culture; however, in the course of time, a male infant was presented to an orphanage nearby, and arrangements were made to correlate a feigned pregnancy with the arrival of this baby boy. Taka's deepest motivation was to preserve the honor of his family in a world where shame is such a powerful cultural negative.

Care and empathy for the plight of this infant were not a primary consideration. In addition, the motivations of his wife were unnoticed and unconsidered. As we discussed in Chapter 4, no child signs up for such a role in the family.

At the tender age of 16, Gwen learned that she was pregnant after a single experience of intercourse with her 17-year-old boyfriend, Jerry. Both were growing up in conservative, religious homes where sexual sins created the greatest amount of guilt by far.

Let's revisit the distinction between guilt and shame. These terms are certainly cousins--guilt is that ugly sensation that you did something wrong and shame is that ugly, more powerful sensation that you are something wrong.

At first, guilt and fear were their common experience. A sense of shame would come later, much more for Gwen than it did for Jerry. To minimize both experiences, privately, they chose to abort the fetus. Complications from the medical procedure left Gwen unable to ever conceive another child.

Years later with a man named Mark as her husband, Gwen pressed for adoption with great intensity. In that process, she found herself rather impatient with the length of time predicted till they would become parents. She was inpatient with agency social workers who sought to be helpful in terms of presenting Gwen and Mark as potential adoptive parents in a portfolio that would be presented to a birth mother (and sometimes a birth father) to consider for the placement of her child.

Years of guilt kept secret as well as underlying shame had their way with Gwen until finally, in conversation with a relinquishment-and-adoption-informed therapist, she came to identify her wish that a successful adoption would mean the end of her guilt, her punishment for that abortion of years ago. She had judged herself quite harshly, and also, she hoped to minimize her secret personal shame. To the degree, of course, that she would be able to face these deeper motivations, her adopted child could grow up free from the role of resolving Gwen's guilt and shame.

As is so often the case, the motivations for a plan for adoption for someone like Mark are quite different from the motivations of his wife. Mark knew that Gwen was unable to conceive before they were married, and he pledged his support to her, no matter how the possibility of family might turn out. In a secondary way, Mark was fine with the idea of bringing a child by adoption into their home, but his primary motivation was that of pleasing his wife.

Simply put, Mark went forward with the plan for adoption because he loved Gwen. But it should be noticed that such a motivation would prove insufficient from the perspective of the adoptee who would reasonably expect the love and affection of both of his parents. Mark had yet to learn about the importance and challenge of the role that he would play in the life of his son.

It has sometimes been said that the better adoptive parents are those who already have birth children because they already know what it means to be a mother and a father, and their motivations for adoption might be more altruistic and therefore less self-interested.

Consider the story of Lisa. An adoptee herself, she took immense joy in becoming a mother to her four children by birth. Never before had she been with people who looked like her--the same nose and ears and eye color, the same hair color, the same interests, and even the same sound of voice.

All of these variables reflected back toward Lisa as a proud and happy mother. For her, mothering was so meaningful and rich an experience of loving and healing that she wanted more. And now, looking to the possibility made sense as a way she could continue the deep pleasure of mothering.

Three relinquished and adopted children later, only then did Lisa realize how much she had been driven to become a mother by both birth and by adoption. The challenge that she still faced was that of bringing an end to her primary role as a mom. Letting her children go off to their own lives and letting go of her primary role of being their mother put a lump in Lisa's throat.

Now she began to see how important these children had been to her, by birth or by adoption, and that her own motivation for mothering so many had been driven by the deep and understandable need to heal her own heart from the sorrows of her own relinquishment. For her, this was a developmental achievement long in coming, a necessary grieving entered into and more accomplished.

Knowing the personal motivations that move us is a clue that most often links us in powerful ways to our own childhood stories. And accordingly, as good adoptive parents will testify, being able over time to put one's motivations into words and reflect more and more fully on them has so much to do with the persons that they have become. Only then is it possible to distinguish in a careful manner what needs adoptive parents will fill for themselves as they respond to the developmental needs of their children.

What might be a most useful motivation for adoption? The answer is simple: pleasure taken in saving and nurturing the physical, emotional, and spiritual life of a child in giving the orphaned child a home. Remember, adoption should first of all be for the child. When this altruistic intention is primary, it sets the stage for a non-defensive and more objective appreciation and understanding of the wounded child taken into a family. Certainly, there is usually a mix of motivations in every narrative of relinquishment and adoption, but when this motivation of enjoying parental care is primary, then other motivations may fall in line.

Attribute # 2- Wise adoptive parenting takes care to protect the marriages of adoptive parents.

As one worn out and frustrated adoptive father put it, "Sometimes these kids can drive a Mack truck right through the middle of our marriage." Splitting up mom and dad is seldom an entirely conscious intention on the part of the child; however, doing so certainly creates a powerful negative drama.

Remember that behavior is always telling in some way; our task is to interpret that behavior as accurately as possible. The behavior of a troubled child who is fearful of closeness to either her adopted mother or adopted father tells her story in a disguised form. Her behavior says many things about her inner conflict with closeness to another. How frightening that is. How foreign it is at times. She shows it and hides at the same time.

And then, when a couple now begins to turn on each other as they parent an adopted child, certainly that adoptee has gained more problematic power in the family by way of her behavior.

Jordan was an adoptive father who, reflecting on his own military upbringing, believed that rules and regulations were always a part of successful parenting. "Sometimes you need to let your children be upset with you, you need to be in charge." This method had worked well with their by-birth children. This simple maxim guided his approach to his newly adopted son from India. But his wife Leah saw things differently. For her, being an adoptive mother meant keeping the peace at all times by being silent, or at other times by bending the rules so as to keep her son calm and comfortable.

It's no surprise that "keeping the rules clear" and "peace at all costs" were very different approaches to parenting that led to conflict between them. Quite understandably, their relinquished and adopted little boy, Eli, quickly figured out that his mother was his protector, even against his father. Accordingly, he would rush to her side whenever he was in trouble and seek her protection from the consequences for his negative behavior.

As this adoption process went on in the early years of his life, little Eli learned that creating conflict between his parents served his purposes of manipulation and protection. And the pillow talk between his mother and father focused more and more on their parenting disagreements. Distance between the two of them as a married couple grew. Things eventually got to the point where Eli could drive that Mack truck through the middle of their marriage.

The story of adopting a child has many variables. Another one might be the very different emotional states of adoptive parents. Post-partum depression is commonly understood in our culture as that sense of loss and despair that mothers by birth sometimes experience. Right alongside the joy of becoming a mother is the darkness of being depressed or immobilized by sadness. This emotional state, often influenced by bouncing hormonal changes, is commonly known and commonly treated.

Much less is known about a mother's post-adoption depression. "I'm so surprised that I have not fallen in love with my child. Sometimes I don't even like her. I don't get it, but that's what's happening."

And then the adoptive father, puzzled by this response on the part of his wife, may become judgmental. Adoptive fathers may pursue their relinquished and adopted children to make up for the troubling limited response of the adoptive mother's care for the child. In such a narrative, guilt and shame deepen the distress of the post-adoption depressed mother.

Pillow talk becomes quite limited, and husband and wife fall asleep without the benefit of healing words to each other. In this case, the adoptee is so innocent and yet so much a point of conflict for this couple. What a tragedy!

Here the challenge for adoptive couples is to stay together. Whether adoptees actively work to split apart a mother and a father or whether other variables come to play, the parenting challenge remains to work toward more or less one parental voice.

Seldom do adoptive parents initially see the importance of protecting their marriage from the conflicts that adopting may create. Sometimes, in the process of planning an adoption, different motivations and different understandings of it become part of the conversation prior to the adoption itself. But usually, conflict within the adopting marriage comes as a surprise. Along the way of attending to the child, attending to each other may be sacrificed.

Attribute # 3- Wise adoptive parenting means that such parents are clearly entitled to their children.

There is such a thing as positive entitlement as a parent. With the term entitled, I mean the strong awareness that a child "belongs to me." The adoptee is clearly appreciated as "my daughter" or "my son." The answer to the inquiry, "To whom do does this child belong?" is not in question. The sufficiently entitled adoptive parent will say without hesitation, "You belong to me." Usually, entitlement develops and strengthens along with discovering, attaching, and caring for the new son or daughter.

Sometimes, however, there is slight hesitation. Physical differences are pronounced because of different genetics. As obvious as it may be, all adoptees face the reality that they are physiologically and psychologically wired to be very different human beings than are the rest of the adoptive family. The fantasy of being a look-alike to one's adoptive child may significantly contrast with the reality. One may think, "I'm not sure this is what I thought it would be, and I'm not sure how much I like it this way."

In the midst of such personal distress, understandably, a sense of entitlement may be compromised. Owning, not as property, of course, but in the healthy sense of "You are mine!" may sometimes be a future goal more than a present experience. And yet, a strong sense of entitlement is critical to the development of good parenting skills.

Recall once more that adoptive mother walking through the airport holding on tightly to the hand of her daughter. As she thought more carefully about this moment, this adoptive mom realized her daughter was not quite hers yet. This fear of losing her was quite difficult to name. When doing so, she was able to see her own hesitation about this little girl being her little girl.

In this narrative, the fantasied birth parents were possible thieves to be feared much more than viewed as partners in the formation of an adoptive family. This was a lesson yet to be learned, but this dynamic compromised the full entitlement that a child needs to experience from his parents. "You belong to me" elicits the wonderful security of knowing that "I belong to you."

Casting first parents in a positive light, whether in fantasy or reality, is sometimes especially difficult when not only second parents but also the grandparents do not see birth parents as acceptable. The challenges of infertility, of continuing a family bloodline, are especially difficult for grandparents of adoptees to face and to accept. "They are not quite one of ours." This negative judgment against them sets the stage for conflict between adoptive parents and their own parents.

And, of course, children get that and know quite well that they are not quite "in" the family narrative. Where there could have been support and encouragement, and most of all inclusion, instead adoptees face negative push-away within the extended adoptive family.

It's so tragic when dis-entitlement becomes the rule of the day. Sometimes children by birth are in the family will or estate planning, and children by adoption are not named in the same legal document. They are not considered equal to children by birth. Countless stories have been told about the nature of this injury to the heart of the relinquished and adopted child.

Attribute # 4-Wise adoptive parenting means engaging the birth parents of their children positively in both fantasy and reality.

These first parents were not able, for whatever reason, to be the parents that these children needed. The task of adoptive parenting is clear--putting birth parents in a positive light serves the adoptee well. What about serving the adoptive parent well?

In fantasy, of course, adoptive parents may create make-believe impressions. They may look upon birth parents as a threat, as people who may return and take back the child given to adoption. Remember also the phrase bad seed. If these beliefs exist, the adoptee may experience the adoptive parents' presenting these birth parents in a positive light as a contrived effort that lacks integrity.

Adoptive parents may understand that how they see these first parents affects the way their children will see themselves as well. But beyond concerns for the self-esteem of the child, adoptive parents are challenged to notice these people, these first parents, in a positive light themselves, even when there seems to be little about which to be positive.

Yet, adoptive mothers who struggle with infertility often quietly envy first mothers' ability to become so easily pregnant. Such envy can drive adoptive parents to push birth parents away, especially when these first parents remind them of their own infertility. In doing so, their envy can remain below the surface, supposedly unnoticed.

When the relinquishment narrative is quite tragic, how accepting can we be? When it involves drugs or alcohol or other derivatives of neglect and abuse, it is so tempting to judge the first parents. Using person-first language is key to accepting these first parents for whom they are with all the difficulties that are described. This becomes the challenge for wise adoptive parents. "Your birth mother was a person who was not able..." is a good way to begin that conversation.

Attribute # 5- Wise adoptive parenting means setting clear boundaries in family life.

I love the story once told to me about the three-year-old adoptee who was discovered, sitting on her bed in conversation with herself. Repeatedly, she said "I can say shoot, but I cannot say shit." (Need we forgive this child's language?) At that very tender age she was quite aware of the boundary for language set by her parents: "Yes" to one word; "No" to another.

Learning to live within a boundary is the first of many developmental achievements in the story of the child. Learning a lesson about acceptable speech becomes one more brick in the wall of security that lets this little one feel safe. She knows where she stands if she says only the "right" things, and she knows that there are consequences when she says the "wrong" thing.

It cannot be said too strongly that "structure creates security," especially for young children. It is not helpful for a child not to know his or her bedtime, a click on the clock that indicates that a child must go to bed. A regimented, structured day-time schedule may sound so military, but to a child, adoptee or otherwise, schedule is essential. "At eight o'clock I brush my teeth, I say my prayers, and I go to bed" offers any child a clear sense of security. Of course, as the child gets older this "day planner" way of living usually subsides, but it is so good when it is initially internalized: "I feel safe because I know what's going to happen next within my protected environment."

Would that it could be so easy! Boundaries that establish rights and wrongs, bedtimes, turns setting tables, clothing that can or cannot be worn to school, or manners with which we manage life experience–all of these will usually create resistance. Seldom is there little pushback to the law and the order of the day. None of us like to be told what to do, old or young.

Recall that closeness is scary in an uncertain world. Boundary setting is a hard-won battle when early-on life experience has compromised the ability to trust. Instead, too often, the adoptee will arch her back.

Our usual parenting methods are reflections of the ways in which we were parented. If Mom was a "yeller," for example, that may be a mother's first line of response to the challenge of disobedience. Or, if Dad ruled with an iron fist, then we fathers will usually default without much thought to similar parenting methods. Adoptive parents may see these default responses as certainly understandable; however, adoptees might interpret such engagements very differently from what parents might intend.

For example, whereas a child by birth might respond to his mother's yelling as part of the context of their ongoing trusting relationship, a child by adoption might experience it in a very different and very negative way. Put simply, the yelling is much more than simply the yelling, and that much more is the strength of relationship.

On the other hand, a child by adoption might respond to discipline of any sort as, first of all, reminiscent of earlier experiences of being yelled at without the strength of relationship. For this adoptee, these parental responses that are not grounded in a trusting relationship may be experienced as another moment of rejection and further abandonment. For example, "Go to your room" may have very different meanings for these two very different childhood experiences.

Accordingly, the adoptive parenting challenge is to wonder how an adoptee experiences these boundaries. Not assuming one knows for sure is the place to begin.

Attribute # 6- Wise adoptive parenting means inviting conversation about relinquishment, the difficulties of abandonment, or the death of first parents.

I often hear about adoptive parents who see themselves quite honestly as open to conversations with their children about the possible early-on hardships of their loss-of-parents narrative. They speak about being quite willing to discuss these difficult stories whenever the adoptee might bring these stories to the family table for conversation.

However, what needs review with this approach is their waiting for that conversation and assuming that it is best engaged at the child's initiative. More careful consideration would mean taking notice of the many times in which children may indirectly allude to their own painful stories. Adoptive parents might then be able to pick up on those moments as opportunities to bring these painful histories more into focus, more to the family table.

This is not the same as leading the conversation. It is paying attention and listening empathically to the adoptee who is carrying that pain. Bringing these stories up in a strong and straightforward manner would usually only create resistance to further conversation. But attending to those indirect hints that a child offers would be very good adoptive parenting practice. From the perspective of the adoptee, parents opening a conversation to further explore how an adoptee thinks and feels about his or her story of parent loss may become a moment of significant empathy.

Understandably hesitant, even nervous about talking, but also wondering and even hoping for something good to include in one's relinquishment and adoption narrative, **the young child may be quite appreciative that Mom or Dad opened the door to talk more about these things: "Well, right, every home isn't like this one. Do you ever wonder if maybe your birth mother might do things differently?"**

We sometimes call this "speaking to the preconscious or even the unconscious." Even if a certain subject is too far a reach for the adoptee to make at one point in time, encouraging future conversation communicates openness to sorting these issues out. And the child knows that you know, even without further conversation.

There may be moments of "No, that is not true! It does not bother me!" when an adoptee experiences the need to deny or at least push away a painful awareness too awful to know right now. For example, after viewing a movie that included the theme of parental loss and adoption, a nine-year-old adoptee was gently questioned by her mother with this inquiry: "Johanna, I'm wondering about something. I'm wondering if watching this movie about adoption bothered you, especially when you saw the little boy crying when he was abandoned."

Certainly, Johanna's mother did well by opening up the conversation as well as communicating her concern, but Johanna was ready to hear none of it. And she let his mother know with some strength that she did not want to "go there." She was nine years old, and not yet prepared to deal with the emotional pain in her own story. Nevertheless, this mother did the right thing, and Johanna knew that her mother knew, even if, once again, there was no conversation.

And, yes, sometimes first parents do pass away, leaving children as orphans. Mothers do die in childbirth. Fathers do contract AIDS and die within months. Loss of life is a tragic reality. Their children are left, abandoned by death, often with little support for the grieving before them.

Some dynamics are different in the case of death because the parent did not choose to relinquish, to "give up" a child to adoption. In this case destiny itself is the broker of tragedy. And again, the children pay the price.

When Tatyana lost her mother to stage-four breast cancer, she was only two years old. She has no memory of her mother or of her father who simply disappeared. Left in an orphanage in Indonesia, her nerves needed to be numbed because the pain of isolation was too awful to deal with in her early years. At around age 5, Tatyana found herself in an adoptive family in Texas.

A significant task for Tatyana was to talk about her fantasies of her first mother, had she lived. Her adoptive mother, Susanna, was wisely quite up to the task of encouraging that conversation: "Tatyana, you just asked about the first part of your life in India. I wonder what

364

your birth mother was like. I wonder what she looked like. If she had the same hair color that you have, or the same talents, or the same silly giggle that we sometimes hear from you. I just wonder what she was like."

What care and openness come from such a comment to a little girl. The freedom to be sad, the freedom to be curious, and the freedom to talk about this person, this forever unknown birth mother–are all gifts from this wise adoptive mother. And again, wondering about her birth mother resulted in a conversation, which began only with the words, "I wonder about that too."

This is a good start towards the necessary grieving still before her. We see then that bringing birth parent narratives to life in words may open the door to substantial conversations. Sometimes adoptive parents, as all others, need to help their children be sad.

Attribute # 7- Wise adoptive parenting means not personalizing angry behavior or rejection by the adoptee.

At times this objective feels impossible to meet, but the effort towards it is important for adoptive parents.

Few friends or relatives will understand good adoptive parenting where children struggle so much with getting close. The judgments of other people, usually not intimately involved with the adoptive parents, may be quite painful. "They must not be very good parents."

Also, the hurts that are absorbed from the child who is fearful of parental love--these negatives need to be held at some distance in order to minimize their toxic effect.

We sometimes use the term *tough* to describe adoptive parents, not in the sense of someone who is a bully, but certainly in the sense of someone who is internally strong and solid. And, as some adoptive parents know all too well, the hard-to-deal-with adoptee can find just the right trigger to pull to wound that adoptive parent. Testing, testing, testing.

Years ago, in the classroom, I would regularly remind students that "Everything has meaning!" or, "Behavior usually tells the truth about a person." **Our task is to discern an accurate interpretation of that behavior.**

You may remember my earlier comments about the white coat in reference to the challenge of maintaining objectivity about whatever lies before us. In this conversation wearing a white coat has to do with looking and responding to a child's behavior in a very rational, calm, and deliberate manner—stating the truth with great clarity and without emotion. Personal anger is carefully disguised and put aside, absorbed in some way.

The opposite of this calm is getting hooked in such a way that tempers rise and conflict escalates. Speaking louder and louder is usually the first sign of this. Adoptive parents might find themselves becoming angry, irrational, and even "at wit's end." Notice immediately that in this scenario power in the family system distributes more to the child and less to the adult.

As the child gains power within the family system and the conflict becomes more difficult to manage, the child, unfortunately, succeeds at manipulations that are in his or her immediate favor.

The antidote to this difficult interaction is for adoptive parents not to personalize the hurtful comments, the destructive behaviors, or the personal attacks with which they are confronted. In the moment, though, as all of us know to some degree, it is so difficult not to personalize the intended injury and rejection that we may experience when a child does battle with us.

Now let's take these notions of not personalizing and bring them to the everyday experience of some adoptive parents. Juliana was adopted from Guatemala at age three, just prior to the time when adoptions from that country ceased because of corruption within its adoption network. She had spent the first two and half years in an orphanage on the outskirts of Guatemala City.

Little is known about her birth history or birth family, as is common in many such international scenarios. And now at age 5, Juliana had become quite powerful in her adoptive family, so much so that other family members, including two sisters by birth, started to walk around on pins and needles. It looked like trouble ahead, not far down the road.

Juliana's most recent behaviors targeted her adoptive mother, Sonora, as the object of her scorn. Her regular personal attacks of "You are not my mother!" were amplified by her stating that she would be much better off in another adoptive family than the one in which she presently lived.

Nothing was good, according to Juliana--the food was bad and her sisters were irritating and both adoptive Mom and Dad didn't understand her. She stated clearly that she would be better off if she had stayed in Guatemala.

The usual warmth and smile of a five-year-old were noticeably absent in her everyday relations with adults.

Certainly, she was the opposite of a "happy camper." It was as if she were deeply distressed on the inside and making sure that everyone on the outside joined her in that distress in one way or another.

When everyone else was upset in day-to-day family life, then Juliana had succeeded at once again reinforcing her throne in the family queendom that she had established. Further behaviors affirmed that throne even more; she had become the most powerful person in the family.

Juliana's next move proved to be very disheartening. One afternoon while she and her sisters were awaiting the return of their parents from a day of work, Juliana snuck away from the babysitter's view and attacked her mother's wardrobe with a sharp pair of scissors. She cut into dress after dress as they hung there before her, silent and defenseless.

Maddening – even that word could not describe the rage that Sonora felt as she pulled out the arrow that Juliana had sunk into her heart. How could a mother not personalize that her wardrobe had been destroyed!

And yet, that precisely is the assignment for wise adoptive parenting, to not take personally the wounds that struggling adoptees sometimes seek to rip open in conflict in order to hurt, to push away adoptive parents who are seeking to care. Not reacting in such an adoptive family scenario may seem humanly impossible–imagine finding your thousand-dollar wardrobe of dresses cut up in pieces!

This would hardly be a time to sit down and calmly asked "Why?" Rather, it would be a moment in which one might work very hard to restrain the impulse to strike back, even to strike the child, because sadly, striking back is getting hooked and getting hooked is losing power.

In this narrative, the adoptee succeeds at expressing her rage about her own life in general, and as well succeeds at reaffirming her throne of power. Here then the adoptive parent is challenged to step away from the deep wound that has been experienced and to put on that white coat and to avoid being hooked by a five-year-old child. Impossible, but it still has to be done somehow, some way.

In adoptive stories such as this one, the only road to objectivity in the middle of the battle is to invoke a strong boundary.

This separation between child and parent can hold the parent in a manner that contains emotion, hold the child, the struggling adoptee, accountable, and seek to understand the behavior.

"Well, it's going to cost you a lot of money to pay us back for the dresses that you destroyed. We will start by taking that $10 out of your piggy bank." Or, "Juliana, you will get another new dress only after Mommy buys one for herself first." **Notice that no reference is made here to the pain inflicted on the disheartened**

adoptive mother. Naming or noticing such a wound only gives more power to the child.

This response is an action, not a reaction. It is quite important to see the difference; an action proceeds from the wisdom of the parent, whereas a reaction proceeds in response to the direct power of the child. Who is then in charge?

As you may see, the difference between acting and reacting is huge. Not taking a child's attack personally is an act of empathy. The child is not allowed to be the enemy of the parent or the family. Instead, the parent wisely wonders what the child is trying to say that he or she cannot find words to say. Verbal exchange for any child is difficult. And not finding the words usually leads to behavior that communicates, sometimes very deeply.

An adoptive parent can become empathic to many things, often painful things, even those that lie behind such negative behavior of cutting up Mom's wardrobe. Not only would this be an aggressive attack against an adoptive mom, it may also be the communication of significant distress as well as the possible dawning of awareness of injuries from her pre-adoptive past. The adoptive parent's empathy opens up the conversation to review these things and build the trust that makes a safe place for the child.

It should be noted once again that success in staying objective and wearing that white coat in conversation with the angry adoptee depends upon the adoptive parents' capacity to absorb the anger of their son or daughter. Taking anger in and noticing it without reacting challenges all of us. But as soon as that anger has its way in breaking down the walls of objectivity that a parent may have in limited ways, as soon as that anger hooks a parent, the opportunity to be objective is lost, if only for the moment.

Attribute # 8- Wise adoptive parenting means being well differentiated from the parenting opinions of other people, especially other family members.

Learning to understand the concept of differentiation is well worth the time because this will lead to a more mature understanding of a healthy human relationship.

Differentiation has to do with the ability to hold onto yourself as well as hold onto your personal perspectives and value judgments when you are with others who may think differently or be judgmental or even rejecting. The well-differentiated person can manage to continue to be herself despite the differing opinions and varying expectations of others.

For example, though opinions about politics may vary greatly, a well-differentiated person can simply say, "I see things differently," without the need to defend one's perspectives or leave the room. In the timeless words of Popeye, "I am what I am and that's what I am. I'm Popeye, the sailor man!"

The experience of other family members being judgmental towards the parenting decisions of adoptive parents is common. But the well-differentiated parent would be able to respond in a calm and thoughtful fashion: "Well, there is another way to look at her behavior." Differentiation would then keep the family power with the parents, exactly where it belongs.

We might say then that the less-differentiated a person is, the more that person will be reactive, judgmental, and unable to really stay in the room. A husband or a wife may say, "I cannot be with you anymore and hold onto myself. When we are together, I lose myself and I need to get myself back. So, I need to leave you." (People usually marry at the same level of differentiation, which is usually the same level of differentiation as that of their own parents.)

A low level of differentiation would possibly translate into over-dependence whereby one says to the other, "I need you to always be available in a certain way so that I can be okay." And, of course, a low level of differentiation usually translates into intolerance and the inability to accept other people for whom they might be.

With regard to relinquishment and adoption, the value of understanding differentiation comes to the fore when adoptive parents hear comments and criticisms about their parenting of their relinquished and adopted children. When adoptees are acting out in some public forum such as the grocery store, people may be very quick to judge that the parents of these children are not very good parents. Being able to say to oneself as an adoptive parent, "Well, I have a different perspective on things" is always challenging.

When young adoptees get in trouble at school for a variety of disruptive behaviors, principals and staff and other students may be quick to cast judgment on these children and then upon their parents: "They should be able to control their children more effectively." There is always plenty of criticism to go around.

What becomes especially difficult for wise adoptive parenting is setting necessary emotional boundaries with their own parents.

Differentiation has to do with being able to say to Grandpa, "I'm sorry, Dad, but we see things differently. If all we do is harsh discipline every day, we may win the battle, but we will lose the war." The war has to do with "winning" more bonding from Sammy and more attachment to Sammy. If that battle is lost, usually the relationship is lost.

So, Mom or Dad tells Grandma, "Our new baby from Romania may have real struggles with attaching to us as her parents. So we do not pass her around from one person to another at Thanksgiving. That may simply frighten her and is not good for her. I hope you understand, Mom." These may be difficult words to speak because of the anticipated blowback from an irritated grandmother, but a well-differentiated adoptive mother will calmly manage her parenting without needing to defend it or leave the room.

Narratives like this one reinforce the critical importance of holding oneself and speaking important truths in times and places where other people may not understand.

Attribute # 9- Wise adoptive parenting means trying not to "go it alone" through the parenting challenges that adoptive parents face.

Sharing the challenges and difficulties of parenting adoptees who do poorly at adopting their parents may feel counterintuitive; however, sharing these stories with other people in similar circumstances may offer significant support and further understanding.

Opening up adoptive family narratives certainly carries some risks. Perhaps the most difficult of these is that of being misunderstood and judged by others who understand little of what is involved in loving children who struggle to love back. Accordingly, finding a setting of trust and non-0judgment is important.

Often post-adoption services include such formal or informal group opportunities for conversation that offers learning and support for the challenges shared by other adoptive parents. But such groups may be hard to identify. Local adoption agencies would be the place to begin such a search. Again, attending such a sharing group may be counterintuitive as parents wish to maintain privacy about family difficulties, but going it alone makes the task of parenting more difficult.

One of the benefits of conversations among adoptive parents is normalizing the difficulties that are encountered. When adoptees struggle to adopt their parents, the dynamics of resistance and ongoing conflict are relatively normal themes that characterize the relationship between parent and child.

Quite understandably, the wounded adoptee may carry a great deal of underlying depression. This may not be the best word because it sounds so clinical and diagnostic. It fails to capture adoptees' ordinary yet real experience of being immensely sad, remembering the losses they've already experienced.

In a very normal, human way these children are mourning. Look at what they have already endured prior to joining an adoptive family. Some have spent years in an understaffed orphanage with barely enough food and clothing. Sometimes neglect and abuse have been part of the narrative of older-age adoptees from countries far away–China, Ethiopia, Haiti, Ukraine, Romania, India, to name a few.

All these variables can be part of the mix in stories of relinquishment and adoption. And when adoptive parents have little knowledge as to what these children may have endured prior to adoption, their parenting becomes a guessing game as to how to understand resistant behavior and how to engage it in a meaningful and productive way. Few adoptive parents are sufficiently trained to engage or adequately supported in their efforts to understand and to empathically meet the deeper needs of these orphans of the world.

Consider, for example, the challenges that Jed and Marianne have had to face with their Korean, now American daughter, Annie. After she was abandoned in an alley near spacious upper-class homes, Annie spent the first 18 months of her life in an orphanage just north of Seoul, Korea, Ilsan by name. Then, through the efforts of Holt's Children's Services, she was placed with Jed and Marianne's family just south of Minneapolis, Minnesota. (This city has one of the largest Korean-American populations in the United States.)

The orphanage called Ilsan is a very well run and well supplied institution serving many of the orphans of northern South Korea. Many of the children there have significant disabilities and need special attention for their survival. Annie was born with a repairable cleft palate.

This was so difficult and shameful in that culture that she was left in that city alley, sad to say.

Jed and Marianne believed that they were quite ready for this adoptive parenting challenge and proceeded with great optimism with their plan for adoption. They planned the customary regimen of surgeries to repair Annie's palate, and they looked forward to life together with this little girl whose impairment would be corrected, leaving only the whisker of a scar.

These medical procedures went without incident and little Annie began to heal physically in the arms of her adoptive parents. This family story started out well with this little girl's improved smile as well as the comfort that she experienced with her parents.

But as the years proceeded, Jed and Marianne found themselves continuously seeking to engage their daughter in a way that would bring more warmth and strength to their relationship with her. Yet she began to resist that offer of care. She took solace in an extended time of sucking her thumb or wearing out pacifiers. As Annie grew older, it was troubling to Jed and Marianne that she seemed to be a little girl without remorse or concern for others. She demonstrated no signs of sadness or regret about her part in hurting other children.

She quickly projected blame onto others without a sense of responsibility for what she may have done. She may have tripped Sally, but "It was Sally's fault that she fell on the sidewalk and cut her knee so much that it bled." Annie would lie to get out of trouble, with no sign of inner conflict about her behavior. Quite understandably, Jed and Marianne became very concerned about their daughter whose behavior was becoming more and more self-centered.

At first, they assumed that their own inexperience at parenting must be the reason for these difficulties. Uninformed about the struggles that are usually set in motion by the loss of first parents and then the loss of the orphanage caretakers at Ilsan, they had very little confidence in the choices they made to help Annie manage her life. Their belief that the blame was theirs as adoptive parents was their first error in sizing up the problems before them.

Annie had been wounded more than they had ever known before they received her from the orphanage at Ilsan. All that was familiar in the first few months of her life had been erased and at the tender age of six months she was placed on new ground, in the orphanage at Ilsan. Set in motion at birth was her need to protect herself from the fearful unknown, from the unpredictable, from the changes in the taste of food, in the sounds of city life, in words spoken in a different language.

And then again, a year or so later, everything that was familiar was once again erased and, after a long and frightening airplane voyage, once again she was faced with the unfamiliar, the unpredictable, the changes in the taste of food, and the sounds of city life, and in words spoken in a different language.

So much transition in her early months of living was more than she could manage without shutting down on the inside to find safety within.

No wonder she resisted Jed and Marianne's outstretched arms and snuggly hugs. It was too frightening to open up once more. Security was only found by blocking these fears and these new people from becoming part her daily life.

Jed and Marianne turned to the resources of the organization called KAAN (Korean American Adoption Network), quite active in the metropolitan Minneapolis community because of the high population of Korean Americans living there. In the setting of an adoptive parent support group, they, for the first time, heard other adoption stories that were eerily similar to their own.

These were the narratives of other parents who had also adopted through Holt's Children's Services. Upon hearing struggles so similar to their own, they realized their experience with Annie was "normal." They were no longer the only parents who thought that they could not parent correctly.

Speaking of their struggles and hearing those of others in the safe non-judgmental space of this group empowered these parents to go back to Annie with more strength and confidence about their parenting. After even one meeting with the group, their hearts were lifted as they saw their struggles with Annie as the norm for the group.

Perhaps because of the "trauma bond" of trying with great effort to succeed as parents with children who struggled to adopt them, they discovered that place of trust where they could learn so much more about the unique qualities of adoptive development after the traumatic transition to new parents.

They gained the great benefit in terms of both knowledge and support in this group setting: knowledge about the unique character of their parenting task, and equally important, emotional support for themselves as parents who loved Annie but were hurt and disappointed in seeking to connect to her heart. Such heartache can certainly be lessened by conversation with other adoptive parents who face similar circumstances. And this, of course, is the opposite of going it alone.

Attribute #10-- Wise Adoptive Parenting means spending time with their children in spiritual conversation.

In our present day and age, this will most likely sound like a quite unusual expectation of parents and especially adoptive parents. If anything, as children observe the behavior of their parents, they often learn that talk about sex or politics or religion may be off the table. Something not discussed. And yet, there is a spiritual need that all of us have, but especially children who have had such a difficult beginning.

This has to do with helping adoptees to construct a framework of understanding the world in which we all live. Here, the hard questions noted above are the front burner inquiries about the nature of our universe as well as of our own souls. I take *soul* to be a reference to that which is deepest within us as we relate to the world around us and the universe for that matter.

Now of course many of us may have put these questions aside, these inquiries about the nature of being alive and being human and being connected in some way to something or someone bigger than life. Our personal spiritual experiences vary so much.

Evangelical Christians speak of a personal relationship with Jesus as central to their spiritual life. They seek and experience God's presence by the work of the Holy Spirit of God.

Jewish brothers and sisters focus carefully on the Old Testament God, Yahweh. The Torah, with its many prescriptions for obedience, sits before them as a map for living life in a spiritual relationship with God.

And the Muslim community looks to Mohammed as the prophet who speaks on behalf of Allah in a manner that offers a prescription for strict obedience and commitment to their understanding of the God of the Old Testament Scriptures.

All of this is to say that children are offered a way of thinking about the world in which they live. Now many parents may simply keep spiritual questions off the table of conversation and never address them with their children. So often it is said, "We will let them decide for themselves when they grow up." But this response falls short of offering children, especially our adoptees, the opportunity to experience a religious way of understanding their spiritual life experiences.

And, of course, here I take the position that we should offer our wounded adoptees every resource possible for their development. As has been said in these pages, some adoptees face a very difficult beginning in their lives. This has been the painful reality that has been addressed over and over, page after page.

For an adoptee, who will certainly question whether and how God may exist, offering that child a way to think and believe is offering that child the gift of a framework for living life. It can have that kind of importance.

Adoptive parents then, wise adoptive parents, will both invite and even create time and space for conversations about these spiritual matters. By way of their own testimonies and by way of their own curiosity about things unknown, adoptive parents have the opportunity to open the door to religious life wherein the spiritual challenges that adoptees face have space for contemplation.

Children pick up right away what they can and cannot discuss with their parents. Even by the tone of voice they may know that certain questions have little room and family life. **Or they may know by the clear absence of religious interest in their families that their own spiritual inquiries have no place for conversation.** They may learn to live without a framework that offers an understanding of our human experience.

For example, let's consider the story of Johnny Ray. He came to his adoptive family after the termination of rights of his own parents by birth. Their ongoing involvement with the struggles of drug addiction cost them the right to parent Johnny Ray. He came to his new home at 12 months of age after experiencing considerable neglect. Diapers that were not changed, irregular bathing, and no schedule to food on the table-- this was hard start for a child.

Johnny Ray was fearful of bonding to his new adoptive parents and in the usual ways of resistance he pushed against the warmth they had to offer. But slowly, way too slowly for the adoptive parents, Johnny Ray's anxieties began to subside. The consistent care and structure of adoptive life was certainly a critical blessing in his development. He tasted good food on a regular basis and he found that spot on his mother's neck where he felt safe.

This is not to say that Johnny Ray was not a rascal of sorts. He was very possessive of his toys and would usually fight to keep them from the hands of other children. Pretty classic behavior given his early on struggles with trust. Lots of people loved him even though it was challenging for him to receive that love.

One afternoon, around age 4, Johnny Ray looked at the moon and asked his father "How does the moon stay up there, Daddy? There is nothing holding it up." What is a father to say to that? How might he respond in a way that is useful and even encouraging to Johnny Ray?

Well, there are no easy answers to questions like this one. But there are thousands of times, thousands of opportunities, when parents have the option of opening up that conversation or closing it down. Opening it up is better.

His father responded, "Johnny Ray, there are lots and lots of things about the world that we do not understand, but I can help with this one. There is something called *gravity* which means that the Earth is like a magnet that keeps pulling on the moon so that it stays where it is when it goes round and round the Earth."

Okay, here we have a simple explanation of a scientific term that a four-year-old can barely understand because it is so cognitive at a rather high level. Johnny Ray could nod his thanks for the comment without getting much from it. But, his father could say just a little more.

"And you know what, Johnny Ray? No one really knows just how the moon got in the sky in the first place. Somehow, God put it there. God is big and God is powerful, more powerful than all your super heroes. God made the world and the moon is part of the world. And, God made you and God is pretty happy with who you are."

In that moment of conversation about the moon and about God, Johnny Ray learned that it was okay to ask his father these kinds of questions. Further, his very existence was affirmed as he was told that God had a big smile for Johnny Ray. Good work for a wise adoptive father!

After some years go by and Johnny Ray begins to think more for himself, he may remember that moment with his dad, wondering about the moon. And he may wrestle with the reality of this Creator, but his parents will have given him an understanding of the world with which he can wrestle.

Five Behaviors Deserving a Wise Response

Difficult behaviors quickly come to mind that are often part of the adoptee's pushback against bonding and attachment. They are: insensitivity to the pain of others, lying, stealing, unfairness, and aggression. We now move into a brief discussion of each of these troubling behaviors along with examples of possible intervention.

Insensitivity to the pain of others: Remember that wooden block flying through the air that hit another child in the day care center? The block had enough velocity to really hurt. How did the daycare attendant respond? She said to the perpetrator of this childhood crime, "Don't throw blocks. You need to use words, not throw things." Her response was not, first, that of assigning a timeout for being a naughty boy; it was first a lesson to be learned. The timeout may have come later, but the first instruction was to use words.

In the context of that vignette is another lesson of great importance. It would take the form of this question; "Johnny, how do you think Dennis felt when that block hit his head?" This would be a beginning lesson about empathy, sensitivity to the pain of others. It involves a guided tour of another's experience, wondering what it is like to be that other boy. And this parental nudge would push right against that lack of empathy that so often characterizes wounded children.

Telling Lies: Twisting or changing the truth to one's immediate benefit is the fastest way to get out of trouble. Children usually are caught lying and must then face the challenge of telling the truth. When adults are seen as people to be feared, lying is that attempt to get around the punishment and/or injury that they anticipate. In the moment, lying is the quickest way out of trouble even if it never works in the long term.

What appropriate discipline might come against not telling the truth? Whatever the consequence may be, a word can be added to the mix of this conversation: "Cindy, why do you think it is so important to tell the truth? Can we wonder about that a minute?" Or, "What do you think would have happened if you had told the truth?" Or, "Can you see that we have a hard time trusting you when you have a hard time telling the truth?" These are separate questions and, of course, they should never be our last. But they get at further conversation that can be helpful. Building trust between parent and child can happen when both become honest partners in conversation.

Stealing: This is a very interesting behavior that some adoptees regularly employ. Often, there is a report of entitlement, as if to say, "I deserve this because I've had such a bad deal so far." Teenage female adoptees often steal makeup, announcing that they deserve it, and that it is too expensive. Might it be a way to imagine her birth mother or to identify with her out there somewhere, as if to become the fantasy? Maybe. It is interesting to wonder about that. These are only guesses, of course, but they seek to understand, to make sense of behavior that is troublesome.

One might add to the mix of conversation the invitation to wonder with the child about the "Why?" behind the stealing. "Sonya, help me understand why you keep stealing things, here around the house, or at the grocery store? Stealing gets you in so much trouble. Respecting other people's stuff is important. How would your life be different if you just didn't do that?"

Engaging the adoptee to wonder about her own behavior and to engage the question of the value of respecting others property–this might lead to interesting and useful.

Unfairness: Wondering what is fair is hardly ever on the radar of wounded children who are seeking to survive as best they can. Questions of justice for others simply do not come to mind. If we think it through, this is quite understandable. In a world that is perceived as dangerous, where personal survival is understood to be primary, "getting whatever you can take" would be the operating principle by which choices are made.

However, justice does come to mind when it gets personal around "what I deserve." Stealing, for example, might be justified as making things fairer in the life of the adoptee. And, when questions around justice, around good everyday fairness in life, are presented for conversation, useful discussions may begin to occur.

Asking what might be fair invites the relinquished and adopted child to look about and take note of the interest of others as they too demand their piece of the pie, especially siblings by both birth and adoption. The practice of sharing things is certainly a learned behavior, much more than it is natural.

Counting out the marbles in the bag and then insisting that they be shared evenly is the beginning of such learning. And then, presenting the idea of fairness can become useful, inviting the child to notice the limits of what is thought to be deserved.

As a child becomes mindful of fairness, in whatever immature way, a reference to fairness to others can be quite useful. Whenever injustice is noticed in dinner table conversation about what happened at school or an instance of unfairness on a television program or a question about someone getting his "fair share" comes up, pointing it out is useful. We teach by how we live and we teach by what we say.

Another example, closer to home for some adoptees, has to do with the very careful way that adoptees take notice of how they are treated by their new parents. Any hints of favoritism towards children by birth, as it is experienced by the adoptee, sets up a negative triangle in which once again the adoptee is the "one person out," the outlier who fits into the family in a more limited fashion.

Adoptees pick this up in a moment as they continue their developmental journey and, understandably, they resent this. It is less than fair to be set aside in any way as an outsider to one's own family. "I don't quite belong" becomes a refrain when such moments of favoritism occur.

Finally, aggression: Passive aggression and active aggression are both methods of expressing deeply felt anger. Aggression can also serve as part of an arsenal of defenses against getting close. During active aggression, the adoptee knows that something is at stake that needs protection, namely himself or herself.

Adoptive parents will hopefully have reasonable ideas about the pain of early-life experiences and corresponding self-perceptions that may drive that behavior. Then they can respond with something like this:

> We get it that at times you may be so angry towards your brother or your sister or your classmate or your teacher or either of us as your parents. But we still need to deal with these things so that you can make your life work better. Stopping yourself from lashing out or doing something that you do not want to do—these are tough lessons to learn, but it is very important that you do. Anger is a difficult thing to manage for all of us. We know that and we want to help you with it.

The above may be a long statement, but it offers the child an invitation to notice the difficulties that come with aggression, passively or actively. We take anger to be understandable because the child has things to truly be angry about, beginning with the all-important loss of parents. And this method of offering reflection in the middle of trouble is most useful and may be a primary way of gently speaking truth to the adoptee.

Very young children become aware of that beginning to their story around ages three or four. The younger child needs structure and perhaps a little exploration, the slightly older child needs structure but more verbal engagement, and the still older child will need structure but more intentional verbal engagement.

We take anger to be a positive expression of self-esteem, an important part of self-development that needs to be respected and understood, but nevertheless managed wisely. This may be the most important and most difficult challenge for some adoptive parents to face in their day-to-day life with adoptees who struggle to accept them as parents, to adopt them, and to allow them to care. Understandably, adoptive parents, especially adoptive mothers, become targets for the rage that may be within the adoptee's heart.

Carissa would not get up to go to school. She refused the use of an alarm clock. Now an eighth grader, Carissa had lots to say about her life with her adoptive parents, and almost all of it was negative. Her older relinquished and adopted brother was quiet; he stayed outside of the gunfire. On a day-to-day basis, Carissa fought with her parents about being ready for school, or doing her homework, or setting th dinner table. Letting her parents be her parents was hardly possible.

And, as these parents looked ahead to the upcoming years of adolescence, they wondered how they might ever successfully manage the conflict. Open, very active aggression by word or deed was Carissa's primary method of managing the expectations of her parents. "I don't care! I'd rather go back to the adoption agency than live with this family!" The ambivalence that she truly carried about allowing them to care had nearly paralyzed her developmental challenges. She was determined to be her own boss, Acting as an incorrigible infant at age 14 kept her as a child impossible to manage.

In the fray of this adoptive family conflict, Carissa had the most power and was using it negatively to poison family life. And this was hardly a time for any lesson to be learned in some cognitive way. Comments about the importance of accepting authority would be useless, untimely, and simply more gasoline on the fire of her irritations.

Until this approach:

Carissa, if you continue to work to defeat us as parents so much that we give in and give up and return you to the adoption agency, as you requested, what will you have accomplished? You would once again be an orphan, a girl with no parents. What do you need from us and what can help? We want to understand why you get so angry.

This comment fortunately mirrored Carissa's ongoing ambivalence. Only then did her anger turn toward tears. And this moment of catharsis, of weeping deeply, of shedding tears not cried for years, began the healing of her broken heart.

These words also gave Carissa an invitation to be reflective. Parents do matter; whether you love them or whether you hate them, they matter. For adoptive parents to matter effectively, they must appreciate and understand the usual ambivalence that their children carry to their adoptive homes. It is often expressed in anger, a more mature form of the underlying primitive rage that may result from the difficult beginnings of their lives. This is the great lesson to be learned in the narrative of difficult adoptions.

In conclusion, **wise parenting is a sustainable goal for adoptive parents.** It need not be perfect; we do it wrong, and we do it wrong, and we do it wrong, and then we do it right. That's good enough; that's what parenting is like.

We learn as we go, but we never fully understand. We never fully appreciate the complex dynamics that are part of adoptive development. When adoptees face unusual injuries in the first days and weeks and years of their lives, it is always an open question how much they can recover from the soul wounds of abandonment and neglect and abuse. But without good care and parental management, there is no question that these children would be much worse off.

Being adopted adds a significant layer of complexity to a child's development, a complexity that most of us who are children by birth cannot appreciate. **Wise adoptive parenting is guided by an empathic appreciation of the struggles that these children by adoption do sometimes bring home.**

Further, it is effective because understanding a child's behavior brings a certain power to adoptive parents. This is to say, when parents love their children and respond to them, especially their troublesome behavior, with their care and understanding of what is going on, they proceed with more confidence in knowing what needs to be accomplished.

And all of this moves these once-orphans further away from the quiet death of their own souls and closer to the life-giving, heart-warming resource of the gentle voices and the warm touch of wise loving parents.

Books to Read

Daniel Hughes wrote a novel titled *Building the Bonds of Attachment: Awakening Love in Deeply Troubled Children* (Jason Aronson, Inc., 2000). This book is about a little girl who struggles deeply with bonding to her adoptive parents. This book is a must first read for adoptive parents who seek an understanding of their wounded children. After observing several adoption failures, Hughes demonstrates parenting methods that are successful in establishing a functioning adoptive family.

Karyn Purvis and her colleagues wrote a book entitled *The Connected Child* (McGraw Hill, 2007) for parents who have welcomed children from other countries and cultures, from troubled backgrounds, and with special behavioral or emotional needs. This text is a valuable resource for parenting young adoptees. The book seeks to be preventative in terms of avoiding struggles with attachment down the road of development. It offers assistance in appreciating the struggles of wounded children and presents strategies for parents that help the wounded child move forward in his or her emotional development.

Questions and Support

Bethany Christian Services, Inc., the largest adoption agency in the United States, offers a wide variety of resources in its effort to expand care for the post-adoption community. Readers can access helpful conversations by contacting Bethany's Post-Adoption Contact Center. Simply call 866 – 309 – 7328. <<**www.Bethany.org/PACC**>>

Mike and Krista Berry, adoptive parents to eight children, live on a farm with them all! They have a blog at <<ConfessionsofanAdoptiveParent.com>>. This resource offers daily words of encouragement to adoptive parents who will identify with many of the parenting challenges that they discuss. With over 100,000 followers, Mike and Kristin have created a national and international community of support for adoptive families.

Mike recently wrote *Confessions of an Adoptive Parent: Help and Hope from the Trenches of Foster Care and Adoption* (Harvest House, 2018). In a very experientially close way, this book honors the struggles of abused children who have lost their parents. The book offers practical recommendations for effective, spiritually focused foster care and adoptive parenting. Written in a positive, very upbeat spirit, the book demonstrates never giving up hope!

And Sherrie Eldridge offers learning and support on a wonderful website at << SherrieEldridgeAdoption.blog>>.